COMPLETE CREATIVE

ORIENTAL COOKING

Beryl Frank

BONANZA BOOKS
New York

Thanks to all of those cooks and librarians and to Deni and Marian, my editors, who helped bring the cooking of the Orient to the cooks of the West — and as always, thanks to Lou.

Contents

Introduction 5

Chapter 1
Appetizers. 6

Chapter 2
Soups 19

Chapter 3
Seafood. 41

Chapter 4
Poultry 65

Chapter 5
Meat 96

Chapter 6
Vegetables and Salads 128

Chapter 7
Eggs and Pancakes 149

Chapter 8
Rice and Noodles. 160

Chapter 9
Doughs and Desserts 184

Chapter 10
Miscellaneous 210

Glossary 227

Index. 236

Introduction

You may never travel to such exotic places as Bangladesh or Hong Kong, but this is no reason to exclude the culinary delights of the Orient from your menus. Oriental cooking is an art in itself, but it can be a learned art which adapts well to Western kitchens.

In a world of constantly changing political boundaries, one thing remains constant. People have to eat. They eat in China, in Thailand, in Korea, and in the Philippines. What they eat usually reflects their own individual culture, as well as the availability of foods in their own areas. Rice and coconuts can be found almost everywhere in Oriental countries, and recipes including both of these basic foods are common throughout Asia. Recipes using both of these basic foods are included in this book. However, the use of the same foods in different ways makes them exciting to prepare.

If you use a current map to locate some of the countries listed here, you may have trouble finding them. Indochina, for instance, includes such countries as Cambodia, Vietnam, and Laos. Indonesia includes the islands of Sumatra, Borneo, and Jawa. India includes the cookery of Pakistan as well—these two adjacent countries have so much similarity in their cuisine that it was not necessary to have a separate section for each of them. Recipes labeled India might also be labeled India-Pakistan.

While the true Oriental cook may prefer to use such special utensils as a wok, a hibachi, or a bamboo steamer, his or her Western counterpart can do equally well with a regular steamer or a series of heavy skillets or heavy saucepans. The recipes offered here are adapted to Western cookware and Western stoves and ovens.

Methods of cooking are somewhat different, however. Cooking in liquid, such as rice cooked in coconut milk, is common in the Orient. So is cooking in oil—both lightly fried foods and deep-fat fried foods are quite usual. Recipes that tell how to cook rice with steam are included, as are ways of cooking with dry heat when preparing toasted sesame seeds.

Special Ingredients

Many recipes use foreign names for their ingredients. Any of the foreign foods are available at your Oriental store. All of them are listed in the Glossary (see Contents for page number) for your convenience.

In order to use the recipes in this book to their best advantage, it is a good idea to read through the Glossary at the back of the book first. This will help to familiarize you with the many new food experiences you will find in Oriental cooking. The more you learn before you start in the kitchen, the happier your gourmet experience will be. Oriental cooking is not hard—just different—and it can be a very exciting experience.

Spelling can be another problem for the novice Oriental cook. Dried shrimp paste, for instance, is spelled in various ways depending on which country is using it. Trasi, terasi, and trassi all mean dried shrimp paste. Regardless of how the word is spelled, it still means dried shrimp paste, and it is used in many different areas of the Orient.

Some recipes call for tamarind pulp in their ingredients. Others call for tamarind liquid. Either way, what is called for is a liquid from the dried tamarind pulp. Check the Glossary to be sure how to make tamarind liquid from the pulp.

Coconut milk is sometimes available in cans at your Oriental store. This is not to be confused with the clear liquid that comes out of the coconut when it is first opened. Coconut milk is made from the pulp of the fruit itself. If you cannot find it in cans, directions for making it are included in this book.

Many people think of curry when talking about Oriental food. In most Oriental recipes, the word curry means sauce. From Burma to India, from Japan to Malaysia, curries—frequently served with rice or noodles—are staples in the Oriental diet. Curry leaves or curry powder are used in many curry dishes, but there are as many varieties of flavors of curry as there are Oriental cooks. You will find curry recipes in many of the food categories, from fish curry to pork curry to curried rice.

The traveler who has been to the Orient will surely enjoy many of the taste delights described in this book. But the gourmet who searches for delicate cuisine and unusual flavors and textures will also enjoy learning about food from the Far East. Oriental cooking is a culinary experience, which will enrich the table and culture of the West.

Meat and Potato Croquettes

INDONESIA   *Yield about 30-36 balls*

When formed into 1-inch-size balls, these are ideal as an appetizer. When made into egg-shaped balls, these croquettes can be a main dish.

3 pounds potatoes, cooked, drained, and
   mashed
1 tablespoon butter
1 small onion, finely chopped
2 to 3 cloves garlic, finely chopped
1 pound ground beef
Salt and pepper to taste
¼ teaspoon nutmeg
4 shallots, finely sliced, including green tops
2 or 3 eggs, separated
Oil for deep frying
Parsley for garnish

Prepare mashed potatoes and set aside. Stir-fry onion and garlic in butter until onion is lightly browned. Add meat, salt, pepper, and nutmeg, stirring constantly until meat browns evenly. Add shallots and cook 2 minutes more.

In a large bowl, combine mashed potatoes, meat mixture, and egg yolks. When all is well blended, form into 1-inch balls and refrigerate for at least 1 hour.

In a small bowl, use a whisk or a fork to beat the egg whites until light and frothy. Dip each meatball into the egg white to coat it thoroughly. This will prevent the meatball from breaking up when fried.

Heat oil in deep fat fryer and fry the meatballs until golden brown. Transfer to a platter, which can be kept warm in the oven until all are fried. Serve hot.

Shrimp Crisps

INDONESIA

Uncooked shrimp crisps, sometimes called prawn crisps, are sold in most Oriental food stores. When used as an appetizer, smaller-size wafers are preferred.

Shrimp crisps
Oil for deep frying

Pour enough oil into wok or frying pan for deep frying. Allow the oil to get hot. Test it with a small piece of the shrimp crisp. Temperature is right if the crisp swells up within 3 seconds of being in the fat.

When the crisps are golden and puffy, remove from the fat to drain on paper towels. If you plan to store these in an airtight container, be sure they are thoroughly cool before sealing.

Hot Fish Balls

THAILAND   *Yield 20 to 25 balls*

4 garlic cloves, peeled and chopped
20 peppercorns
4 coriander roots, finely chopped
Pinch of sugar
3 dried chilies
1½ pounds cod fillets, skinned
1 tablespoon all-purpose flour
1 tablespoon soy sauce
⅓ cup vegetable oil

Using a mortar, pound the garlic, peppercorns, coriander roots, and chilies to a paste. Gradually add the fish, continuing to pound the mixture to a paste. Lastly, put in flour and soy sauce and pound the mixture for another minute. Shape into 1-inch balls.

Use either a wok or a deep-fat fryer and heat the oil. Drop a few of the fish balls into the fat. When golden brown all over, remove them from the fat with a slotted spoon. Drain on paper towels and put on a platter to keep warm. When all of the fish balls are fried, serve at once.

Stuffed Soybean Cake

THAILAND	Yield 12 servings

Oil for frying
4 ounces pork, finely minced
3 cloves garlic, crushed
¼ teaspoon salt
⅛ teaspoon pepper
1 tablespoon fresh coriander, chopped
2 teaspoons fish sauce
12 cubes bean curd

In a medium-size skillet, heat enough oil to cover the pan. Add pork, garlic, salt, and pepper and cook until pork is well done, stirring frequently. Add coriander and fish sauce; then remove from heat.

Cut dried bean curd into 12 cubes. Make a hole in the center of each square big enough to hold some of the pork stuffing. When the bean curd is stuffed, deep fry in heated oil. Drain on paper towels. Just before serving, refry the bean curds and serve hot. Garlic and vinegar sauce may be served with these.

Pork and Crab Balls

THAILAND	Yield 12 servings

8 ounces pork, ground
2 ounces pork fat, ground
6 ounces crab meat, flaked and picked over for bones

2 tablespoons coriander leaves, finely chopped
1 teaspoon salt
¼ teaspoon ground black pepper
2 tablespoons beaten egg
1 tablespoon cornstarch
6 sheets dried bean curd skin or wonton pastry
Oil for deep frying

Mix the ground pork, pork fat, and crab meat together until well blended. Add the coriander leaves, salt, pepper, and beaten egg. Put in the cornstarch and blend well.

Use slightly warm water to soften the bean curd skin. When it is easy to handle, cut it into 4-inch squares. Place 1 scant tablespoon of the meat filling in the center of each square. Gather up the edges and tie with a plastic-covered wire twist. Steam the balls for 10 to 12 minutes over boiling water. Remove wire twist.

Deep fry the balls in hot oil until golden brown all over. Drain on paper towels and keep warm until ready to serve. These may be served with a spicy dip.

Galloping Horses

THAILAND	Yield 4 to 6 servings

5 cloves garlic
2 or 3 tablespoons oil
2½ pounds mixed lean and fat pork
3 tablespoons roasted peanuts, coarsely ground
2 tablespoons sugar
1½ tablespoons fish sauce
2 small fresh pineapples
Coriander leaves
1 fresh chili, cut in slivers

Place garlic cloves in a press until well crushed. Then, fry garlic in oil until light brown. Add the pork, peanuts, sugar, and fish sauce. Stir this mixture until the pork is well cooked, dry and dark brown in color.

Peel and core the pineapples and cut them into mouth-size pieces, about 1-inch square. Spoon the pork mixture on top of each piece of fruit. Arrange on a platter and decorate with coriander leaves and chili slivers.

Fried Prawns

BURMA	Yield 4 servings

16 large prawns, peeled
1 teaspoon salt
1 teaspoon ground turmeric
1 teaspoon chili powder
2 tablespoons sesame oil
2 tablespoons peanut oil
Thin bamboo skewers

Mix salt, turmeric, and chili powder together and thoroughly coat prawns with the mixture. Bend prawns into a semicircle and put on skewer through top and tail. Thread 4 prawns to a skewer. Heat both kinds of oil in a shallow pan. Fry prawns until golden on both sides. Serve at once.

Fried Bread with Pork, Beef, or Shrimp

THAILAND	Yield 28 pieces

1 cup raw pork, beef, or shrimp,
   coarsely ground
2 tablespoons onions, finely chopped
1 teaspoon salt
½ teaspoon pepper
2 eggs
7 slices bread, crusts removed and quartered
Vegetable shortening or oil

Season your choice of pork, beef, or shrimp with onions, salt, pepper, and eggs. Be sure the meat is blended well with the rest of the ingredients. Spread this mixture on each quarter piece of bread.

Melt 2 or 3 tablespoons of shortening in a skillet. Allow the fat to get very hot; then lower the flame. Place each piece of meat-covered bread into the fat, meat side down. When the meat side is nicely browned, turn to brown the other side. Remove and drain on paper towels. Keep warm until all of the pieces are fried. Serve at once.

Curried Nuts

INDIA	Yield 2 cups

¼ cup olive oil
1 tablespoon curry powder
1 tablespoon Worcestershire sauce
⅛ teaspoon cayenne pepper
2 cups nuts (assorted are best)

Combine oil and seasonings in medium-size skillet. When mixture is hot, add nuts; stir constantly until nuts are completely coated.

Line baking pan with brown paper. Spread out nuts. Bake at 200 °F for 10 minutes. Nuts should be crisp.

Savory Pastries

INDIA	Yield 32 to 36 pastries

Pastry

1½ cups plain flour
¾ teaspoon salt
1 tablespoon ghee or oil
½ cup warm water

Filling

1 tablespoon ghee or oil
1 clove garlic, finely chopped
1 teaspoon fresh ginger, finely chopped
2 medium onions, finely chopped
2 teaspoons curry powder
½ teaspoon salt
1 tablespoon vinegar or lemon juice
½ pound ground beef or lamb
1 teaspoon garam masala
2 tablespoons fresh mint or coriander leaves, chopped
Oil for frying

In a large bowl, sift together the flour and salt. Combine the ghee and water with the dry ingredients, mixing thoroughly. If needed to form a workable dough, add a little extra water. Knead the dough until it is elastic to the touch, about 10 minutes. Cover and set aside while preparing the filling.

To make the filling, fry garlic in hot ghee with half the onion until onion is transparent. Mix in the curry powder, salt, and vinegar. Next, add ground beef and stir constantly until meat changes color. Reduce the heat, add hot water, and cover. Cook until all liquid has been absorbed and meat is tender. Stir frequently to prevent sticking to the pan. Then add the garam masala and fresh mint. Allow mixture to cool and then mix in the remaining onion.

Shape the dough into 1-inch pieces. On a lightly floured board, roll one piece into a 6-inch circle. Cut the circle in half. Working with one half at a time, fold the dough around your dampened hand to a cone shape. Brush the edges with water to seal. Fill the cone with some of the meat mixture and close the opening by pinching together.

Heat oil for deep frying. Put a few pastries at a time into the fat. When golden brown on all sides, remove from the fat; drain on paper towels. Transfer finished pastries to an oven dish to stay hot until all are cooked and ready to eat.

Onion Fritters

INDIA *Yield 6 to 8 servings*

This filling and delicious first course may be made ahead, several hours before being served. If this is done, refry fritters about 1 minute in hot oil just before serving to have them piping hot.

Batter

1 cup unsifted chick-pea flour
2 teaspoons peanut or corn oil or melted vegetable shortening
1 teaspoon ground cumin
1½ teaspoons Kosher salt
1-2 green chilies, seeded and minced
½ cup warm water

Onions

2 medium-size onions, peeled and thinly sliced
Peanut or corn oil, enough to fill a fryer 2 inches

Use a large bowl to sift the flour. Using your fingers, rub the 2 teaspoons oil into the flour, until no more lumps of fat can be seen. Add cumin, salt, and chilies. Gradually, add the water while constantly beating the mixture. Use electric beater or wire whisk. Beat the batter vigorously for 10 minutes; cover and let rest in a warm place for at least ½ hour.

After the batter has rested, add the onions and coat thoroughly. This will make the mixture coarse and lumpy. Heat oil in frying pan until very hot but do not allow to smoke. Drop the onion batter mixture from a large spoon (about 2 tablespoons at a time). Fry about 6 at a time, keeping the heat medium-low for slower cooking. Each batch will take about 10 minutes until they are golden brown and crisp. Remove the finished fritters with a slotted spoon and drain on paper towels. Keep warm until ready to serve.

Kabobs with Raisin Stuffing

INDIA   *Yield 20 or more*

The kabob

1 pound lean ground beef
2 teaspoons garlic, finely chopped
1½ teaspoons fresh gingerroot, finely chopped
1 teaspoon ground cumin
1 teaspoon ground coriander
1 teaspoon paprika
1 teaspoon garam masala
½ teaspoon black pepper
¼ cup bread crumbs
1 tablespoon sweet butter
1 large egg, lightly beaten
1¼ teaspoons Kosher salt

Stuffing

2 tablespoons blanched almonds, chopped
2 tablespoons seedless raisins
2 tablespoons light vegetable oil for frying

In a large bowl, mix all of the ingredients for the kabobs. When thoroughly mixed, cover and set aside for at least ½ hour. This may be made and refrigerated up to two days in advance.

Put the well-chopped almonds and raisins together. Divide the prepared kabob mixture into equal portions. Shape into cocktail-size sausages, about 1½ inches long and ½ inch thick. Make a lengthwise slit in each sausage and fill this with stuffing. Pinch the meat together to seal the stuffing inside. (This too can be done ahead and refrigerated until ready to fry the kabobs.)

Heat the oil in a large frying pan; add the kabobs. Cook them for about 8 to 10 minutes, until they are browned all over. Serve piping hot.

Wonton

CHINA   *Yield about 120 wonton*

½ pound pork, minced
¼ cup fresh mushrooms, minced
1 tablespoon scallion, minced
¼ teaspoon salt
⅛ teaspoon freshly ground black pepper
1 egg yolk
Wonton squares
Peanut oil

Mix minced pork, mushrooms, and scallion with salt, pepper, and egg yolk. Place ½ teaspoonful of the mixture in center of wonton square. Fold one corner up over the filling at an angle to make two askew triangles. Pull the bottom corners of the triangles gently down below their base. Overlap the tips of the two corners slightly and pinch them together. Fry in hot peanut oil and drain. Serve with Chinese mustard or catsup mixed with a little horseradish.

Stuffed Mushrooms

CHINA   *Yield 24 mushrooms*

24 large mushrooms, stems removed
1 pound ground meat
4 tablespoons chopped scallions
3½ tablespoons soy sauce, divided
⅛ teaspoon salt
Freshly ground black pepper to taste
1½ tablespoons flour
1¼ cups beef broth

Wash mushrooms, remove stems, and put mushrooms aside. Chop the meat and scallions together, until fine. Add 1 tablespoon soy sauce, salt, pepper, and flour. Shape mixture into small balls and stuff mushrooms.

Heat large skillet to medium heat. Add remaining soy sauce and beef broth. Place mushrooms in skillet stuffed-side-up; cover and let cook for about 20 minutes, or until meat is done.

Appetizers Wrapped in Bacon

CHINA	Yield 4 servings

8 slices bacon, cut in half
1 pound chicken livers, cut in half
1 6-ounce can whole water chestnuts, drained
   and sliced

Lay bacon slices flat; place chicken livers and water chestnuts on top and roll up. Secure with toothpicks. Place appetizers in small amount of hot oil in frying pan or wok and cook until bacon is browned.

Cocktail Meatballs

CHINA	Yield 4 servings

1 20-ounce can pineapple chunks
1 jar red cherry jelly or preserves
¼ cup catsup
3 whole cloves
1 stick cinnamon
1 teaspoon salt
1 teaspoon cornstarch
1 tablespoon soy sauce
1 pound ground chuck, made into cooked
   meatballs

Drain pineapple and reserve juice. Combine juice with jelly or preserves, catsup, cloves, cinnamon, and salt. Heat to boiling. Dissolve cornstarch in enough liquid (either water or a small amount of the pineapple juice mixture) to make a smooth paste and stir into the boiling mixture. Cook until cornstarch thickens and clears.

Add the pineapple chunks and soy sauce. Pour over the cooked meatballs in a chafing dish and serve warm.

Chicken Wings

CHINA	Yield 8 to 12 servings

1 10-ounce bottle soy sauce
2 teaspoons freshly grated ginger or 1 teaspoon
   powdered ginger
2 cloves garlic, minced
⅓ cup brown sugar
1 teaspoon dark mustard
24 chicken wings
Garlic powder

Mix together soy sauce, ginger, garlic, brown sugar, and mustard. Blend well. Marinate chicken wings in mixture for two hours or longer. Drain wings, reserving marinade. Bake 1½ hours at 350°F, turning and basting with marinade frequently. Sprinkle with garlic powder and place under broiler for a minute or two just before serving to get crispy.

This may also be served as a main dish (makes 4-5 servings).

Oriental Chicken Livers

CHINA	Yield 4 servings

8 ounces chicken livers, cut in half
⅓ cup soy sauce
½ cup flour
1 small onion, sliced, or onion flakes

Marinate chicken livers overnight in soy sauce. Remove livers from marinade and dredge in flour. Heat small amount of oil in frying pan and fry livers and onion until browned.

This may also be served as a main dish (serves 2).

Scallops

CHINA	Yield about 25 appetizers

1 cup soy sauce
1 tablespoon lemon juice
2 teaspoons fresh gingerroot, finely chopped, or substitute powdered ginger
2 tablespoons sugar
1 pound scallops, cut into bite-size pieces

In large saucepan combine soy sauce, lemon juice, ginger, and sugar. Bring to a boil. Add scallops and cook over medium-high heat until all the liquid has evaporated.

Sweet-and-Sour Sauce

CHINA	Yield about 1¼ cups

4 tablespoons catsup
¼ cup brown sugar
2 tablespoons soy sauce
3 tablespoons wine vinegar
2 tablespoons dry white wine
2 tablespoons cornstarch, dissolved in ½ cup cold water

Combine catsup, sugar, soy sauce, vinegar, and wine in saucepan. Bring to a boil. Add the cornstarch dissolved in water to the sauce. Cook over low heat, stirring constantly, until sauce has thickened. Serve this with chicken, beef, pork, or seafood.

Sweet-and-Sour Plum Sauce

CHINA	Yield about 1½ cups

½ cup water
1 cup plum jelly
2 tablespoons catsup
2 tablespoons vinegar

Place ingredients in saucepan and stir. Bring to boil. Serve warm.

Egg-Roll Skins

CHINA	Yield about 24 skins

18 eggs
3 tablespoons cornstarch
3 teaspoons salt
2¼ cups water
Oil

Beat eggs. Add cornstarch and salt. Beat in water. Heat oil in bottom of 8-inch frying pan or wok and pour about ¼ cup of batter into pan. Fry lightly, turn, and fry on other side.

Vegetarian Egg Rolls

CHINA	

Experiment with this recipe. These are very good.

Vegetables such as:
    cabbage
    bok choy
    celery

carrots
fresh mushrooms
onions
scallions
green pepper
bean sprouts

The sauce

Apricot preserves
Plum preserves
Soy sauce
Dijon mustard
Peanut butter

Use as many of the above vegetables as you wish, in whatever amounts you desire. Shred or finely chop all the vegetables. Stir-fry quickly in small amount of oil. Add soy sauce to taste, garlic pow-der, and some peanut butter. Fill egg-roll skins, or wonton skins (for cocktail size), and fry in oil in wok or deep frying pan. Serve immediately or freeze and warm in oven before serving.

Make sauce by combining amounts of above ingredients to taste. Some prefer the sauce somewhat sweet, while others like it sharp.

Egg Rolls I

CHINA *Yield 8 egg rolls*

Dough

½ **pound flour**
1 ½ **cups water**
Salt
1 ½ **teaspoons peanut oil**

Egg rolls II

Filling

½ pound green cabbage
1 leek
1 medium onion
1 8-ounce can bamboo shoots
1 4-ounce can mushrooms
4 tablespoons oil
4 ounces ground beef
4 ounces ground pork
2 cups fresh bean sprouts
4 tablespoons soy sauce
2 tablespoons sherry
Salt
Cayenne pepper

Peanut oil
Beaten egg yolks
6 cups oil for deep frying

Place flour in a bowl. Slowly stir in water, making sure that you always stir in the same direction. Add salt and 1½ teaspoons peanut oil and cover bowl. Let rest for 30 minutes.

Meanwhile, prepare filling. Wash and drain cabbage and leek and cut into thin slices. Chop onion. Drain bamboo shoots and cut into fine strips. Drain and coarsely chop mushrooms. In skillet, heat 4 tablespoons oil and add ground meats; cook until lightly browned. Stir in cabbage, leek, onion, and bamboo shoots. Cook for 5 minutes. Add mushrooms and bean sprouts and cook for an additional 2 minutes. Season to taste with soy sauce, sherry, salt, and cayenne pepper. Remove from heat and set aside.

Brush an 8-inch skillet with peanut oil. Pour in ⅛ of the egg-roll dough; tilt skillet to spread batter evenly. Over low heat, cook until set. Turn out onto moistened paper toweling. Cover with another moistened paper towel. Continue until all dough is used up.

Cut egg-roll rounds into 6-inch squares. Divide filling among the 8 egg rolls. Fold two opposite corners of egg rolls toward the middle. Starting with corner closest to you, roll up egg roll. Brush inside of opposite corner with small amount of

beaten egg yolk; seal egg roll. Heat oil in deep frypan. Add rolls and fry until done. Put paper toweling on cake rack; place egg rolls on rack and drain. Keep them warm and serve on preheated platter.

Egg Rolls II

CHINA *Yield about 2 dozen*

You can purchase ready-made egg-roll skins in supermarkets or Oriental specialty stores.

Dipping batter

1 egg
1 tablespoon cornstarch
1½ teaspoons baking powder
1 cup flour
1 tablespoon sugar
2 teaspoons salt
1¼ cups milk
1¾ cups water

Filling

1 cup bamboo shoots, shredded
½ pound bean sprouts, rinsed and well drained
1½ cups water chestnuts, shredded
3½ cups cooked chicken, slivered
¾ cup barbecued pork, slivered
¾ cup fresh parsley, finely chopped
1 cup fresh mushrooms, chopped
½ cup scallion, finely chopped
Salt and freshly ground black pepper to taste
Oil

Beat egg slightly. Sift together dry ingredients. Mix with egg. Slowly stir in milk and water and stir until smooth.

All filling ingredients should be cut finely. Mix filling ingredients (except oil) together and sauté in a little oil for about 10 minutes, stirring occasionally. Let mixture cool. Spoon about ½ cup onto egg-roll skin. Fold like an envelope. Dip in batter and fry in hot oil for about 5 minutes, turning carefully to brown both sides. Serve with Chinese mustard and/or duck sauce.

Shrimp Hors d'Oeuvres

CHINA	*Yield 6 servings*

6 tablespoons oil
1 pound small cleaned shrimp
Salt to taste
1 tablespoon sherry, or to taste

Heat oil; stir-fry shrimp just until color changes. Drain; sprinkle with salt and sherry.

Shrimp Toast

CHINA	*Yield 16 shrimp toasts*

¼ teaspoon sesame-seed oil
¼ teaspoon soy sauce
Pinch of white pepper
Pinch of salt
½ pound uncooked shrimp, cleaned, deveined
8 slices 2-day-old white bread, sliced thin
1 quart vegetable oil

Add sesame-seed oil, soy sauce, pepper, and salt to shrimp; mix thoroughly. Cut 32 rounds from bread slices. Spread shrimp mixture evenly on 16 rounds. Top each circle with another round; press edges together.

Heat oil in deep pot until very hot. Drop each round into oil; turn to brown evenly. Takes approximately 2 minutes. Drain on paper toweling.

Pineapple Cocktail Barbecue

CHINA	*Yield 6 to 8 servings*

1 can pineapple chunks (approximately 16 ounces), drained; reserve syrup
1 jar red-cherry preserves or jelly (approximately 10 ounces)
¼ cup catsup
3 whole cloves
1 stick cinnamon
1 teaspoon salt
1 teaspoon cornstarch
2 teaspoons water
1 tablespoon soy sauce
Meatballs, cooked, made from 1 pound ground chuck

Combine pineapple syrup with cherry preserves, catsup, cloves, cinnamon, and salt. Heat to boiling. Dissolve cornstarch in water until it makes smooth paste. Stir into boiling sauce. Cook until cornstarch thickens and turns clear.

Add pineapple chunks and soy sauce. Pour over meatballs. Keep warm in chafing dish. Serve with toothpicks.

Salted Chicken

CHINA	*Yield 12 servings*

1½ tablespoons salt
1 tablespoon rice wine
2 small slices gingerroot
2 scallions, cut into 1-inch pieces
1 whole chicken, 2½ to 3 pounds
Cold water
1 cup chicken stock
¼ teaspoon salt
1 tablespoon sesame oil

15

Mix together salt, wine, gingerroot, and scallions. Rub chicken with mixture; let stand 30 minutes. Place chicken in pot; cover with cold water. Bring to boil; simmer 40 minutes over medium heat. Remove from pot; chill. Remove skin; cut into pieces approximately 2 inches long and 1 inch wide.

Mix together stock, ¼ teaspoon salt, and sesame oil. Pour over chicken. Garnish with additional scallions if desired.

Chicken Wings in Oyster Sauce

CHINA   *Yield 4 servings*

3 tablespoons oil
2 cloves garlic, crushed
8 chicken wings, each divided into 3 parts
2 tablespoons soy sauce
3 tablespoons oyster sauce
1 tablespoon sugar
½ cup water

Preheat wok. Goat bottom and sides with oil. Rub bottom and sides with garlic; discard garlic. Add middles and tips of wings; brown on both sides. Add rest of wing pieces; brown.

Mix together soy sauce and oyster sauce; stir into chicken. Stir in sugar and water. Cover wok; cook over medium-low heat for 15 minutes.

Sweet-and-Sour Spareribs

CHINA   *Yield 24 to 28 pieces*

5 tablespoons soy sauce
2 tablespoons sherry
2 cloves garlic, minced
1 teaspoon sugar
1½ pounds spareribs
1 tablespoon cornstarch
2 tablespoons sugar
1 tablespoon vinegar
1 teaspoon cornstarch
Oil for cooking

Combine 3 tablespoons soy sauce, 1 tablespoon sherry, garlic, and 1 teaspoon sugar; blend well.

Have butcher cut crosswise through bones of spareribs at about 1- to 1½-inch intervals. Cut bones apart. Pour soy-sauce mixture over spareribs. Let stand at room temperature 1 hour; stir occasionally. Blend in 1 tablespoon cornstarch.

Blend together 2 tablespoons sugar, 2 tablespoons soy sauce, 1 tablespoon sherry, vinegar, and 1 teaspoon cornstarch together in saucepan. Cook over medium heat, stirring constantly, until thickened. Set aside.

Heat approximately 3 inches oil in deep pot.

Drain marinade from spareribs. Add one portion of meat at a time to hot oil; cook until well browned. Drain on paper toweling. Place cooked spareribs into cooked sauce; coat well. Cover; chill. Serve spareribs at room temperature.

Abalone Appetizer

CHINA   *Yield 5 to 6 servings*

1 teaspoon fresh gingerroot, grated
1 tablespoon soy sauce
1 tablespoon sherry
1 can abalone, drained, cut into bite-size pieces

Mix together ginger, soy sauce, and sherry. Pour over abalone. Refrigerate several hours.

Cucumber Hors d'Oeuvres

CHINA	Yield 6 servings

2 tablespoons oil
3 small red chili peppers, seeded, cut into very
    thin slices
4 medium to large cucumbers, cut into 2-inch
    lengths, quartered, seeded
1 teaspoon soy sauce
2 tablespoons sugar
¼ teaspoon salt
1 tablespoon vinegar

Heat oil in skillet. Add chili peppers; stir-fry 4 seconds. Add cucumbers; stir-fry 30 seconds. Add soy sauce, sugar, and salt; stir until well blended. Refrigerate at least 24 hours; remove cucumbers from liquid. Sprinkle with vinegar.

Ground-Beef Filling for Egg Rolls

CHINA	Yield about 24 egg rolls

1 pound ground beef
¼ cup margarine
4 cups cabbage, very finely shredded
½ cup scallion, finely chopped
1 cup celery, finely chopped
2 cups fresh bean sprouts
¼ cup soy sauce
1 tablespoon sugar (or to taste)
Salt to taste
Freshly ground black pepper to taste

Brown beef in margarine until just browned. Add rest of ingredients; cook 5 minutes, stirring frequently. Adjust seasonings if necessary. Drain; cool. Use purchased egg-roll skins as a shortcut.

Water Chestnuts with Bacon

CHINA	Yield about 20

⅓ to ½ pound bacon
1 6-ounce can water chestnuts
1 tablespoon soy sauce
1 tablespoon dry sherry
Toothpicks

Wrap ½ slice bacon around each water chestnut; fasten with toothpick. Place water chestnuts in ovenproof dish; brush with mixture of soy sauce and sherry. Bake at 350°F 15 to 20 minutes.

Cocktail Kabobs

CHINA	Yield 40 to 50

1 15¼-ounce can pineapple chunks, drained
1-pound package brown-and-serve sausages,
    cooked according to package directions, cut
    into thirds
1 8-ounce can water chestnuts, halved
2 green peppers, cut into ¾-inch squares
¼ pound small mushrooms, stemmed
Reserved syrup from drained pineapple
4 tablespoons soy sauce
3 slices fresh gingerroot
3 tablespoons brown sugar
2 tablespoons dry sherry

Alternate pieces of pineapple, sausage, water chestnuts, green pepper, and mushrooms on toothpicks.

Combine remaining ingredients; heat in skillet. Add kabobs. Cover; simmer 10 minutes. Remove from skillet and serve warm.

Shrimp Wrapped in Bacon

JAPAN	*Yield 4 servings*

8 cleaned shrimp with tails intact
8 slices bacon

Wrap shrimp with bacon; fasten with toothpicks. Bake in 350°F oven for 15 to 20 minutes.

Simple Fish Appetizer

JAPAN	*Yield 5 to 6 servings*

1 6-ounce can tuna
1 teaspoon soy sauce (more, if desired)
2 tablespoons chopped onion

Drain tuna. Mix with soy sauce and chopped onion; spread on rice crackers (or another cracker of your choice).

Skewered Fish Meat

JAPAN	*Yield 3 servings*

6 pieces white fish meat, each about 2 ounces
Salt
7 ounces white miso (soybean paste)
½ cup rice wine or sherry
2 tablespoons sugar

Sprinkle fish meat lightly with salt; refrigerate for 12 hours.

Mix soybean paste, rice wine or sherry, and sugar together until well blended. Drain fish, place in mixture, and refrigerate for 24 hours.

Thread fish on skewers; broil in oven, on grill, or on a hibachi.

Fried Chicken Balls

JAPAN	*Yield 4 servings*

½ large onion, chopped
1 pound chicken, chopped finely
1 tablespoon sugar
1½ tablespoons mirin (sweet rice wine)
2 tablespoons soy sauce
1 egg
2 tablespoons oil
3½ tablespoons water
1½ tablespoons sherry

Soak chopped onion in water; squeeze out moisture. Combine chicken and onion with sugar, mirin (or sherry mixed with sugar: 1 part sugar to 2 parts sherry), 1 tablespoon soy sauce, and egg. Stir until thoroughly mixed. Roll into bite-size balls.

Heat oil in pan; brown meatballs on all sides. Combine water, sherry, and remaining 1 tablespoon soy sauce. Add to meat in pan; cook until liquid is almost evaporated.

Chicken Liver Teriyaki

JAPAN	

Chicken livers, as many as are needed
Equal amounts of soy sauce, sugar, and water
Soy sauce or mustard for dipping

Marinate livers in mixture of soy sauce, sugar, and water. Skewer the livers; place on hibachi or grill, turning while cooking. When done, dip livers into soy sauce or mustard and enjoy. Use approximately 4 livers per person.

Milk Soup

INDONESIA   *Yield 2 to 3 servings*

2 tablespoons butter or margarine
2 tablespoons chopped onions
1 teaspoon chopped garlic
1 bay leaf
Dash of ground coriander
1 teaspoon salt
2 cups chicken broth
1 small stalk Chinese cabbage, chopped
1 cup coconut milk

Melt butter in a saucepan; gently sauté the onions and garlic. Put in spices and chicken broth and bring to a boil. Add cabbage and reduce heat to medium. Cook a few minutes, until the cabbage is just tender. Then, put in the milk and stir constantly until soup comes to a boil once more. Serve at once.

Chicken Soup

INDONESIA   *Yield 6 to 8 servings*

3- to 4-pound chicken
2 quarts water
2 teaspoons salt
1 small onion, peeled and quartered
2 cloves garlic, peeled and finely sliced
1 tablespoon ginger powder
Dash of white pepper
7 ounces soybean paste
4 sticks celery, cut into ½-inch pieces
1 cup sherry
4 hard-boiled eggs, shelled and cut in half
Chopped chives for garnish

Wash chicken inside and out and dry with paper towels. In a soup pot, bring the water to a boil. Add salt. Add the chicken and simmer for an hour

Chicken soup

or until chicken is tender. Remove chicken from broth. Discard skin and bones of the chicken and cut meat into bite-size pieces. Set aside and keep warm.

Add onion, ginger, and pepper to broth. Cook over low heat for 15 minutes. In a small bowl, mix soybean paste, celery, and sherry.

Place chicken in preheated, individual soup dishes. Add some broth to each dish. Add a portion of the soybean-paste mixture to each dish. Top with half a hard-cooked egg. Garnish with chives and serve at once.

Curry Soup

INDONESIA   *Yield 2 to 3 servings*

1 teaspoon ground chestnuts or cashews
½ cup meat or chicken, cubed
2 tablespoons butter or margarine
¼ teaspoon curry powder
1 cup beef broth
½ cup potatoes, peeled and diced
½ cup green beans, sliced
½ cup carrots, diced
1 bay leaf
1 cup coconut milk
Salt to taste
1 tablespoon dried onion flakes, sautéed in
   2 teaspoons oil

Stir nuts and meat in the melted butter along with the curry powder. Slowly pour in the beef broth and bring to a boil. Put in the vegetables and the bay leaf and cover. Reduce heat to medium and cook about 10 minutes or until the vegetables are tender. Add the milk and extra salt if desired. Once again, bring the soup to a boil. Garnish with onion flakes and serve at once.

Beef Balls with Noodles

INDONESIA   *Yield 4 to 6 servings*

12 ounces egg noodles, parboiled and set aside
   to drain

Beef balls

2 onions, grated
2 cloves garlic, crushed
1 tablespoon oil or margarine
1½ pounds ground beef
4 slices slightly stale bread, diced
1 egg, beaten lightly
½ teaspoon nutmeg
1 teaspoon salt
¼ teaspoon freshly ground pepper

Broth

1 onion, peeled and thinly sliced
2 cloves garlic, crushed
1 tablespoon oil
4 cups chicken stock (canned will do)
1-inch piece green ginger, scraped and bruised
4 shallots or spring onions, sliced
4 stalks celery, sliced
4 cabbage leaves, finely shredded
Celery leaves or parsley for garnish

In a small skillet, lightly brown onions and garlic in the oil. Combine them in a large bowl with the rest of the beef balls ingredients in the order given. When completely blended, form into balls, making between 12 and 18, depending on the size. Set aside.

To make the broth, stir-fry onion and garlic in bottom of large saucepan. Add soup stock and ginger and bring to a boil. With a slotted spoon, lower meatballs into stock and allow to return to a boil. Reduce heat to medium and cook for 15 minutes or until meat is cooked through. Add the vegetables and cook 5 minutes more or just until they are slightly crunchy in texture.

Divide noodles into individual soup bowls. Put 2 or 3 meatballs on top, along with some of the vegetables. Fill to the top of the bowl with the broth. Garnish with celery leaves or parsley.

Noodles in Broth

INDONESIA	Yield 4 to 6 servings

6 ounces egg noodles, parboiled and set aside
  to drain
2 cloves garlic, thinly sliced
1 onion, peeled and thinly sliced
1 tablespoon oil or margarine
7 cups water
2 slices fresh ginger
1 pound chicken breasts
Salt and freshly ground pepper to taste
4 cabbage leaves, shredded
1 cup bean sprouts, cleaned
2 shallots or spring onions including green tops,
  cut in ½-inch pieces
¼ cup snipped celery tops
¼ cup fried onion flakes

Stir-fry garlic and onion slices in oil in the bottom of a deep saucepan. Add water, chicken breasts, and salt and pepper to taste. When this comes to a boil, reduce the heat and cook for 20 minutes or until the chicken is tender. Remove the chicken and allow to cool. When you can handle the chicken, remove bones and cut breast meat into strips. Set aside.

Add cabbage, bean sprouts, and shallots to the stock and simmer for 2 minutes. Put cut up chicken strips in and continue to simmer until chicken is hot. Adjust salt and pepper to taste.

Divide the noodles into individual soup bowls. Fill each bowl with piping hot soup stock and garnish with celery tops and onion flakes. Serve at once.

Prawn and Eggplant Soup

INDONESIA	Yield 4 servings

4 ounces fresh prawns, shelled, deveined, and
  chopped into small pieces
2 tablespoons peanut oil
1 medium onion, finely chopped
2 cloves garlic, finely chopped
2 fresh red chilies, seeded and chopped
1 ripe tomato, peeled and chopped
2 daun salam or curry leaves
2 cups chicken stock
1 medium eggplant
1 cup coconut milk
½ teaspoon brown sugar
1 teaspoon salt

In a large saucepan, fry onion, garlic, and chilies until onions are golden. Add tomato and daun salam leaves and sauté for 5 minutes. Mash the tomato to a pulp while frying. Add soup stock, bring to a boil, and then allow to simmer.

Peel and dice the eggplant and add to the simmering stock. Cook for 10 minutes or until eggplant is tender. Add the coconut milk, sugar, and salt. Stir continuously while all the ingredients heat through. Pour into bowls and serve with rice and curries.

Vegetable Soup

INDONESIA	Yield 2 to 3 servings

2 ears corn, husked and sliced from the cob
2 tablespoons onions, chopped
1 teaspoon chopped garlic, optional
2 tablespoons sugar
1 teaspoon salt
3 cups water

2 bouillon cubes, optional
4 ounces spinach

Put all ingredients except the spinach into a saucepan. Bring to a boil; reduce heat and simmer for 2 minutes. Add spinach and cook for 2 more minutes. Spoon into soup bowls.

Chicken Rice Soup

THAILAND *Yield 4 to 6 servings*

5 cups chicken stock
2 large boneless chicken breasts, skinned and cut into ½-inch cubes
¼ pound boneless pork loin, cut into ½-inch cubes
1½ cups rice, cooked
2 celery stalks, with leaves, cut into ½-inch lengths
2 scallions, chopped
Nam pla (fish sauce) to taste
Freshly ground black pepper
1 tablespoon vegetable oil
4 cloves garlic, peeled and finely chopped
¼ pound bacon, cut into ½-inch squares

Cream of chicken soup

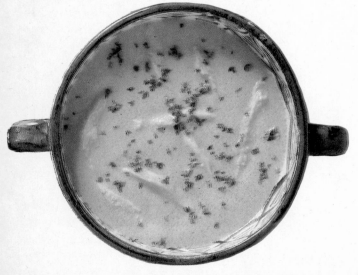

Add the chicken and pork to boiling stock; cook until meat turns white, at least 10 minutes. Add the rice and simmer for 5 minutes. Remove from heat. Add celery, scallions, nam pla, and pepper. Check the seasonings and add more if needed.

In a small skillet, fry garlic in oil until golden brown. Drain and set aside the garlic. Then fry the bacon until crisp.

Ladle the soup into individual bowls and garnish with garlic and bacon.

Pork and Chicken Soup

THAILAND *Yield 6 servings*

1 pound sweet pork (see Index), divided in 2 parts
6 cups water
2 chicken legs
1 teaspoon peppercorns
1 whole coriander plant, including root
½ teaspoon salt
5 dried Chinese mushrooms
3 ounces cellophane noodles
3 tablespoons chopped spring onions, including leaves
3 tablespoons chopped fresh coriander leaves
1 red chili, seeded and sliced, optional

Prepare pork; divide in half and set aside.

In a large saucepan, place water, chicken legs, peppercorns, well-washed coriander, and salt. After the water has come to a boil, reduce heat and simmer for 20 minutes until chicken is tender.

Cover the mushrooms in hot water while the chicken is cooking. Cut off stems and add them to the broth. Slice the caps thinly and set aside. Soak noodles in hot water for 15 minutes. Drain well and slice into 2-inch lengths.

Remove cooked chicken legs from the broth. Cut the meat into small pieces and discard the skin and bones. Cook the soup down to about 4 cups; strain.

Dice half the pork and set aside. (Use the other half as a side dish of sweet pork.) Add 2 cups of the pork stock to the chicken stock. Allow to come to a boil; then add noodles and mushrooms and simmer for about 10 minutes. Add the chicken, pork, spring onion, and coriander. Serve at once, garnished with chili slices.

Pork with Bamboo Shoots Soup

THAILAND	*Yield 4 to 6 servings*

2½ pounds bamboo shoots, finely sliced
Saltwater
2½ pounds pork, cut into 1½-inch squares
10 cloves garlic
Pepper
Coriander seeds
Enough chicken stock to cover meat and
    vegetables, about 4 to 5 cups
Nam pla
Palm sugar or light brown sugar to taste

Place bamboo shoots in salted water and boil until the shoots become light yellow. Drain and set aside. Prepare the pork in squares.

Pound the spices together with a mortar and pestle. Then mix thoroughly with the meat in a large saucepan. Add the soup stock, bamboo shoots, nam pla, and sugar. Cover the saucepan and cook the soup until the pork is quite tender; at least 1 hour. Serve piping hot.

Prawn Soup with Lily Buds

THAILAND	*Yield 6 to 8 servings*

3 ounces cellophane noodles
30 dried lily buds
8 dried Chinese mushrooms
4 or 5 cloves garlic, peeled
3 whole fresh coriander plants, including roots
1 pound small raw prawns, well washed and
    drained
3 tablespoons peanut oil
1 medium onion, peeled and sliced
8 cups water
6 spring onions, sliced diagonally
4 tablespoons fish sauce
1 tablespoon light soy sauce
1 teaspoon sugar
2 eggs

Soak noodles in a bowl with warm water. Soak the lily buds and dried mushrooms in a bowl of hot water for 30 minutes. After they have soaked, pinch off the ends of the lily buds. The Thais and Chinese tie a knot in each lily bud. You may prefer to cut them in two. Discard the stems of the mushrooms and thinly slice the caps. Cut noodles to about 2 inches long.

Place garlic and washed coriander in electric blender, reserving some coriander leaves for garnish. Add 2 tablespoons water and purée.

Shell and devein the prawns, saving the shells and heads. Heat 1 tablespoon oil in a large saucepan. Fry the shells and heads until the shells turn bright pink. Add water; cover and simmer for 20 minutes. Strain the stock into a large bowl and discard shells.

Heat remaining 2 tablespoons oil in clean saucepan. Fry onions until transparent; add garlic and coriander paste, stirring until oil separates from the mixture. Put in prawns and stir-fry for 3 minutes. Add the hot stock, lily buds, mushrooms, and noodles. Bring all to a boil and then lower heat; simmer for 5 minutes. Add spring onions, fish sauce, soy sauce, and sugar. Gradually pour beaten eggs into the boiling soup. Serve at once, garnished with coriander leaves.

Tapioca Soup

THAILAND *Yield 4 to 6 servings*

4½ cups chicken stock
¾ cup ground raw pork
Dash of nam pla or soy sauce to taste
½ cup small or instant tapioca
¾ cup canned or frozen crab meat, flaked
Pepper to taste
5 or 6 lettuce leaves, sliced in strips

Place soup stock and pork in a saucepan and bring to a boil. Season with nam pla to taste. At this point, add the tapioca and simmer for at least 15 minutes or until the pork is cooked through. (If you use instant tapioca, add for the last 5 minutes of this simmer.) Add the flaked crab meat and again bring to a boil. Add pepper and more nam pla if desired. Serve in individual bowls, each one garnished with shredded lettuce.

Transparent Vermicelli Soup

THAILAND *Yield 4 to 6 servings*

¼ pound wun sen, soaked in water for
    10 minutes
2 coriander roots, finely chopped
2 garlic cloves, peeled and chopped
1 teaspoon freshly ground black pepper
½ cup ground pork, firmly packed
5 cups water
3 large shrimp, shelled and deveined
⅓ cup dried shrimp, optional
1 ounce dried squid, sliced, optional
½ onion, peeled and sliced
2 tablespoons tree ears, soaked in warm water
    for 20 minutes

1 egg
Few scallions, finely chopped to garnish

Separate the wun sen and drain; then cut it into 2-inch lengths. Grind the coriander roots, garlic, and pepper to a fine paste. Continue pounding the mixture as you add the pork. When the paste is smooth, shape into small balls about ½ inch in diameter.

In a large saucepan, bring water to a boil; add pork balls and cook for 5 minutes. Add the shrimp. If any scum rises to the surface, spoon it off. Allow to simmer for 5 minutes, stirring constantly.

Add remaining ingredients, except for egg and scallions, and continue to simmer for 5 more minutes. Gradually stir in the egg, and then remove the soup from the heat. Garnish with scallions and serve at once.

Clear Soup

BURMA *Yield 4 servings*

Add cabbage, cauliflower, bean sprouts, or noodles to this if you choose. It is tasty clear or with vegetables.

6 cups water
¾ pound pork bones
5 peppercorns, crushed
3 cloves garlic, peeled and crushed
2 teaspoons soy sauce
Salt and pepper to taste
Finely chopped celery and/or
Finely chopped scallions plus tops for garnish

Measure the water into a large saucepan. Add pork bones, peppercorns, garlic, and soy sauce and bring to a boil. Then reduce the heat and simmer for about 30 minutes. Remove the bones from the soup. Season to taste. Serve in warmed soup bowls and garnish with celery and/or scallions.

Soup with Fresh Greens

BURMA	*Yield 4 servings*

This soup can be as varied as the greens you use in it. Any fresh green vegetable will do from watercress to spinach to mustard leaves. It's quick and easy too.

5 cups water
1 medium onion, peeled and sliced
3 cloves garlic, peeled and sliced
3 tablespoons pounded dried shrimp
½ teaspoon shrimp paste, optional
2 teaspoons soy sauce
1 teaspoon salt
½ pound green leaves, washed and drained

Bring the water, onion, and garlic to a boil. Reduce the heat and add shrimp, shrimp paste, soy sauce, and salt. Stir well to blend all the flavors. Then, put in the green leaves. Boil all together for just 5 minutes. Add extra seasonings if desired. Serve at once.

Radish and Fish Soup

BURMA	*Yield 4 servings*

A substitute for the long white radishes can be white turnips. Other substitutes can be spinach, eggplant, or okra.

½ pound white fish fillets, cut into chunks
1 teaspoon salt
½ teaspoon turmeric powder
2 tablespoons vegetable oil
1 medium onion, peeled and pounded or finely grated
3 cloves garlic, peeled and crushed
½-inch piece of fresh gingerroot, peeled and pounded
½ teaspoon chili powder
4 tomatoes, chopped
½ teaspoon shrimp paste, optional
1 tablespoon shrimp-flavored soy sauce
5 cups cold water
5 sprigs coriander leaves
3 tablespoons dried tamarind pulp
6 tablespoons hot water
¾ pound long white radishes including green tops, peeled and thinly sliced

Rub the fish with salt and turmeric and set aside.

Heat the vegetable oil and lightly brown onion, garlic, ginger, and chili powder, stirring well to mix the flavors. Add the fish and stir-fry until the pieces are well coated. Next add tomatoes, shrimp paste, and soy sauce. Add water and coriander and bring to a boil. Reduce heat to a simmer for 15 minutes.

In a bowl, pour the hot water over the tamarind pulp and knead to get the flavor. Strain off the liquid and discard the pulp. Add the tamarind liquid and radishes to the soup pot and simmer for 15 minutes more. Check the seasoning and add any if needed. Allow the soup to stand for at least 30 minutes.

When ready to serve, reheat just to the boiling point and serve at once.

Pumpkin or Squash Soup

BURMA	*Yield 4 to 6 servings*

1 cup uncooked shrimp, shelled and deveined
6 cups beef broth
1 large onion, finely chopped
2 teaspoons anchovy paste
2 cloves garlic, minced
4 cups pumpkin or winter squash, cut into small squares
¼ teaspoon ground dried chili peppers
Salt to taste

Dice the raw shrimp very finely. Put into saucepan with the beef broth, onion, anchovy paste, and garlic. Bring this mixture to a boil. Add the remaining ingredients. When mixture has again come to a boil, reduce heat and simmer for 15 minutes. Serve at once.

Cucumber and Mung Bean Soup

INDIA	*Yield 6 to 8 servings*

¾ cup yellow split mung beans, cleaned and washed
⅛ teaspoon turmeric
3 cups water
¾ cup grated potatoes
2 cups grated cucumbers (about 2 large cucumbers)
1½ teaspoons Kosher salt
4 tablespoons ghee or light oil
¾ teaspoon cumin seeds
¼ teaspoon black pepper
Juice of ½ lemon
2 tablespoons minced fresh coriander leaves

In a large saucepan, place beans, turmeric, and water. Bring to a boil; reduce heat and simmer for 30 minutes. Stir the soup from time to time. When cooking time is finished, transfer soup to a bowl and purée with electric beater or wire whisk. Add enough hot water to make 5 cups in all. Return to saucepan.

Bring the puree to a boil along with the potatoes, onions, cucumbers, and salt. Simmer about 5 minutes. In a small frying pan, heat the ghee. Put in the cumin and black pepper just until coated with ghee. Remove from heat. Pour this mixture on top of the soup. Add lemon juice and coriander leaves and serve at once.

Mulligatawny Soup

INDIA	*Yield 4 to 6 servings*

Mullaga means pepper and tanni means water and broth. The combination of flavors used here was first created about two centuries ago in India for the British.

3 to 4 tablespoons butter or oil
1 large onion, chopped
1 carrot, chopped
1 or 2 stalks celery, chopped
1 medium sour cooking apple
1 tablespoon curry powder or paste
1½ tablespoons flour
1 tablespoon tomato purée
4 to 5 cups stock
1 bay leaf
3 or 4 sprigs parsley
Pinch of thyme
Salt and pepper
2 tablespoons shredded coconut
1 teaspoon sugar
4 to 6 tablespoons cooked rice
2 teaspoons lemon juice
4 to 6 slices lemon
Paprika

Melt butter. Add onion, carrot, celery, and apple; stir well. Cook gently 5 to 6 minutes. Add curry; cook a few minutes. Add flour; mix well. Cook a few minutes to brown slightly. Add tomato purée and stock; blend well. Bring slowly to boil; reduce heat. Add herbs, seasoning, coconut, and sugar; simmer 30 to 45 minutes with lid on pan. Remove bay leaf. Blend soup in electric blender or put through fine food mill; return to pan. Add rice; adjust seasoning. Reheat; add lemon juice just before serving. (If preferred, rice can be served separately.) Serve hot with slice of lemon; sprinkle with paprika.

Lentil and Vegetable Soup

INDIA	*Yield 4 to 6 servings*

1 cup yellow split peas or red lentils, soaked overnight and drained

6 cups water

1 tablespoon tamarind pulp

1 cup hot water

1 pound mixed vegetables such as eggplant, carrots, and beans

2 tablespoons ghee or oil

1 tablespoon ground coriander

2 teaspoons ground cumin

½ teaspoon ground black pepper

½ teaspoon ground turmeric

1 peppercorn-size grain of asafetida

2 green chilies, seeded and sliced

2½ teaspoons salt

½ teaspoon black mustard seeds

1 small onion, finely sliced

Place lentils in 6 cups water and cook until soft. At the same time, soak tamarind pulp in hot water. When the water cools, squeeze the tamarind pulp and strain, keeping only the seasoned liquid. Add this to lentils. Prepare vegetables by cutting into small bite-size pieces.

In a small skillet, heat 1 tablespoon ghee. Stirring constantly, fry the ground spices and asafetida for 2 minutes. Put them in with the lentils, along with the chilies, salt, and vegetables.

Mulligatawny soup

27

This will cook for about 30 minutes or until vegetables are soft.

In the remaining tablespoon of ghee, fry the mustard seeds and onion slices until onion is brown. Add this to the soup mixture and simmer for 2 minutes more. Serve at once.

Lime Soup

INDIA *Yield 6 to 8 servings*

1 cinnamon stick, 3 inches long, broken into
   3 pieces
6 whole cloves
3 green cardamom pods
1 teaspoon black peppercorns
4 tablespoons ghee or oil
2 medium-size onions, peeled and chopped

5 medium-size potatoes, peeled and cubed
¼ teaspoon turmeric
6 cups homemade beef, vegetable, or chicken
   broth
¼ cup firmly packed fresh coriander leaves or
   2 tablespoons dried coriander leaves
Kosher salt to taste
⅔ cup coconut milk
⅓ cup heavy cream
Juice of 1 small lime or lemon

Tie cinnamon, cloves, cardamom, and peppercorns in a piece of cheesecloth and crush spices together with a wooden mallet.

Heat the ghee in a large saucepan; add onions and potatoes. Stir often and cook for 10 minutes. Add the turmeric, broth, and spice bag. When soup has come to a boil, reduce heat and simmer for about 30 minutes. Turn off heat and add coriander leaves and salt. Allow to cool. When broth is cool, remove spice bag and purée in a blender, food processor, or food mill.

Reheat the soup and add coconut milk and heavy cream. Simmer until all liquid is heated. When serving, garnish each individual soup bowl with a little lime juice on top.

Cream Chicken Soup

INDIA *Yield 4 to 6 servings*

3 to 4 pounds whole soup chicken
6 cups water
1 leek, cut into coarse pieces
2 dried pepper pods
10 peppercorns
Salt to taste
3 egg yolks
1 cup cream
1 tablespoon curry powder

Soup with vegetables and meat dumplings

Pinch of sugar
Chopped parsley for garnish

Wash chicken inside and out and drain. Place in a pot with cold water. Bring to a boil. Add pepper pods, peppercorns, and salt. After mixture comes to a boil, skim off the top. Boil until the chicken is tender, 30 minutes or more. Remove chicken from the pot and allow to cool. Strain the broth.

Remove the skin and loosen the meat from the bones. Cut white meat only into small pieces. (Reserve dark meat for another meal.) Keep white meat warm.

In a pot, stir egg yolks, cream, curry, and sugar. Place in a double boiler. Add 3 cups lukewarm chicken broth. Beat this mixture as it heats into a creamy mass. Pour into preheated soup dishes. Divide chicken into bowls and garnish with parsley.

Wonton soup

Pepper Water

INDIA   *Yield 4 to 6 servings*

Rasam, or pepper water, is frequently served in southern India. It can be a course by itself or an accompaniment to the meal.

1 tablespoon dried tamarind pulp
1 cup hot water
2 cloves garlic, peeled and sliced
1 peppercorn-size grain of asafetida
1 teaspoon ground black pepper
1 teaspoon ground cumin
4 cups cold water
2 teaspoons salt
2 tablespoons chopped fresh coriander leaves
2 teaspoons oil
1 teaspoon black mustard seeds
8 curry leaves

Allow tamarind pulp to soak in hot water for 10 minutes. Squeeze and strain, keeping only the seasoned liquid. Bring the tamarind liquid, garlic, asafetida, pepper, cumin, water, salt, and coriander leaves to a boil in a saucepan. Reduce heat and simmer for 10 minutes.

Heat the oil in a small frying pan; sauté mustard seeds and curry leaves until leaves are brown. Add this to the simmering soup. Serve at once.

Soup with Dumplings

PHILIPPINES   *Yield 6 to 8 servings*

Dough

3 cups flour
¼ teaspoon salt
3 egg yolks, beaten lightly
¼ cup water

Filling

1 cup ground pork (½ pound)
1 egg yolk
½ teaspoon salt
Dash of pepper

Broth

2 cloves garlic, peeled and crushed
½ medium onion, chopped
1½ cups shrimp, shelled and deveined
About 3 tablespoons lard or oil
Salt to taste
3 cups shrimp juice (pound heads of shrimp,
    squeezing out juice, adding enough water to
    make 3 cups)
1 chicken, cooked and cut into small pieces
3 quarts chicken broth
Salt and pepper to taste
2 tablespoons chopped parsley

To make the dough, combine the flour and salt; make a well in center of mixture and add the egg yolks. When well mixed, gradually add water. Knead until dough is elastic. Pat down very thin on a floured board. Cut into 3-inch triangles.

Mix all of the filling ingredients in a bowl in the order given. Spoon 1 teaspoon into the center of each triangle, folding the dough over the filling. Seal the edges of the dough and set aside.

To make the broth, melt lard and sauté garlic, onion, and shrimp until brown. Add salt and shrimp juice; bring to a boil for 1 minute. Add chicken and broth. When all has come to a boil again, drop in the prepared dumplings. Check seasonings, adding salt and pepper if needed. Lower heat and allow to simmer for 20 minutes. Add more pepper if desired. Dish into soup bowls and garnish with chopped parsley.

Sour Soup of Beef

PHILIPPINES   *Yield 6 to 8 servings*

1 pound shank beef
1 pound soup bones
8 ounces pork chop with fat removed
Water to cover the meat and bones
1 medium onion, peeled and sliced
2 underripe tomatoes, sliced
2 teaspoons salt

Celery soup

1 tablespoon dried tamarind pulp
1 cup boiling water
1 large sweet potato, peeled and diced
1 giant white radish, sliced
2 cups shredded greens (such as spinach)
Fish sauce to taste
Lime or lemon wedges

Cover the beef, bones, and pork with water in a large soup pot. Add onions, tomatoes, and salt. After this has come to a boil, cover and reduce heat to a simmer. Cook until the meat is tender. Lift out the meat and set aside to cool.

While this is cooking, pour boiling water over tamarind pulp. When cool, squeeze to dissolve the pulp and strain into the simmering soup. Discard the seeds and fiber of tamarind.

Thinly slice the pork and dice the beef. Remove and discard the bones from the broth. Return the meat to the soup, adding the sweet potatoes and radish. When the sweet potato is almost soft, put in the greens and season the soup to taste with fish sauce. Simmer for 5 minutes more or until the leaves are soft. Garnish each soup bowl with a wedge of lemon or lime.

Egg Drop Soup

CHINA   *Yield 4 servings*

4 cups chicken broth, homemade or canned
1 tablespoon cornstarch
¼ cup cold water
1 tablespoon soy sauce
Pinch of grated fresh gingerroot, or a sprinkle of powdered ginger
Few sprinkles freshly ground pepper
2 eggs, slightly beaten
1 tablespoon fresh parsley, coarsely chopped

Garnish

A few cooked pea pods, or a small amount chopped scallions

Bring chicken broth to a boil. Dissolve cornstarch in water, stir into broth, and bring to a boil again. Add soy sauce, ginger, and pepper. Holding eggs above soup, slowly pour them into soup in a slow steady stream while whisking eggs into soup to form long threads. Turn off heat, add parsley, and garnish soup with pea pods or chopped scallions. If desired, warm chow mein noodles can be served with this soup.

Soup with Vegetables and Meat Dumplings

CHINA   *Yield 4 to 6 servings*

Meat dumplings

2 slices bread
½ pound lean ground beef
Salt
White pepper
5 cups beef bouillon

Soup

¾ head savoy cabbage (green cabbage can be substituted), sliced
1 leek, sliced
2 ounces fresh mushrooms, sliced
1 celery stalk, sliced
1 tablespoon oil
1 small onion, chopped
2 ounces frozen peas
4 ounces egg noodles
Salt
White pepper
1 tablespoon soy sauce
3 tablespoons sherry

Soak bread in small amount of cold water. Squeeze as dry as possible and mix with ground beef and salt and pepper to taste. Bring bouillon to a boil. Using 1 teaspoon of meat mixture, form little dumplings and drop into boiling broth. Reduce heat and simmer for 10 minutes.

For soup, slice cabbage, leek, mushrooms, and celery. Heat oil in a large saucepan. Add onion and cook until golden. Add sliced vegetables and cook for 5 minutes. Remove dumplings from beef broth with a slotted spoon, drain on paper toweling, and keep warm. Strain broth and add to vegetables. Add peas and noodles and simmer for 15 minutes. Return dumplings to soup. Season with salt, pepper, soy sauce, and sherry. Serve immediately.

Egg-Flower Soup

CHINA	Yield 4 servings

4 cups chicken broth
½ medium onion, chopped
½ cup celery, sliced
Pinch of salt
1 egg, beaten
½ cup spinach, chopped

Place chicken broth in pot and bring to boil. Add onion, celery, and salt. Bring to boil again. Stir in beaten egg. Add spinach and let simmer for 1 minute.

Black-Mushroom Soup

CHINA	Yield 8 servings

¼ cup dried black mushrooms
1 clove garlic, crushed
1 tablespoon sesame oil
8 cups rich chicken broth
1 piece of gingerroot, size of hazelnut
2½ tablespoons soy sauce
½ cup cooked chicken, finely diced
½ cup cooked ham, finely diced

½ cup bamboo shoots, diced
½ cup scallions, finely chopped

Soak mushrooms in warm water until soft and spongy, about 10 minutes. Squeeze out liquid and chop very fine. Crush garlic and sauté in oil for 2 or 3 seconds; remove from oil and set aside. Sauté the mushrooms in the same pan for about 5 minutes.

In soup kettle, bring chicken broth to boil. Add mushrooms, garlic, ginger, and soy sauce. Simmer about 4 hours. Strain the broth and add chicken, ham, bamboo shoots, and scallions. Simmer until heated through.

Sharks'-Fin Soup

CHINA	Yield about 8 servings

¾ pound dried sharks' fins
1 tablespoon oil
2 tablespoons fresh gingerroot, sliced
¼ cup scallions, sliced
1 tablespoon sherry
3 quarts chicken broth, divided
2 tablespoons cornstarch
1 teaspoon soy sauce
¼ cup water
½ pound crab meat

Wash sharks' fins and cover with cold water. Drain, cover with fresh water, and boil 3 hours. Drain, add fresh water, and boil again for 3 hours. Drain and let dry.

Heat oil in large saucepan. Sauté the ginger and scallions for 3 minutes. Add the sherry, 1 quart of the chicken broth, and the sharks' fins. Cook over medium-high heat for 15 minutes. Drain off any remaining liquid. Add the remaining broth; bring to a boil. Mix together the cornstarch, soy sauce, and water. Slowly stir into the soup. Stir in the crab meat. Heat through.

Crab Soup

CHINA	*Yield 4 to 6 servings*

2 tablespoons oil
½ pound crab meat
¼ teaspoon salt
2 medium tomatoes, chopped coarsely
1½ teaspoons fresh gingerroot, chopped
5 cups chicken broth
2 eggs, beaten
1½ tablespoons vinegar
1½ tablespoons sherry
1½ tablespoons soy sauce
3 scallions, sliced

In large pot, heat oil. Sauté crab meat, salt, tomatoes, and ginger for 5 minutes. Add chicken broth and cook over low heat 10 minutes. Beat eggs, and add vinegar, sherry, and soy sauce. Pour into the soup slowly. Stir in the scallions and let soup simmer for about 3 minutes.

Wonton Soup

CHINA	*Yield 6 servings*

Dough for dumplings

4 ounces flour
Salt
1 tablespoon milk
2 tablespoons oil
1 small egg

Filling

4 ounces fresh spinach, chopped
4 ounces ground pork
½ tablespoon soy sauce
⅛ teaspoon powdered ginger

Soup

5 cups chicken broth
2 tablespoons chopped chives

In bowl, stir together flour and salt. Add milk, oil, and egg. Knead dough until it is smooth. On a floured board, roll out dough until it is paper thin. Cut into 3-inch squares. Cover with a kitchen towel while you prepare the filling.

Thoroughly wash spinach; remove coarse stems. Place in bowl and barely cover with boiling water; let stand for 3 minutes. Drain well and coarsely chop. Add ground pork, soy sauce, and ginger. Blend thoroughly. Place 1 teaspoon of filling on each dough square, giving filling a lengthy shape. Fold over dough from one side and roll up jelly-roll fashion. Press ends of roll together to seal.

Bring chicken broth to a boil. Add wontons and simmer over low heat for 20 minutes. Spoon soup into bowls. Garnish with chopped chives.

Hot-and-Sour Soup

CHINA	*Yield 5 to 6 servings*

¼ cup cloud ears
¼ cup golden needles
¼ pound pork, shredded into 1½-inch-long strips
3 tablespoons cornstarch
2 teaspoons sherry
½ cup water
3 tablespoons white-wine vinegar (or to taste)
White pepper to taste
½ teaspoon hot oil
2 teaspoons sesame-seed oil
4 cups chicken stock
Salt to taste
1 tablespoon soy sauce
2 bean curds, each cut into 8 pieces
1 egg, beaten
2 scallions, chopped

Soak cloud ears and golden needles in hot water about 15 minutes or until noticeably increased in size; drain. Shred cloud ears. Cut golden needles in half. Combine pork with 1 tablespoon cornstarch and sherry.

Mix 2 tablespoons cornstarch with water; set aside.

Combine vinegar, pepper, hot oil, and sesame oil in bowl; set aside.

Bring chicken stock, salt, and soy sauce to boil in large soup pot. Add pork; boil 1 minute. Add cloud ears, golden needles, and bean curds; boil 1 minute. Add cornstarch mixture; stir until thickened. Lower heat. Add vinegar mixture. Taste; adjust seasoning if necessary. Slowly stir in egg. Garnish with scallions.

Clam Soup

CHINA	*Yield 5 to 6 servings*

2 cups chicken broth
2 cups clam juice
2 cups minced clams
1 small onion, minced
2 tablespoons fresh parsley, minced
2 tablespoons soy sauce
1 tablespoon sherry

In large saucepan, combine chicken broth and clam juice. Add clams and onion and bring to a boil. Simmer for 10 minutes. Add parsley, soy sauce, and sherry and heat through.

Celery Soup

CHINA	*Yield 4 servings*

1 heaping tablespoon dried Chinese mushrooms
2 small celeriac roots, with green tops (celery stalks may be substituted)

4 tablespoons oil
½ pound pork shoulder, cut into 1½-inch-long, ½-inch-thick strips
2 small onions, minced
1 clove garlic, minced
3 cups hot chicken broth, from cubes or homemade
2 quarts salted water
1 ounce Chinese transparent noodles
2 tablespoons soy sauce
⅛ teaspoon ground ginger

Soak mushrooms in cold water 30 minutes.

Cut off celeriac tops; set aside. Brush celeriac roots under running cold water. Peel; cut into ½-inch cubes. Heat oil in saucepan. Add pork; brown on all sides, stirring constantly, about 3 minutes. Add onions, garlic, and celeriac root; cook 5 minutes. Drain mushrooms; cut in halves, or quarters if very large. Add to saucepan. Pour in broth. Cover; simmer over low heat 25 minutes.

Meanwhile, bring salted water to boil in another saucepan. Add noodles. Remove from heat immediately; let stand 5 minutes. Drain noodles. Five minutes before end of cooking time of soup, add coarsely chopped celeriac tops. Season to taste with soy sauce and ground ginger. Place noodles in soup tureen or 4 individual Chinese soup bowls. Pour soup over noodles. Serve immediately.

Chicken Vegetable Soup

CHINA	*Yield 4 to 6 servings*

6 cups chicken broth
½ cup bean sprouts
¼ cup water chestnuts, thinly sliced
1 scallion, minced
½ cup bok choy, sliced (use leafy part also)
3 Chinese mushrooms, soaked and drained and sliced

½ cup snow pea pods
½ cup cooked, diced chicken
2 teaspoons soy sauce
1 tablespoon sherry
Pepper to taste

Bring chicken broth to boil in soup pot. Add vegetables and chicken and simmer about 1 minute. Add soy sauce and sherry. Add pepper to taste. If desired, cellophane noodles or very fine egg noodles may be added.

Chrysanthemum Soup

INDOCHINA   *Yield 4 servings*

Use chrysanthemum choy, a cultivated, edible form of the flower, available in Oriental groceries.

½ cup ground pork
Freshly ground black pepper to taste
2 tablespoons plus 1 teaspoon fish sauce
1 shallot, peeled and finely chopped
6 cups chicken stock
1 pound chrysanthemum choy
2 scallions, cut into 2-inch lengths

In a bowl, mix the pork, pepper, 1 teaspoon fish sauce, and shallot. Allow to stand for about 15 minutes. Take 1 teaspoon of meat mixture and shape into a small ball. Continue until all of meat is used and rolled.

Bring the soup stock to a boil and add the pork balls. Cook for 12 minutes. Put in remaining fish sauce and black pepper to taste.

Line a warmed soup tureen with chrysanthemum choy and scallions. Over this, pour the hot stock and the meatballs. Rice and fish sauce make a nice accompaniment for this soup.

Melon and Dried Shrimp Soup

INDOCHINA   *Yield 4 to 6 servings*

½ cup dried shrimps
6 dried Chinese mushrooms
1 pound melon (any variety) or cucumbers
8 cups chicken stock
1 to 2 tablespoons fish sauce
6 thin slices fresh ginger
2 tablespoons Chinese wine or dry sherry

Soak dried shrimps in water overnight. Drain.

Soak mushrooms in hot water for 30 minutes. Discard the stems and slice the caps finely.

Peel the melon and scrape out the center portion with seeds. Cut into bite-size pieces.

In a saucepan, place stock, fish sauce, ginger, mushrooms, and dried shrimp. Bring all to a boil and then reduce heat. Simmer for 30 minutes. Remove and discard ginger slices. Add the melon and simmer for 5 minutes more. Then, add the wine and stir once. Dish into individual serving bowls.

Duck Soup

INDOCHINA   *Yield 8 servings*

1 3- to 5-pound duck
1 tablespoon salt
¼ teaspoon freshly ground black pepper
5 shallots, peeled and crushed
5 cups water
1 cup dried bamboo shoot, soaked in hot water for 2 hours
1 lump rock sugar
¼ cup fish sauce
½ pound medium rice vermicelli
1 tablespoon chopped scallion, green parts only

1 tablespoon chopped coriander leaves
Nuoc Cham (see Index)

Rub the duck with salt, pepper, and crushed shallots. Set aside for at least 1 hour.

Bring water to a boil in a large saucepan. Add the duck and prepared bamboo shoot. Return to boil and then simmer for 15 minutes. Skim off any scum that may form. Then, add the rock sugar; cover and simmer for 1 hour.

Next, add the fish sauce and simmer covered for another 30 minutes or until bamboo shoot is tender.

Cook the rice vermicelli in another pan according to package directions for just 5 minutes. Drain and rinse. Remove the duck from the soup and cut into 8 pieces. Divide the vermicelli into 8 soup bowls and put a piece of duck on top. Cover with the hot soup. Garnish with scallion and coriander leaves and serve with Nuoc Cham.

Pork and Lotus Root Soup

INDOCHINA   *Yield 4 servings*

1 pound lean pork ribs, cut into short lengths
1 pound fresh lotus root or 8 slices canned lotus root
3 spring onions, sliced, including greens
½ teaspoon salt
6 cups water
1 to 2 tablespoons fish sauce

Peel fresh lotus root and cut into slices. Along with prepared spring onions, place lotus root in saucepan with salt, water, and pork ribs. Bring to a boil. Then cover the pan, reduce heat, and simmer for at least 1½ hours. Just before serving, add fish sauce to taste. Serve with hot white rice as an accompaniment.

Cold Noodle Soup

KOREA   *Yield 4 to 6 servings*

1 pound fresh wheat noodles
Boiling water
½ pound cooked beef brisket or top round
4 cups chicken stock
8 whole black peppercorns
2-inch piece of fresh gingerroot, peeled
1 to 2 teaspoons salt
1 teaspoon soy sauce
4 dried chilies
24 cucumber slices
1 large, hard pear, peeled, cored, and thinly sliced
3 hard-cooked eggs, shelled and cut in half lengthwise
Prepared mustard and vinegar to taste

Cook noodles in boiling water for 5 minutes. Drain and set aside to cool.

Slice the meat into strips about 2 inches long by ½ inch wide.

Place all ingredients in a saucepan except the noodles. Reduce heat after mixture has come to a boil and simmer for 5 minutes. Allow to get cold; remove peppercorns, ginger, and chilies.

Divide noodles into individual serving bowls. Divide cucumber and pear slices as well, alternating the slices in layers on top of the noodles. Place a half egg on top of each bowl. Spoon the cold soup over all that is in the bowl. Top with mustard and vinegar. This soup is served cold.

Oxtail Soup

KOREA   *Yield 6 to 8 servings*

1 oxtail, cut into 8 pieces
8 cups water
2 slices fresh ginger
1 teaspoon salt

Dipping Sauce

3 tablespoons light soy sauce
1 tablespoon sesame oil
1 tablespoon toasted crushed sesame seeds
¼ teaspoon ground black pepper
3 tablespoons spring onions, finely chopped
3 teaspoons garlic, finely chopped
1 teaspoon ginger, finely chopped

Put oxtail, water, 2 slices ginger, and 1 teaspoon salt into a saucepan and bring to a boil. Reduce heat and simmer for about 2 hours or until the meat is tender to the fork. Lift off any froth or scum that forms during the cooking. Remove oxtail and cut meat from the bones and into bite-size pieces; return meat to broth.

Combine the sauce ingredients in a bowl; mix well until all flavors blend. Serve dipping sauce with the soup.

Soup of Soybean Sprouts

KOREA   *Yield 4 to 6 servings*

1 pound soybean sprouts, washed, drained, and tails pinched off
1 pound lean steak, cut into thin strips
1 tablespoon soy sauce
1 tablespoon sesame oil
¼ teaspoon ground black pepper
2 cloves garlic, peeled and crushed
8 cups water
Finely chopped green leaves of 2 spring onions

Prepare bean sprouts, chopping them if they are too long. Marinate the meat in soy sauce, sesame-seed oil, pepper, and garlic for 30 minutes. Heat wok or large saucepan and stir-fry beef until it browns nicely. Add water and bean sprouts and bring to a boil. Cover and simmer for 30 minutes. Remove from heat and add onion leaves. Let stand covered for 5 minutes. Adjust seasoning with soy sauce and salt if desired and serve at once.

Spiced Fish Soup

KOREA   *Yield 4 servings*

If you don't like food spicy and hot, skip this one.

1½ pound cod fillets, skinned and cut into large chunks
3 cups water
2 tablespoons vegetable oil
1 medium onion, peeled and finely chopped
2 tablespoons scallions, chopped
2 teaspoons garlic, crushed
1 teaspoon fresh gingerroot, crushed
2 to 6 teaspoons chili powder, according to taste
2 to 3 teaspoons salt
1 cup zucchini, thinly sliced
1 medium green pepper, cored, seeded, and finely sliced

Cover cod chunks with water and bring to a boil. Lower the heat and simmer for 5 minutes. Set aside.

In a medium-size skillet, heat the oil. Put in all ingredients except the zucchini and green pepper. Stir-fry for 1 minute. Add the zucchini and pepper and continue to stir-fry for 1 minute more. Place this mixture in the saucepan with the fish and simmer gently until well heated. Serve at once.

Coconut Milk Soup

MALAYSIA   *Yield 4 to 6 servings*

2 cups thin coconut milk
2 medium onions, peeled and sliced

6 curry leaves
2 fresh red or green chilies, seeded
½ teaspoon ground turmeric
1½ teaspoons salt
2 tablespoons prawn powder
1½ cups thick coconut milk
2 tablespoons lemon juice

Place coconut milk, onions, curry leaves, chilies, and seasonings in a large saucepan. Bring to a boil and then simmer for 15 minutes. Add thick coconut milk, stirring constantly with a wooden spoon. When all is heated, remove from burner. Add lemon juice and stir to blend. Spoon over boiled rice and serve with a dry curry.

Spiced Chicken Soup

MALAYSIA　　　　　　　*Yield 4 to 6 servings*

6¼ cups water
1 small chicken, quartered
4 jumbo shrimp, cleaned, deveined, and cut in half
Salt and pepper to taste
2 kemiri nuts, chopped
4 shallots, peeled and chopped
2 garlic cloves, peeled and chopped
1 teaspoon ginger powder
Pinch of turmeric powder
Pinch of chili powder
Vegetable oil for frying
1 tablespoon light soy sauce
1¼ cups bean sprouts, cleaned
1 potato, peeled and sliced into very thin rounds
Lemon slices
Coriander leaves

Use a large saucepan and bring water to a boil. Put in chicken, shrimp, and salt and pepper to taste. When water has again come to a boil, reduce heat and simmer for 40 minutes. Remove chicken and shrimp from broth. Take meat from chicken bones and discard bones. Peel shrimp, discard heads, and cut shrimp into 4 or 5 pieces. Set aside.

Pound the kemiri, shallots, and garlic to a smooth paste. Mix in ginger, turmeric and chili powder.

In a wok or deep frying pan, heat about 2 tablespoons oil. Stir-fry the spice paste for a few seconds. Add 1 cup reserved liquid, soy sauce, chicken, and shrimp and allow to simmer for 10 minutes. Put in remaining broth and simmer for another 10 minutes. Add the bean sprouts and adjust seasoning to taste. Continue to simmer for 3 minutes.

Fry potato slices in a skillet until crisp on both sides. Divide potatoes equally into soup bowls. Spoon soup over the potatoes. Garnish with lemon slices and coriander if desired.

Lobster Soup

JAPAN　　　　　　　*Yield 4 servings*

6 ounces lobster meat
2 teaspoons salt
1½ teaspoons soy sauce
4½ cups dashi
2 medium cucumbers, sliced thin
8 dried mushrooms
4 pieces lemon rind

Mince the lobster meat, pour ½ teaspoon of the salt over it, and boil. Gradually add ¾ teaspoon of soy sauce and ¼ cup of dashi to the lobster.

Peel and slice the cucumbers. Boil the mushrooms in ¼ cup of dashi and ¾ teaspoon of salt. Into each of 4 bowls place pieces of boiled lobster, cucumbers, and mushrooms.

Heat together 4 cups of dashi, ¾ teaspoon of salt, and ¾ teaspoon of soy sauce; pour some into each bowl. Garnish lobster soup with floating lemon rind.

Meatball Soup

JAPAN	*Yield 4 servings*

½ pound ground beef or pork
2 eggs
1 tablespoon flour
2 teaspoons freshly grated ginger or 1 teaspoon
   ground ginger
5 cups beef or chicken stock
1 teaspoon soy sauce
Pinch of salt
3 carrots, parboiled and sliced ¼ inch thick
Very thin spaghetti, enough for 4 small
   servings, cooked and drained
4 sprigs of parsley

Mix together beef or pork, eggs, flour, and ginger. Set aside. Mix the stock with the soy sauce and salt. Bring to a boil. Add the carrots. Make very small meatballs from the meat mixture; drop them gently into the boiling soup, and boil gently for about 15 minutes.

Divide the spaghetti into 4 individual bowls; add the soup and meatballs. Garnish with parsley.

Clam Soup

JAPAN	*Yield 4 servings*

16 small clams
4 cups boiling water
½ teaspoon salt
¾ teaspoon rice wine or sherry
1 tablespoon soy sauce
Lemon slices for garnish

Thoroughly wash the clams. Put them into boiling water; boil them until the shells crack. Put in the salt, rice wine or sherry, and soy sauce. Serve the clam soup with a garnish of lemon slices.

Clear Soup

JAPAN	*Yield 4 servings*

This is a nice soup to start off with before enjoying a dinner of Sukiyaki or Tempura.

4 cups chicken broth
1 teaspoon soy sauce
1 teaspoon sugar
Pinch of salt
1 cup chicken, cubed
1 scallion, chopped fine
Few sprigs of parsley

Combine chicken broth, soy sauce, sugar, and salt; bring to a boil.

In each of 4 bowls put a few cubes of chicken, a few pieces of scallion, and parsley for garnish. Pour soup into bowls; serve without spoons.

Oyster Soup with Miso

JAPAN	*Yield 4 servings*

8 ounces shucked oysters
3½ ounces miso (soybean paste)
4 cups dashi
¾ teaspoon cornstarch
Cold water
½ teaspoon red pepper

Wash oysters; set aside. Blend the miso and dashi; bring to a boil. Gradually add oysters to the boiling mixture.

Mix the cornstarch with enough cold water to make a smooth paste; add this to the oyster mixture, stirring constantly. Simmer until done. Flavor with red pepper.

Miso Soup with Egg

JAPAN	*Yield 4 servings*

4 cups chicken broth
¼ cup white miso (soybean paste)
¼ teaspoon salt
1 egg, beaten
2 teaspoons sherry or sweet rice wine (sweet
    sake)
Lemon-peel twists

Bring broth, miso, and salt to a boil. While slowly mixing the soup, gradually pour in the egg. Remove from heat; stir in the sherry or sake. Place a twist of lemon peel in each bowl before adding soup.

Egg-Flower Soup with Water Chestnuts

JAPAN	*Yield 6 servings*

1 quart chicken broth
½ cup finely chopped water chestnuts
2 eggs, beaten
¼ teaspoon pepper

Bring chicken broth to a boil. Add water chestnuts, cover, and simmer for 4 minutes. Add beaten eggs slowly while stirring soup. Add pepper; stir through once.

Oyster Soup

JAPAN	*Yield 4 servings*

8 ounces shucked oysters
4 cups dashi
¾ teaspoon cornstarch
Small amount of cold water
½ teaspoon Tabasco

Wash the oysters. Add them to the boiling dashi; cook until the oysters are done. Mix the cornstarch with enough cold water to make a smooth paste; add to soup. Flavor with the Tabasco.

Baked Snapper

INDONESIA	*Yield 4 to 6 servings*

1 3- to 4-pound snapper
1 medium onion, peeled and chopped
2 cloves garlic, peeled
1 teaspoon fresh ginger, finely chopped
2 tablespoons tamarind liquid
1 tablespoon dark soy sauce
1 tablespoon oil
1 teaspoon salt
1 teaspoon ground turmeric
3 tablespoons fresh coriander leaves, finely
  chopped
Banana leaves or foil for wrapping

Wash the fish and pat dry with paper towels. Score the flesh diagonally on each side. Use a blender or food processor to mix onion, garlic, ginger, tamarind liquid, soy sauce, oil, salt, and turmeric. When blended smooth, rub into body of fish on both sides. Rub remaining mixture into body cavity for extra flavor. Lay fish on banana leaves in a baking dish and sprinkle with coriander. Fold leaves to cover fish and secure with skewers. If banana leaves are unavailable, use foil.

Bake at 375°F for 35 to 40 minutes or until the fish flakes when tested with a fork. Reseal the fish after testing and serve closed. When opened, it will have a delightful fragrance.

Fish Curry

INDONESIA	*Yield 4 to 6 servings*

2 pounds fish fillets
Juice of half a lemon
Sprinkle of salt
Flour for dredging
3 tablespoons oil
1 large onion, peeled and chopped
1 large apple, peeled, cored, and diced
4 tablespoons butter or margarine
1½ tablespoons curry powder
1 cup clear fish broth
2 tablespoons raisins

Wash the fillets, wipe dry, and put on a platter. Sprinkle with lemon juice and salt and dredge in flour. When fish is floured on both sides, heat oil and cook fillets in a skillet until they are golden brown on both sides. Set aside and keep warm.

Melt the butter in a small saucepan and cook onions and apples until onions are transparent. Add curry powder and fish broth and simmer until apples are soft. Return fish to skillet, add the broth, and simmer 10 minutes or until the fish is tender. Place in a serving dish and sprinkle with raisins. Serve hot.

Fish in Brown Bean Sauce with Vegetables

INDONESIA	*Yield 4 to 6 servings*

1½ pound fish steaks (any firm fish such as
  mackerel)
Salt
2 small onions
6 sweet chili peppers, seeded and cut in strips
½ cup fresh green beans, sliced diagonally
1 cup sliced, canned bamboo shoots
2 cloves garlic, peeled and finely chopped
1½ teaspoons fresh ginger, finely grated
2 tablespoons bean sauce (tauco)
4 tablespoons peanut oil

1 teaspoon dried shrimp paste, optional
1 tablespoon light soy sauce
⅔ cup water

Cut fish into serving pieces. Salt on both sides and set aside.

Peel onions. Cut one onion in 8 long sections. Then slice each section in half. Separate the layers. Set aside. Prepare peppers, beans, and bamboo shoots; set each aside separately. Chop remaining onion very fine and mix with garlic, ginger, and bean sauce; set this aside also.

Remove excess moisture from fish with paper towels. Brown both sides of each piece of fish in peanut oil on high heat. Set aside. To remaining fat, add onion, ginger, garlic, and bean sauce mixture. Stir constantly until onions are soft. Add shrimp paste and green beans and stir for 2 minutes. Add peppers and remaining onion and stir-fry for 1 minute more. Put in bamboo shoots, soy sauce, and water and stir well. Cover and reduce heat to simmer for 3 minutes. Then add the fish. When fish is heated through, serve at once. Delicious over white rice.

Fish in Coconut Milk and Spices

INDONESIA   *Yield 6 servings*

1½ pound fish steaks, 6 portions (tuna or
    mackerel)
Salt to taste
Juice of ½ lemon
2 onions, finely chopped
3 cloves garlic, peeled and crushed
2 teaspoons fresh ginger, finely grated
1 teaspoon ground turmeric
½ teaspoon dried shrimp paste
1 teaspoon sambal ulek or chili powder
1 stalk lemon grass or 2 strips lemon rind
1 teaspoon salt

1½ cups thin coconut milk
2 tablespoons fresh basil, chopped
¼ cup tamarind liquid
1 cup thick coconut milk

After washing, rub fish with salt and lemon juice and set aside.

In a saucepan, combine onions, garlic, ginger, turmeric, shrimp paste, chili, lemon rind, and 1 teaspoon salt with the thin coconut milk. Simmer uncovered until onions are quite soft and coconut milk has thickened. Next, add fish, basil, and tamarind liquid. Allow to simmer until fish is tender, 10 to 15 minutes. Stir in thick coconut milk, continuing to stir until all is hot through. Serve at once.

Fish with Peanut Sauce

INDONESIA   *Yield 4 to 6 servings*

2 large fish steaks
Lemon juice
Salt
Black pepper
Oil for frying
2 tablespoons light soy sauce
2 tablespoons peanut sauce (see Index)
½ cup thick coconut milk
1 tablespoon tamarind liquid or vinegar
1 tablespoon chopped fresh coriander leaves

Wash and dry fish steaks; cut into serving pieces. Rub each piece on both sides with lemon juice, salt, and pepper. Let sit for at least 15 minutes. Before frying fish, dry again with paper towels.

Heat oil and brown fish on both sides. Remove all but 1 tablespoon of oil. Mix the remaining liquid ingredients together and put into a pan. Place the fish over the sauce. Sprinkle coriander on top and cover. Simmer for 5 minutes more and serve at once.

Shrimp Rolls

THAILAND *Yield 4 to 6 servings*

2 bean-curd leaves
4 or 5 heaping tablespoons pork fat, finely
  diced
Boiling water
2 pounds whole raw shrimp, shelled, washed,
  and finely minced
3 cloves garlic, peeled and finely chopped
2 teaspoons salt
1 teaspoon ground pepper
4 tablespoons flour
2 eggs, beaten
Oil for deep frying

Pour water over bean-curd leaves and set aside to soften. Cover pork fat with boiling water; drain well and set aside.

Place prepared shrimp in a large bowl. Mix with garlic, adding salt, pepper, and flour. Add beaten eggs to this mixture. Add the prepared pork fat and mix again. Divide into 2 portions. Wrap each portion, like a sausage, in bean-curd leaves. Steam for 10 minutes and allow to cool.

When cool, cut into slices and fry in hot oil until brown and crisp on the outside. Although these shrimp rolls are good by themselves, they are even better when served with your favorite sweet-and-sour sauce.

Whole Fried Fish with Ginger Sauce

THAILAND *Yield 2 to 3 servings*

Ginger sauce

8 dried Chinese mushrooms
Hot water
6 tablespoons vinegar

Fish curry (Indonesia)

Curried shrimp (India)

6 tablespoons sugar
¾ cup water
2 tablespoons soy sauce
2 tablespoons spring onion, finely chopped
1 tablespoon cornstarch
1 tablespoon cold water
4 tablespoons red ginger, chopped

The fish

1 whole fish, about 2 pounds
Flour seasoned with salt
Oil for frying

Prepare the sauce first. Soak the mushrooms in hot water for 30 minutes. Trim off and discard tough stems. Finely slice mushroom caps. Boil the mushrooms, vinegar, sugar, water, and soy sauce together for 5 minutes. Add the spring onion. Blend cornstarch with cold water and gradually stir it into the sauce. When the sauce is clear and thick, remove it from the heat and add the red ginger. Simmer until fish is ready.

Keeping the head on the fish, trim fins and tail. Dry the cavity with paper towels. Slash the fish diagonally on both sides to form diamond shapes in the meat. Dip it in seasoned flour. Deep-fry in hot oil until fish is fork tender. Remove to a serving dish. Spoon ginger sauce over the fish.

If other dishes are served as a main course along with the fish, this will serve more than the 2 or 3 people listed above.

Fish in Red Sauce

THAILAND *Yield 4 to 6 servings*

1½ pounds fish fillets
4 tablespoons oil
2 onions, peeled and finely chopped
4 ripe tomatoes, chopped
2 tablespoons vinegar

Salt and pepper to taste
2 or 3 fresh chilies, seeded and chopped
3 to 4 tablespoons fresh coriander leaves,
    chopped

Fry onions in oil until they are golden. Add tomatoes, vinegar, salt, pepper, and chilies. Cover and simmer the sauce for 20 minutes until it is thick. Add fish and cover again. Cook for 10 to 15 minutes or until fish is fork tender. Garnish with coriander leaves and serve hot.

Fried Fish with Tamarind

THAILAND   *Yield 4 to 6 servings*

1 whole fish, about 2 pounds
Salt
Lard or oil for frying
3 cloves garlic, peeled and crushed

3 tablespoons soy sauce
1 tablespoon palm sugar
2 tablespoons fish sauce
4 tablespoons tamarind liquid
1 tablespoon fresh ginger, finely shredded
3 spring onions, cut into 1-inch pieces
3 tablespoons fresh coriander leaves, chopped
3 fresh red chilies, sliced

Have fish cleaned and scaled but keep the head on. Trim off fins and tail. Salt the cavity of the fish and then wipe it dry with paper towels. Heat lard and fry fish on both sides until brown and tender, 5 to 10 minutes. Drain on paper towels. Put on a warmed platter and cover with foil to keep warm.

Pour off excess fat, leaving about 1 tablespoon in pan. Lightly brown garlic. Add soy sauce, sugar, fish sauce, and tamarind liquid and bring to a boil. Now add ginger and spring onions. Cook for 1 minute, stirring. Spoon mixture over the fish. Garnish with coriander leaves and chilies and serve at once.

Lobster Indian-style

Shrimp balls

Shrimp Bombay

Fish in Coconut Cream

BURMA *Yield 4 to 6 servings*

1 teaspoon dried chili peppers
2 pounds fish fillets, cut into 1-inch squares
1 medium onion, peeled and chopped
1 heaping teaspoon powdered ginger
3 cloves garlic, peeled and minced
2 tablespoons lemon juice
1½ teaspoons salt
1 tablespoon cornstarch
½ teaspoon turmeric
1 medium onion, peeled and sliced
¾ cup oil
1 cup coconut cream

Pound the first five ingredients until very fine. You may use an electric blender or food processor. To this pounded mixture, add lemon juice, salt, cornstarch, and turmeric. When well mixed, shape into small balls and set aside.

Shrimp curry

Use a large skillet to brown onion slices in oil. Remove onions and set aside to drain on paper towels. Add fish balls to oil and cook until brown. Remove. Drain all but 1 tablespoon of oil from the skillet. Add coconut cream and bring to boiling point. Add the fish and reduce heat to simmer for 15 minutes. Place on warmed platter and garnish with browned onions.

Shrimp Curry with Tomatoes

BURMA   *Yield 4 servings*

1 ¼ pounds shrimp, shelled and deveined
2 tablespoons shrimp-flavored soy sauce
½ teaspoon salt
½ teaspoon turmeric powder
¼ cup vegetable oil
1 large onion, peeled and pounded
4 cloves garlic, peeled and crushed
½-inch piece fresh gingerroot, peeled and pounded
½ teaspoon chili powder
3 tomatoes, chopped
2 tablespoons chopped coriander leaves
¼ cup water
Coriander leaves for garnish

Marinate shrimp with soy sauce, salt, and turmeric. Marinate for at least 15 minutes.

Heat vegetable oil with onion, garlic, ginger, and chili powder until spices are fragrant but not dry. Add the shrimp, tomatoes, and coriander. Cover the pan and cook for 5 minutes. Gradually add the water, cover again, and simmer for 15 minutes. The shrimp should be nicely pink and the water absorbed. Place in a warm serving dish and garnish with coriander leaves.

Spiced Fried Fish with Onions

BURMA   *Yield 4 servings*

1 ½ pounds white fish fillets, cut into 4-inch squares
½ teaspoon turmeric powder
1 tablespoon shrimp-flavored soy sauce
2 tablespoons dried tamarind pulp
6 tablespoons hot water
7 tablespoons vegetable oil
2 medium onions, peeled and sliced
1 ½ teaspoons chili powder

Rub the fish lightly with turmeric and soy sauce. Set aside.

Prepare tamarind by covering pulp with hot water. Soak 10 minutes. Knead to extract flavor (squeeze until tamarind mixes with the water) and strain, discarding pulp.

Heat oil in large skillet. Fry onions over brisk heat until crisp and light brown. Remove onions from oil and drain on paper towels.

Pour off half the oil. Add chili powder, then fish, and fry quickly for 1 minute over high heat. Add tamarind liquid, cover, and simmer for 20 minutes. Check liquid as fish cooks and add more oil if needed to prevent sticking.

Transfer to a warm serving platter. Garnish with reserved onions and serve hot.

Steamed Fish Parcels

BURMA   *Yield 10 servings*

The native way to prepare the parcels is in banana leaves. If you can't obtain banana leaves, use aluminum foil as a substitute.

1 ¼ pounds thick white fish fillets (cod, haddock, etc.) cut into 3 x 1 ½ inch pieces

2 teaspoons salt
½ teaspoon turmeric powder
3 small onions, peeled
2 cloves garlic, peeled and crushed
1-inch piece of fresh gingerroot, peeled and
    pounded
½ teaspoon chili powder
1 tablespoon rice flour
⅔ cup coconut milk
2 teaspoons vegetable oil
½ teaspoon powdered lemon grass
Banana leaves or foil for wrapping
10 bok choy leaves, washed and cut in half

Rub the fish all over with 1 teaspoon salt and turmeric. Set aside.

Thinly slice 1 onion and pound or chop the remaining onions. Make a paste of the onions, remaining salt, garlic, ginger, chili powder, and rice flour. Add coconut milk to onion paste; add oil, lemon grass, and sliced onions. Mix well.

Cut foil or banana leaves, if available, into 10, 7-inch squares. Place a piece of bok choy on each piece of foil. Top with some of the paste mixture and 1 piece of fish. Add more paste to this and cover with another piece of bok choy. Fold foil over the filling to form a sealed parcel. Steam these parcels over boiling water for 20 minutes.

Baked Spiced Fish

INDIA   *Yield 4 servings*

1¼ cups unflavored yogurt
1 medium onion, peeled and chopped
1 garlic clove, peeled and chopped
1 tablespoon vinegar
1½ teaspoons cumin powder
Pinch of chili powder
1½ pounds fish fillets (sole or haddock,
    preferably)
Juice of 1 lemon

1 teaspoon salt
1 lemon slice
Coriander leaves

Mix yogurt, garlic, clove, vinegar, cumin, and chili powder together. An electric blender or food processor is good for this. Work the ingredients into a well-blended sauce.

Score the fish and place in an ovenproof dish. Dot with lemon juice and sprinkle with salt. Pour the prepared marinade over the fish, cover, and refrigerate overnight.

When ready to cook, cover fish with foil. Bake at 350°F for 30 minutes. Garnish with lemon slice and coriander.

Curried Shrimp

INDIA

1½ teaspoons vinegar
1 clove garlic, minced
1½ teaspoons ground coriander
½ teaspoon salt
½ teaspoon turmeric
¼ teaspoon cumin
¼ teaspoon dry mustard
⅛ teaspoon freshly ground pepper
⅛ teaspoon ground ginger
1 small piece stick cinnamon
Dash of cayenne pepper
1 cardamom seed
1 bay leaf
1 pound fresh, large shrimp, peeled, deveined
1½ tablespoons butter
½ cup onions, chopped
½ sweet green pepper, chopped
½ cup coconut milk
1 tablespoon all-purpose flour
1½ teaspoons lemon juice

Combine vinegar, garlic, coriander, salt, turmeric, cumin, mustard, pepper, ginger, cinnamon, cayenne pepper, cardamom, and bay leaf in medium-size bowl. Add shrimp; mix well. Cover; refrigerate 2 hours.

Melt butter in chafing dish over direct flame. Add onions and green pepper; cook, stirring occasionally, until tender. Remove cinnamon stick, cardamom seed, and bay leaf; add shrimp mixture. Cook, stirring occasionally, 10 minutes or until shrimp are tender.

Combine coconut milk and flour; stir into shrimp mixture. Cook about 3 minutes, until sauce thickens and comes to a boil. Stir in lemon juice. Serve with rice, toasted coconut, plumped raisins, peanuts, and chutney.

Fish Curry with Tomato

INDIA	Yield 4 servings

1 pound fish fillets or fish steak
2 tablespoons ghee or oil
1 medium onion peeled and finely chopped
2 cloves garlic, peeled and finely chopped
2 tablespoons fresh coriander leaves or mint, chopped
1 teaspoon ground cumin
1 teaspoon ground turmeric
½ to 1 teaspoon chili powder to taste
1 large, ripe tomato, chopped
1 teaspoon salt
1½ teaspoons garam masala

Wash fish in cold water and cut into serving pieces. Heat ghee in a saucepan. Fry onion, garlic, and coriander on a low setting until onion is soft and golden in color. Add cumin, turmeric, and chili powder and stir for 1 minute. Add tomato, salt, and garam masala. Continue stirring until tomato has cooked down to a pulp. Add lemon juice and more salt if needed. Place fish in frying pan, spooning sauce over it. Cover and simmer for 10 minutes. Especially good over cooked white rice.

Fish Fillets

INDIA	Yield 4 servings

1 pound fresh or frozen fish fillets
½ cup flour
2 teaspoons curry powder
¼ teaspoon salt
½ cup butter or margarine
½ cup chopped blanched almonds
Chives, chopped
Chutney

Thaw fish if frozen; pat dry with toweling.

Mix flour, curry powder, and salt well. Thoroughly coat each piece of fish with mixture.

Heat butter in large skillet. Brown fish over moderate heat about 4 minutes per side. When fish flakes easily, it is done through. Remove fillets; put them onto a heated serving dish.

Add almonds to butter left in skillet; stir until browned. Pour over fish. Garnish with chopped chives; serve chutney as a relish.

Pan Fried Fillet of Sole

INDIA	Yield 6 servings

The hidden ingredient here is carom, which adds a special flavor. The fish should be marinated for at least 24 hours before cooking.

6 whole skinless, boned fillets, about ½ pound each

Marinade

1 teaspoon Kosher salt
2 tablespoons lemon juice
1 tablespoon garlic, finely minced
½ teaspoon carom seeds, crushed

Crumb coating

¼ cup flour
2 large eggs, beaten
2½ cups bread crumbs
½ teaspoon Kosher salt
½ teaspoon black pepper
Peanut or corn oil for frying

Dry each fillet with a paper towel and place in a bowl. Mix the marinade ingredients together and rub over each fillet. Cover and let stand in the refrigerator for 24 to 48 hours.

Just before frying, place 3 bowls on countertop. Put flour in one, beaten eggs in the second bowl, and bread crumbs and seasonings in the third. Dip each fillet in the flour, then the eggs, and finally the bread crumbs, making sure they are thoroughly breaded. Place on waxed paper until all fillets are covered.

Heat oil in a frying pan about ¾ inch deep. Gently add 2 or 3 fillets to oil. When brown on one side, about 3 minutes, turn with a large spatula until brown on the other side. Drain on paper towels. Then transfer finished fillets to warm serving dish and put in a low oven to keep warm until all fillets are cooked. Serve hot with your favorite relish.

Lobster Indian-Style

INDIA   *Yield 4 to 6 servings*

1 carrot, scraped and cut in 4 pieces
1 leek, coarsely cut
4 or 5 quarts water
1 tablespoon salt
1 live 3-pound lobster
4 tablespoons butter

1 onion, peeled and finely chopped
1 piece of celery root, diced
½ bunch each parsley, dill, and chervil
2 cups white wine
2 teaspoons flour
½ cup cream
1 teaspoon curry
Pinch sugar

In a large pot, bring water with salt, carrot, and leek to a boil. Boil for 10 minutes. Place lobster, head first, into the boiling water. Boil for 15 minutes. Remove lobster. Cut in half lengthwise, and take meat carefully out of the shell. Remove the innards. Cut legs open and remove meat. Rinse lobster meat under cold water and pat dry. Discard water.

Heat butter in a pot. Steam lobster meat with onion, celery, and herbs for 5 minutes. Add white wine. Bring to a boil and then simmer for 20 minutes. Remove lobster and place in a pre-heated serving dish. Keep warm.

Strain the liquid into a different pot to make the sauce. Mix flour with a little cold water and stir into the sauce. Boil for 5 minutes. Mix cream with curry and add. Season to taste with sugar, adding salt if needed. Pour sauce over the lobster and serve at once.

Shrimp Bombay

INDIA   *Yield 4 to 6 servings*

1 pound fresh shrimp
1 cup water
1 teaspoon salt

Sauce

2 tablespoons butter or margarine
1 shallot, peeled and finely cut
1 green pepper, seeded and diced
2 teaspoons curry powder
2 tablespoons flour

1 cup shrimp broth
Scant 1 cup beef broth
2 tablespoons tomato paste
½ cup cream
Pinch sugar
Pinch salt
Parsley for garnish

Rinse shrimp in cold water and drain. Place in 1 cup boiling water with salt. Boil shrimp until pink and drain, reserving the broth. Shell and devein the shrimp.

Heat butter or margarine in a pot. Add shallot and green pepper and cook for 3 to 5 minutes. Sprinkle with curry and then stir in flour. Pour in reserved shrimp broth and beef broth. Stir constantly for about 5 minutes. Remove from the heat.

Mix the tomato paste and cream together. Add the mixture to the hot sauce. Season to taste with sugar and salt. Return sauce to stove at a simmer and add shrimp. Heat only until the shrimp is hot through. Place in a serving dish and garnish with parsley. Delicious with a side dish of rice.

Shrimp Balls

INDIA	*Yield 4 to 6 servings*

1 pound canned shrimp
2 onions, peeled and finely chopped
½ bunch parsley, finely chopped
3 branches fresh mint or ½ tablespoon dried mint
1 slice fresh white bread, minus crusts and crumbed
1 teaspoon salt
Pepper to taste
½ teaspoon ground ginger
1 egg
4 tablespoons lemon juice
6 tablespoons flour
1 teaspoon ground coriander

Dash of tabasco sauce
2 tablespoons cold water
4 tablespoons oil
Lemon slices for garnish

Drain liquid off shrimp. In a bowl, mix shrimp, onions, parsley, mint, bread crumbs, salt, pepper, and ginger. Add egg and lemon juice. Mix ingredients well. With a spoon, beat them into a smooth mass. Let rest at room temperature for 30 minutes.

Stir flour, coriander, tabasco, and cold water to a thick, smooth dough. Form the shrimp mixture into round balls 1 inch thick. Heat oil in a skillet. Roll shrimp balls in the flour mixture and fry on each side for 5 minutes, until golden brown. Garnish with lemon and serve at once.

Fish with Ginger

PHILIPPINES	*Yield 4 servings*

1½ to 2 pounds flathead or other delicate white fish
3 tablespoons oil
3 tablespoons fresh ginger, finely chopped
1 teaspoon ground black pepper
Rice washings (the water in which rice has been washed prior to cooking the rice)
Salt to taste
4 spring onions
1 sprig coriander leaves for garnish

Tomato sauce

---

2 tablespoons pork fat, chopped
2 cloves garlic, peeled and crushed
1 medium onion, peeled and chopped
2 tomatoes, chopped
2 tablespoons red misu (salted bean curd paste)
1 tablespoon vinegar
¼ teaspoon ground black pepper

Have fish cleaned and scaled. Rub cavity with salt and then rinse lightly.

In a large skillet, heat oil; fry ginger until soft and golden. Add pepper and stir. Place fish in pan with enough rice water to almost cover. Season with at least ½ teaspoon salt and place a spring onion on top. Cover the skillet and simmer for about 15 minutes, or until fish is tender. Transfer to a serving dish. Garnish with uncooked onions and coriander leaves. Pour liquid around the fish. Serve with white rice and tomato sauce.

To make tomato sauce, heat pork fat, garlic, and onions in a medium skillet. Stir until the onions are soft. Add tomatoes and continue stirring until the tomatoes cook down. Add remaining ingredients and stir well. Simmer for several minutes and serve.

Hot Pickled Fish

PHILIPPINES   *Yield 4 to 6 servings*

2¼ pounds cleaned white fish (red snapper, sea bass, etc.)
Salt
Flour for coating
3 tablespoons oil
3 cloves garlic, peeled and ground
1 teaspoon grated fresh gingerroot
1 large onion, peeled and thinly sliced into rings
1 large green pepper, cored, seeded, and sliced into thin strips
1 tablespoon cornstarch
1¼ cups water
3 tablespoons cider vinegar
1½ tablespoons brown sugar

Slice the fish into steaks; pat dry and sprinkle lightly with salt and flour.

Heat 2 tablespoons oil in skillet. Fry fish until it is crisp and brown. Set aside.

Add remaining oil to pan with garlic and ginger. Fry until brown. Then add onion and green pepper. Stir-fry for one minute, remove from pan, and set aside.

Make paste of the cornstarch with ¼ cup of water. Add to pan with remaining water, vinegar, and sugar. Stir constantly over a low heat until thickened. Add the fish and bring to a boil. Cover and simmer for 5 minutes more. Return onions and green pepper and stir until heated through. Lift fish to a warm serving dish. Arrange vegetables around it. Check remaining sauce, adding seasoning if required. Pour over the fish and serve.

Shrimp in Coconut Milk

PHILIPPINES   *Yield 6 servings*

1½ pound raw shrimp
2 cups thick coconut milk
1 tablespoon garlic, finely chopped
1 teaspoon ginger, finely chopped
1 teaspoon salt
¼ teaspoon black pepper

Do not shell shrimp, but wash well and drain. In a saucepan, place the shrimp and remaining ingredients listed. Bring this mixture to a boil, stirring constantly. Reduce heat and simmer for 15 minutes, continuing to stir. Serve at once over hot white rice.

Shrimp Curry

PHILIPPINES   *Yield 4 to 6 servings*

4 tablespoons butter
2 onions, peeled and finely chopped
1 tablespoon curry powder
1 ounce candied ginger, finely cut
½ cup beef broth
½ cup coconut milk

Shrimp with bean sprouts

Cantonese shrimp and beans

Chinese fish

Curried shrimp (China)

53

½ cucumber, diced, unpeeled
1 pound shrimp, cooked, shelled, and deveined
Juice of ½ lemon
1 tablespoon soy sauce
1 teaspoon cornstarch
¼ cup water
Dash of cayenne pepper

Heat butter and cook onions until they are golden. Add curry and ginger. Pour in beef broth and coconut milk. When hot, add cucumber and shrimp. Season with lemon juice and soy sauce. Simmer.

Mix cornstarch in water and add to pan. Stir until the sauce thickens slightly. Season with cayenne pepper to taste and serve at once.

Shrimp with Bean Sprouts

CHINA *Yield 4 servings*

1 green pepper (or a red, ripe one), cut into ¼-inch strips
1 cup bean sprouts
1 teaspoon ginger, grated
2 tablespoons vegetable oil
6 ounces cooked shrimp
1 tablespoon dry sherry
2 teaspoons soy sauce
Salt

Fish curry (Malaysia)

Crispy fried noodles

12 ounces fine egg noodles
2 cups vegetable oil for frying

Combine green pepper, bean sprouts, and ginger. Heat oil in a wok; stir-fry vegetables about 2 minutes. Push aside. Add shrimp; stir-fry until heated. Combine shrimp and vegetables; add sherry and soy sauce. Salt to taste. Serve hot with crispy fried noodles.

To make the fried noodles, cook noodles in boiling, salted water according to package directions. Drain; rinse thoroughly in cold water. Dry on paper towels. Fry handfuls of noodles in oil at 375°F, turning frequently, about 5 minutes. Drain on paper towels.

Cantonese Shrimp and Beans

CHINA	Yield 6 servings

1½ pounds frozen raw, peeled, deveined
   shrimp
1½ teaspoons chicken-stock base
1 cup boiling water
¼ cup green onion, thinly sliced
1 clove garlic, crushed
1 tablespoon salad oil
1 teaspoon salt
½ teaspoon ginger
Dash of pepper
1 (9-ounce) package frozen cut green beans,
   thawed
1 tablespoon cornstarch
1 tablespoon cold water

Dissolve chicken-stock base in boiling water.

Cook onion, garlic, and shrimp in oil 3 minutes; stir frequently. If necessary, add a little broth to prevent sticking. Stir in salt, ginger, pepper, beans, and broth; cover. Simmer 5 to 7 minutes, until beans are cooked but still slightly crisp.

Combine cornstarch and water. Add to shrimp; cook until thick and clear, stirring constantly.

Chinese Fish

CHINA	Yield about 4 servings

1 whole trout, about 1 pound
1 whole carp, about 3 pounds
Juice of 1 lemon
Salt
White pepper
2 slices lean bacon
Margarine to grease pan
4 large leaves savoy cabbage (if unavailable,
   use regular cabbage)
1 pound fresh mushrooms
2 pieces sugared ginger
3 tablespoons soy sauce
Pinch of ground anise
1 cup hot water
2 teaspoons cornstarch
2 tablespoons bacon drippings
Juice of half a lemon

Garnish

2 tablespoons chopped parsley
Lemon slices

Have fishmonger scale and clean out the insides of the fish, but leave whole. At home, wash fish thoroughly under running water, pat dry, and rub with lemon juice. With sharp knife, make shallow incisions in backs of both fish and rub with salt and pepper. Cut bacon into small strips and insert one strip in each incision. Grease ovenproof baking dish with margarine and line with cabbage leaves. Place fish on top. Slice mushrooms and sugared ginger. Mix together and spoon over fish.

Sprinkle with soy sauce and ground anise. Pour in small amount of hot water. Cover with lid or aluminum foil and place in preheated oven at 350°F. Bake for 30 minutes. While baking, gradually add rest of hot water and baste fish with pan drippings.

Remove fish and cabbage leaves from pan. Arrange on a preheated platter. Bring pan drippings to a boil, scraping all brown particles from bottom of pan and adding some more water, if necessary. Blend cornstarch with small amount of cold water, add to pan drippings, and stir until sauce is smooth and bubbly. Correct seasonings if necessary, and serve separately. Melt and heat bacon drippings. Pour over fish and sprinkle with lemon juice. Garnish fish with chopped parsley and lemon slices.

Curried Shrimp

CHINA   *Yield 4 servings*

1 pound fresh shrimp, shelled, cleaned
Juice of 1 lemon
1 egg white
1 tablespoon cornstarch
2 cups sesame-seed or vegetable oil
1 tablespoon dried Chinese mushrooms
1 can (approximately 6 ounces) bamboo shoots
1 medium onion, chopped
½ teaspoon ground ginger
1 green pepper, sliced thin
2 teaspoons curry powder
1 teaspoon sugar
2 tablespoons soy sauce
8-ounce can tiny peas, drained
2 tablespoons rice wine or sherry

Sprinkle shrimp with lemon juice. Blend egg white and cornstarch; coat shrimp with mixture. Heat oil in heavy, deep skillet or deep-fryer. Fry shrimp 2 to 3 minutes; remove with slotted spoon. Set aside; keep warm.

Break mushrooms into small pieces; cover with boiling water. Let soak 15 minutes.

Drain bamboo shoots; reserve liquid. Cut shoots into thin strips. Pour 2 tablespoons oil used for frying into skillet, Add bamboo shoots and onion; cook until transparent. Pour ½ cup reserved liquid from bamboo shoots. Season with ground ginger. Add green pepper; cook 5 minutes. Pepper should be crisp. Add curry powder, sugar, and soy sauce.

Drain soaked mushrooms. Add mushrooms, peas, and shrimp to skillet. Fold in carefully; heat through.

Heat wine in small saucepan; pour over dish just before serving.

Crab Rangoon

CHINA   *Yield about 95 filled squares*

¼ pound crab meat, chopped
¼ pound cream cheese
¼ teaspoon A-1 sauce
⅛ teaspoon garlic powder
Wonton squares
1 egg yolk, beaten
Oil for deep frying

Blend chopped crab meat with cream cheese, A-1 sauce, and garlic powder. Put ½ teaspoon of mixture in center of each wonton square. Fold corners of the square over, moisten edges with beaten egg yolk, and twist together. Fry in oil until lightly browned. Drain and serve hot.

Hot-Mustard Shrimp

CHINA   *Yield 2 to 3 servings*

3 tablespoons powdered mustard
¼ teaspoon salt
1 teaspoon sugar

1 teaspoon horseradish
¾ cup flat beer
1 pound shrimp, cleaned
4 tablespoons melted butter
Duck sauce

Mix mustard, salt, sugar, and horseradish together. Add enough beer to make a smooth paste. Gradually add rest of beer to make sauce thin. Let mixture stand for 1 hour. If it becomes too thick, add more beer or cold water.

Dip shrimp in mustard sauce, skewer, and brush with melted butter. Grill on hibachi or grill for approximately 8 minutes. Turn frequently for even browning. Serve with duck sauce.

Sweet-and-Sour Fish

CHINA	Yield 4 servings

3 to 3½ pounds fish fillets (carp, bass, or fish of
   your choice)
4 tablespoons onions, finely chopped
2 teaspoons fresh gingerroot, chopped
Pinch of salt
¼ teaspoon freshly ground black pepper
1 teaspoon soy sauce
1 teaspoon sherry
½ cup cornstarch (more if needed)
Fat for deep frying

Sweet-and-sour sauce

¾ cup cider vinegar
1 tablespoon cornstarch
1 green pepper, cut into julienne strips
1 carrot, peeled, cut into julienne strips
2 teaspoons fresh gingerroot, chopped
4 scallions, sliced into ½-inch pieces
2 tablespoons sweet pickle relish
Salt to taste
¼ cup sugar

Sprinkle fish with onions, gingerroot, salt, pepper, soy sauce, and sherry. Let stand 30 minutes. Roll in cornstarch; let stand 10 minutes.

Heat fat in deep-fryer or deep skillet over medium-high heat. Fry the fish 10 to 15 minutes or until done. Drain. Serve with sweet-and-sour sauce.

To make the sauce, mix all ingredients together. Cook over low heat, stirring constantly, until thickened.

Deep-fried Fish with Vegetables

INDOCHINA	Yield 4 to 6 servings

1½ pounds white fish fillets, cut into finger
   pieces
1 tablespoon egg white
1 teaspoon salt
1 tablespoon cornstarch
6 tablespoons oil
1 clove garlic, peeled and crushed
½ teaspoon fresh ginger, finely grated
2 cups white Chinese cabbage, sliced
6 spring onions, cut in 2-inch lengths
2 tablespoons fish sauce
½ cup water
1 teaspoon extra cornstarch

Dip fish in egg white, then in a mixture of salt and cornstarch. Heat oil and fry fish on high heat. Do not crowd the pan. Each batch should cook 2 minutes. Drain on paper towels and keep warm.

Leaving just 1 tablespoon oil in frying pan or wok, stir-fry garlic, ginger, and cabbage for 1 minute. Stir-fry spring onions with the other vegetables for 1 minute more. Add fish sauce and water and bring to a boil. Mix cornstarch with cold water and pour in. Continue strirring until sauce thickens. Arrange a platter with a bed of rice, the thickened sauce, and fish pieces on top; serve piping hot.

Fish with Coconut Cream

INDOCHINA   *Yield 4 servings*

1 pound fish fillets
2 large, dried chilies
15 cloves garlic, peeled
3 tender lemon leaves
1 teaspoon laos powder, optional
2 stalks lemon grass, finely sliced, or 2 strips
   lemon rind
1 cup thick coconut milk
3 cups thin coconut milk
1 tablespoon fish sauce
2 tablespoons roasted peanuts, finely chopped
Fresh basil leaves for garnish
5 or 6 small dried chilies
Oil for frying

Cut fillets into serving pieces. Remove stalks and seeds from large, dried chilies; soak in hot water for 10 minutes. With mortar and pestle, pound chilies, garlic, lemon leaves, laos powder, and lemon grass to a fine paste.

Place thick coconut milk in saucepan and cook about 10 minutes until oil floats on top. Add pounded mixture and stir constantly until well blended. Add fillets to mixture, coating well. Then add thin coconut milk and fish sauce and simmer for 10 minutes. Last, add the peanuts and stir for 1 minute more. Garnish with basil and small chilies that have been fried for 15 seconds in hot oil.

Raw Fish Salad

INDOCHINA   *Yield 4 to 6 servings*

2 pounds fresh fish, boned and finely chopped
1 teaspoon salt
½ cup water

Juice of 5 or 6 lemons
5 medium onions, peeled and finely chopped
5 cloves garlic, peeled and finely chopped
3 or 4 fresh pimientos, finely chopped
2 tablespoons fennel or shallots, finely chopped
Lettuce leaves

Place minced fish in a large bowl. In another bowl, mix salt, water, and lemon juice. Pour liquid over fish and allow to stand for at least 15 minutes. Press out the water from the fish; bring water to boil and put in saucepan. Set aside the water to cool. Add cooled water to fish, followed by onions, garlic, pimientos, and fennel. Mix well. Serve on a bed of lettuce with your favorite green salad.

Simmered Pineapple with Fish

INDOCHINA   *Yield 4 servings*

2 tablespoons vegetable oil
1 pound fish steaks
1 shallot, peeled and sliced
1 cup fresh pineapple, cut into 1-inch squares
6 tablespoons fish sauce
¼ cup sugar
Freshly ground black pepper

Heat 1 tablespoon oil in skillet; fry fish until lightly browned on both sides. In a separate skillet, heat remaining oil. Add shallot slices and fry until lightly browned. Add pineapple squares and cook for 3 minutes. Lift out shallots and pineapple and discard juice.

In medium-size saucepan or flameproof casserole, place half of the pineapple mixture. Add fish steaks and cover with remaining pineapple, fish sauce, sugar, and pepper. Cover and simmer for 25 to 30 minutes. Serve at once.

Cod fillets in shrimp sauce

Fried Oysters

KOREA   *Yield 4 servings*

1 pound oysters, washed and shelled
½ cup flour
2 eggs, beaten
¼ cup oil
1 teaspoon salt

Vinegar soy sauce

½ cup soy sauce
1 tablespoon sugar
3 tablespoons vinegar
Pine nuts, finely chopped, for garnish

Dredge each oyster in flour. Just before frying, dip oysters in the egg and place gently in heated fat. When nicely browned all over, remove to drain on paper towels. Salt lightly. Keep cooked oysters warm until all are ready. Serve with vinegar-soy sauce.

To make the sauce, mix soy sauce, sugar, and vinegar in a small bowl until sugar is completely dissolved. Sprinkle with chopped pine nuts and serve.

Fried Fish

KOREA   *Yield 4 to 6 servings*

6 small fillets of fish, washed and dried
2 tablespoons light soy sauce
2 tablespoons toasted, crushed sesame seeds
Pinch of ground black pepper
2 tablespoons spring onions, finely chopped
2 teaspoons sesame oil
2 tablespoons vegetable oil

In a bowl, combine soy sauce, sesame seeds, pepper, spring onions, and sesame oil. Dip each fillet in the mixture, coating both sides. Heat vegetable oil in frying pan and fry for a few minutes on each side until fish is golden brown. Serve at once.

Salted Fish

KOREA   *Yield 4 servings*

1 pound perch or mackerel, skinned and boned
¼ cup water
1 tablespoon sugar

Eel kabobs

4 tablespoons soy sauce
Dash of pepper to taste
1 scallion, chopped with greens
1 clove garlic, peeled and minced
½ teaspoon candied ginger

Prepare the fish by cutting it into small squares. In a saucepan, place the fish with remaining ingredients and stir gently until all flavors blend. Cook over medium heat for 5 to 10 minutes or until fish is tender. Serve hot with white rice.

Fish Curry

MALAYSIA   *Yield 4 to 6 servings*

2 pounds fish fillet, cod or red perch preferred
2 tablespoons lemon juice

2 teaspoons salt
2 tablespoons curry
3 tablespoons flour
4 tablespoons peanut oil
1 tablespoon butter or margarine
3 onions, peeled and thinly sliced in rings
4 tablespoons milk
1 tablespoon flour
¼ cup peanuts
½ teaspoon ground ginger
½ cup cream

Cut fish into 2-inch cubes and put on a platter. Sprinkle with lemon juice. Cover and allow to soak for 10 minutes. Then, sprinkle on both sides with salt and 1 tablespoon curry. Coat with flour. Fry in hot peanut oil for 3 minutes, until light brown. Remove, place in a heated dish, and keep warm.

Heat butter in a second skillet. Place onion rings in milk, then in 1 tablespoon of flour. Fry in the

Fish tempura

Steamed whole fish

Steamed rock lobster

61

hot fat for 5 minutes, until golden brown. Keep warm.

Break peanuts in half. Add them to the fish skillet along with ginger, cream, and the remaining curry. Simmer for 2 minutes. Pour over fish. Garnish with onion rings and serve.

Fish with Sweet-and-Sour Sauce

MALAYSIA	Yield 4 to 6 servings

1 teaspoon gingerroot, finely chopped
Salt and pepper to taste
1½ pounds bass, cleaned and wiped dry with
   paper towels
2 teaspoons cornstarch
Fat for deep frying
2 tablespoons tomato ketchup
1 cup water
1 teaspoon sugar
Salt and pepper
1 small cucumber, finely minced
Parsley greens for garnish

Add salt and pepper to gingerroot. Marinate the fish in this mixture for 15 minutes. Sprinkle 1 teaspoon cornstarch over fish and let stand for 15 to 20 minutes more. Heat fat in a deep frying pan and fry the fish until it is golden brown. Remove from fat and drain on paper towels. Put on a heated serving plate.

Put remaining cornstarch together with rest of ingredients in a saucepan. Allow the sauce to thicken over medium heat, stirring occasionally. Pour over the prepared fish and garnish with parsley greens.

Spiced Coconut Fish

MALAYSIA	Yield 4 servings

1 pound fish fillets, washed, cleaned, and scaled
½ cup desiccated (dehydrated) coconut
¾ cup hot water
1 clove garlic, peeled
½ inch fresh ginger
1 teaspoon ground cumin
1 teaspoon ground coriander
1 teaspoon garam masala
1 teaspoon salt
1½ tablespoons lemon juice
1 tablespoon fresh coriander leaves, chopped
Banana leaves or foil

Cut fish into 4-inch lengths. In a blender or food processor, or with mortar and pestle, combine coconut, hot water, garlic, ginger, cumin, coriander, garam masala, and salt until all is very finely ground. Add lemon juice and coriander leaves.

On a square of foil or banana leaves, place 1 fillet. Spoon 2 to 3 teaspoons of coconut mixture on top. Wrap to make a sealed parcel. Continue in this way until all the fish is used. Steam the parcels over boiling water for 15 minutes. Serve at once, piping hot, with white rice.

Eel Kabobs

JAPAN	Yield 2 to 3 servings

2 eels, about 1 pound each

Marinade

¾ cup rice wine or sherry
3 teaspoons honey
5 tablespoons soy sauce

Skin eels, cut off heads, and, with a very sharp knife, remove eel fillets from bone. Cut into 1½-inch pieces; place in deep bowl. Combine rice wine (or sherry), honey, and soy sauce. Heat. Pour marinade over eel pieces. Let marinate for 30 minutes.

Light coals in your barbecue grill; wait until white hot. Thread eel pieces on metal skewers; place on grill. Turn skewers occasionally; baste with marinade. Grill for 15 minutes. This can also be done under the oven broiler or on a hibachi.

Cod Fillets in Shrimp Sauce

JAPAN	*Yield 4 servings*

4 cod fillets, about 6 ounces each
Juice of 1 lemon
Salt
White pepper
2 tablespoons butter
1 medium onion, sliced
2 tablespoons chopped parsley
½ cup dry white wine

Shrimp sauce

2 tablespoons butter
1½ tablespoons flour
1 cup hot beef broth
½ cup dry white wine
6 ounces fresh mushrooms
4 ounces fresh shrimp
2 teaspoons lemon juice
Salt
2 egg yolks

Garnish

Lemon slices
Parsley

Sprinkle cod fillets with lemon juice. Let stand for 10 minutes. Season to taste with salt and pepper. Heat butter in large skillet. Add fish; brown well for about 10 minutes on each side. Add sliced onion; cook until golden. Stir in chopped parsley. Pour in white wine; simmer for another 5 minutes. Remove cod fillets to preheated platter; keep them warm. Reserve pan drippings.

To prepare sauce, melt butter in a saucepan. Stir in flour; pour in hot beef broth, as well as reserved pan drippings. Add white wine. Let simmer over low heat. Cut mushrooms into thin slices and add, together with shrimp, to sauce; simmer for 15 minutes. Season to taste with lemon juice and salt. Remove small amount of sauce; blend with egg yolks. Return to sauce; stir thoroughly. Heat through, but do not boil, since yolks will curdle.

Pour sauce over cod fillets. Garnish with lemon slices and parsley.

Fish Tempura

JAPAN	*Yield 4 to 6 servings*

2 pounds fresh fish fillets
Salt to taste
Lemon juice
½ recipe Basic Tempura Batter
Oil
Chili-horseradish sauce
Soy sauce

Basic tempura batter

2 cups all-purpose flour, sifted
3 egg yolks
2 cups ice water

Chili-horseradish sauce

1 cup mayonnaise
⅓ cup chili sauce
3 tablespoons horseradish

Cut the fish fillets into bite-size pieces and drain well on paper toweling. Prepare other ingredients. Season the fish with salt and squeeze desired amount of lemon juice over fish. Make up the batter.

Sift flour 3 times. Combine the yolks and water in a large bowl over ice and beat with a whisk until well blended. Gradually add the flour, stirring and turning the mixture with a spoon. Don't overmix. Keep the batter over ice while frying. Makes approximately 4½ cups.

Place all the fish in the batter. When ready to fry, remove the fish from the batter with a fork and drain slightly. Heat the oil in a wok, an electric skillet, or deep-fat fryer to between 350 and 375°F. Fry the fish, a few pieces at a time, for about 5 minutes, turning to brown evenly. Remove the fish from the oil with a slotted spoon and drain well on paper toweling. Keep fish warm until all is cooked. Serve with chili-horseradish sauce or just dipped into soy sauce. Use this batter for vegetables also, or meat, or seafood. Skim off loose particles of food as they appear, to keep the oil clean. Keep the batter cold.

To make chili-horseradish sauce, combine all ingredients in small bowl and mix thoroughly. Chill well before serving.

Steamed Rock Lobster

JAPAN *Yield 6 servings*

3 (8-ounce) packages frozen South African rock lobster tails
6 large mushrooms, cut into slices
6 scallions, cut into long, thin strips
1 cup celery, thinly sliced
1 bunch broccoli, trimmed and cut into florets
1 tablespoon soy sauce
1 envelope dehydrated chicken broth
¼ cup water

Remove thin underside membrane from lobster tails with scissors. Push bamboo skewer lengthwise through tail to prevent curling.

Place colander over boiling water in large pot, or use steamer. Place lobster tails in colander; place vegetables on top and around tails.

Combine soy sauce, broth, and water; brush over tails and vegetables. Cover pot; steam 20 minutes or until vegetables are crisp-tender and lobster meat loses translucency and is opaque.

Steamed Whole Fish

JAPAN *Yield 3 servings*

1½ pounds whole fish (flounder, pike, trout, or sea bass)
1 teaspoon salt
½ teaspoon freshly ground pepper
¼ teaspoon powdered ginger
3 cups water
2 teaspoons mixed pickling spices (more, if you prefer it spicier)
2 bay leaves
2 cloves garlic, cut in half
2 tablespoons chopped scallion

Garnish

Lemon slices
Tomato
Parsley

Have fish scaled and cleaned and head removed, if you prefer. Lightly score the skin so seasonings will flavor the fish. Combine salt, pepper, and ginger; rub on fish thoroughly.

Pour water into large frying pan or wok; add pickling spices, bay leaves, garlic, and scallion. Place rack in pan so that the fish will sit above the liquid, in order to allow the steam to circulate. Place the fish on the rack, cover, and let simmer for approximately 30 minutes, or until fish is tender.

Garnish fish with lemon slices, tomato, and parsley.

Chicken with Soy Sauce

INDONESIA   Yield 4 servings

1 3-pound chicken
Salt
2 tablespoons dark soy sauce
2 shallots, peeled and finely sliced
2 garlic cloves, peeled and crushed
½ teaspoon chili powder
Juice of ½ lemon or lime
2 teaspoons sesame-seed oil
Oil for basting

Gently rub the outside of the chicken with salt. Roast at 375°F for 45 minutes or until chicken is golden brown all over. Allow to cool.

Divide the chicken into four pieces. Use a mallet to beat the chicken flesh and loosen the fibers. Mix together the remaining ingredients to form a marinade for the cooked chicken. Allow the chicken to marinate for 1 hour, turning the pieces from time to time.

When ready to serve, place the chicken under the broiler. Brush each piece with oil and broil just long enough to heat through.

Chicken Grilled on Skewers

INDONESIA   Yield 4 to 6 servings

1½ pounds chicken breasts, boned and skinned
2 red chilies
2 medium onions, peeled and chopped
3 teaspoons fresh ginger, finely chopped
2 tablespoons lemon juice

1½ teaspoons salt
2 tablespoons light soy sauce
2 tablespoons dark soy sauce
2 tablespoons sesame oil
2 tablespoons palm sugar
½ cup thick coconut milk

Cut chicken into small squares. Set aside.

Preferably in a blender or food processor, make a paste of the chilies, onions, ginger, lemon juice, salt, and soy sauce. When smooth, pour paste into a bowl and stir in oil and sugar. Add chicken, making sure that each piece is covered with the marinade. Cover and marinate for at least 1 hour. (If prepared the night before, it can be kept in the refrigerator overnight.)

Place pieces of chicken on skewers, leaving half the skewer free at the blunt end. Grill 2 inches from heat for 5 to 8 minutes, or until chicken is crisp and brown. Brush once with extra oil during the grilling period.

Place remaining marinade in saucepan with coconut milk. Simmer, stirring constantly, until smooth. Serve in a small bowl with the chicken.

Balinese-style Fried Chicken

INDONESIA   Yield 4 servings

1 onion, peeled and roughly chopped
2 cloves garlic, peeled
1 teaspoon fresh ginger, chopped
3 fresh red chilies, seeded and chopped
4 kemiri nuts
1 tablespoon dark soy sauce
1 2½-pound frying chicken
Peanut oil, at least ½ cup
2 teaspoons palm sugar

2 tablespoons lemon juice
½ teaspoon salt
1 cup coconut milk

Make a smooth paste, preferably in blender or food processor, of onion, garlic, ginger, chilies, kemiri nuts, and soy sauce.

Quarter the chicken and dry each piece with paper towels. Heat ½ cup peanut oil in wok or frying pan and brown chicken pieces quickly on both sides. Remove chicken and drain on paper towels.

Pour off excess oil, leaving 1 tablespoon in pan. Fry the prepared paste in this for a few minutes, stirring constantly. While stirring, add sugar, lemon juice, salt, and coconut milk, and allow to come to a boil. Put chicken into this sauce and simmer for 25 minutes, until chicken is tender and sauce has thickened. Serve with rice.

Skewered Chicken

INDONESIA	Yield 6 or more servings

4 whole chicken breasts

Marinade

½ cup walnuts, chopped
Juice of 1 lemon
1 cup hot chicken broth
1 teaspoon salt
Generous dash of white pepper
1 onion, peeled and diced
1 clove garlic, peeled and crushed
2 tablespoons oil

½ cup cream
Parsley for garnish

Skin and bone the chicken. Cut meat into ½- to 1-inch wide strips.

Prepare the marinade by mixing walnuts, lemon juice, chicken broth, salt, and pepper in a bowl. Add onion, garlic, and oil to mixture. Set aside ⅓ of the marinade for later use. Place chicken strips in marinade and allow to sit for at least 3 hours.

Drain chicken and place meat on 4 skewers. Put skewers on a flat pan and cook in broiler for 20 minutes, turning once. Mix reserved marinade with cream and serve separately. Remove chicken from skewers and put on preheated platter. Garnish with parsley and serve hot.

Chicken in Mild Sauce

INDONESIA	Yield 4 to 6 servings

1 2½- to 3-pound chicken, cut in serving pieces
4 candlenuts or macadamia nuts
3-inch piece green ginger, finely chopped
2 onions, peeled and finely chopped
3 cloves garlic, peeled and finely chopped
2 tablespoons coriander
½ teaspoon cumin
1 piece lemon grass
2 salam leaves, optional
2 tablespoons oil
Salt and pepper to taste
4 cups coconut milk
2 tablespoons tamarind juice

Blend nuts, ginger, onions, and garlic into a fine paste. In a large saucepan, stir-fry the paste, coriander, cumin, lemon grass, and salam leaves in the oil long enough to bring out the aroma and flavor of the spices. Season the chicken with salt and pepper and add to saucepan. Allow to simmer for 10 minutes. Slowly pour coconut milk over the chicken and stir as it comes to a boil. Reduce heat to medium and continue cooking until chicken is tender to the fork. Add additional salt and pepper if needed. Last, add tamarind juice and serve at once.

Skewered chicken

Chicken Ginger with Honey

THAILAND   *Yield 4 to 6 servings*

Most of the work for this dish is done the day before.

5 scallions, cut into ½-inch pieces
1 ¼ cups fresh gingerroot, shredded
2 tablespoons vegetable oil
3 boneless chicken breasts, skinned and cut into
    bite-size pieces
3 chicken livers, chopped
1 onion, peeled and sliced
2 tablespoons tree ears, soaked in warm water
    for 20 minutes
2 tablespoons soy sauce
1 tablespoon honey

Cover the cut spring onions in a bowl with cold water. Allow to soak. Mix gingerroot with some

cold water to reduce the hot taste. Squeeze and rinse under cold running water. Drain.

Fry the chicken and liver pieces in heated oil for 5 minutes. Remove from pan and drain on paper towels. Add onion to fat, followed by garlic and tree ears, and stir-fry for 1 minute. Return chicken to pan.

Mix the soy sauce and honey together well. Pour over the chicken. Add ginger and continue cooking for 2 to 3 minutes. Last, add the drained spring onions. Transfer all of this to a bowl, cover, and refrigerate overnight. When ready to serve, reheat until chicken pieces are hot through.

Chicken Kai Yang

THAILAND   *Yield 4 to 6 servings*

1 3-pound roasting chicken, cut into serving
    pieces
6 cloves garlic, peeled

2 teaspoons salt
2 tablespoons black peppercorns
4 whole plants fresh coriander, including roots
2 tablespoons lemon juice

Crush garlic with salt. Coarsely crush peppercorns. (Use either mortar and pestle or blender.) Wash coriander carefully, drain, and finely chop entire plant. Mix all seasonings together and rub into the chicken pieces well. Allow to stand for at least 1 hour. Better still, cover and refrigerate overnight.

Grill the chicken pieces under a hot grill, turning every 5 minutes. When chicken is tender and skin crisp, the chicken is done.

Garlic Chicken

THAILAND   *Yield 4 servings*

4 boneless chicken breasts, skinned
3 garlic cloves, peeled and crushed

1 tablespoon freshly ground black pepper
2 tablespoons soy sauce
1 teaspoon sugar
1 teaspoon salt
1 teaspoon sesame-seed oil
Vegetable oil for shallow frying

With a sharp knife, cut the surface of the chicken breasts on both sides. In a bowl, mix all of the remaining ingredients, except vegetable oil, well. Rub this mixture into the chicken breasts and allow to marinate for at least 2 hours.

Using your wok or skillet, heat about 5 tablespoons vegetable oil. When hot, add 2 pieces of chicken and cook for about 4 minutes per side until both sides are golden brown. Remove from the pan and drain on paper towels. Proceed in the same way with the remaining chicken. Add more oil when needed.

Cut each piece of cooked chicken in half with a sharp knife. Return to skillet and cook until edges are no longer pink. Serve at once.

Grilled chicken

Chicken with Yellow Bean Sauce

THAILAND	Yield 3 servings

1 large chicken breast
1 tablespoon egg white, slightly beaten
2 teaspoons water chestnut flour or cornstarch
Oil for deep frying
1 tablespoon lard
1 tablespoon yellow bean paste
1 teaspoon sugar
2 tablespoons Chinese wine or sherry
½ teaspoon sesame oil

After skinning and boning the chicken breast, dice the meat into small pieces. Pour egg white over the chicken meat and add flour or cornstarch. Mix to make a batter. Heat oil and deep-fry chicken just until the color changes. Since these are small pieces, they will cook fairly quickly. Remove from frying pan and drain on paper towels.

In the hot lard, fry the bean paste for a few seconds. Add remaining ingredients and mix well. Return the chicken to the frying pan and allow to heat through in the sauce. Serve with white rice.

Chicken Curry

BURMA	Yield 4 to 6 servings

2 small frying chickens, cut into serving pieces
2 teaspoons curry powder
2 tablespoons soy sauce
Pinch of saffron
2 large onions, peeled and finely chopped
½ teaspoon ground dried chili peppers
3 cloves garlic, peeled
¼ cup oil
2½ cups water
1 teaspoon cinnamon

1 heaping teaspoon salt
3 bay leaves

Wipe chicken pieces dry with paper towels. Combine curry powder, soy sauce, and saffron; rub all pieces of the chicken with this mixture. Set aside.

Pound onions, chili peppers, and garlic very fine. Heat oil in large skillet and brown this onion mixture. Add the chicken, making sure each piece is seasoned with the onion mixture. Add remaining ingredients, cover, and simmer gently for at least 1 hour. When chicken is tender, remove from heat and serve.

Chicken with Noodles and Coconut

BURMA	Yield 6 to 8 servings

This is typical of Burmese cooking because of the split-pea and lentil flours. You may substitute chick-pea flour for the split-pea flour. You can make the Burmese flours easily with your blender, food processor, or mortar and pestle.

1 3½-pound chicken, cut into large pieces
1 tablespoon salt
½ teaspoon turmeric powder
3 quarts water
7 tablespoons vegetable oil
4 medium onions, peeled and pounded
4 cloves garlic, peeled and crushed
1-inch piece of fresh gingerroot, peeled and pounded
2 teaspoons chili powder
5 tablespoons split-pea flour
5 tablespoons lentil flour
1⅔ cups thick coconut milk
2 pounds fresh or dried egg noodles

Indian boats

To serve

6 tablespoons oil
12 cloves garlic, peeled and sliced crossways
3 hard-cooked eggs, shelled and quartered
2 onions, peeled and sliced
5 scallions, including green tops, finely
 chopped
1 tablespoon chili powder, optional
2 lemons, quartered

Rub chicken with salt and turmeric. Place the chicken in a large can or kettle with water. Bring to a boil, then simmer for 25 minutes. The chicken will be cooked but still firm. Remove chicken but continue to simmer the liquid.

Remove skin and bones from chicken and add to liquid. Cut the chicken meat into chunks.

Using a large skillet, heat oil and add onions, garlic, ginger, and chili powder. Stir-fry for 5 minutes. Add chicken meat and continue stir-frying for 10 minutes. Turn off the heat.

Mix the flours to a paste with 1 cup of the cooking liquid. Strain remaining liquid into pan with chicken. Slowly stir in the flour paste and bring to a boil. Reduce heat and add coconut milk. Simmer for 20 minutes. Mixture should be consistency of thick pea soup. Adjust seasonings, cover pan, and set aside.

Cook noodles, drain, and keep hot. In a small frying pan, fry small quantities of noodles until crisp. When all are fried in this way and drained on paper towels, place in a serving bowl. Add garlic to pan and stir-fry until golden and crisp. Transfer to small bowl.

Reheat chicken mixture and place in serving bowl. Surround this with noodles and other accompaniments, such as oil, hard-cooked eggs, onions, and scallions.

Chicken with Fresh Coconut

INDIA *Yield 4 servings*

½ cup ghee
1 large onion, peeled and sliced
2 cloves garlic, peeled and sliced
4 whole cardamoms
4 whole cloves
1-inch piece of cinnamon stick
2 teaspoons garam masala
1 teaspoon turmeric powder
1 teaspoon chili powder
1 teaspoon salt
1 3-pound chicken, skinned, boned, and cut
    into 8 pieces
Flesh of ½ fresh coconut, thinly sliced
1 tablespoon tomato paste
1¼ cups water

In a large pan, melt ghee. Fry onions and garlic until both are soft. Add spices and salt and stir-fry for 3 minutes more. Add the chicken pieces and brown on both sides, about 10 minutes. Add coconut, tomato paste, and water. Bring to a boil, stirring constantly. Lower the heat, cover, and simmer for 45 minutes. When chicken is fork tender, serve at once.

Chicken with Lentils

INDIA *Yield 4 servings*

This recipe should be made from two types of dried beans. If you cannot find chenna dal or moong dal, substitute the more familiar lentil.

½ pound chenna dal
½ pound moong dal
5 cups water

¾ cup ghee
2 large onions, peeled and sliced
4 cloves garlic, peeled and sliced
6 whole cloves
6 whole cardamoms
2 teaspoons garam masala
2½ teaspoons salt
1 3-pound chicken, skinned, boned, and cut
    into 8 pieces
1 pound frozen whole leaf spinach
4 large tomatoes, chopped

After washing the dals, place them in a saucepan with water. Bring to a boil, then cover and simmer for 15 minutes. While the dals are cooking, melt ghee in a large skillet. Fry the onions and garlic until soft. Add the spices and salt and stir-fry for 3 minutes. Add the chicken pieces and brown on both sides. Drain cooked chicken on paper towels.

Add spinach and tomatoes to skillet and fry gently for 10 minutes. Mash the dals in cooking water and stir into spinach. Return chicken to the pan. Cover and simmer for 45 minutes or until chicken is tender. Serve at once.

Chicken Curry I

INDIA *Yield 4 to 6 servings*

1 frying chicken, cut into serving pieces
2 tablespoons vegetable oil
2 tablespoons butter or margarine
2 cups cooked barley
1 medium onion, minced
2 cups chicken broth
Salt and pepper to taste
2 teaspoons curry powder
1 teaspoon marjoram
1 cup plain yogurt
1 tomato, peeled, seeded, cut into bite-size
    pieces

71

Brown chicken in oil and butter in a large skillet. Remove chicken from pan; place on bed of barley in Dutch oven or flameproof casserole.

In the same skillet, cook onion in the remaining oil and butter until transparent. Remove; place on top of chicken. Pour 1½ cups broth over chicken and barley. Sprinkle with salt, pepper, curry powder, and marjoram. Cover; cook over low heat 30 minutes. Remove cover. Add yogurt, tomato, and ½ cup broth if needed. Cook uncovered, 20 to 30 minutes, until chicken is tender.

Chicken Curry II

INDIA	*Yield 4 to 6 servings*

1 2½- to 3-pound frying chicken
4 tablespoons margarine
1 onion, peeled and finely chopped
2 cups beef broth
2 apples, peeled, cored, and diced
2 teaspoons curry
2½ tablespoons cornstarch
4 tablespoons powdered milk
1 teaspoon salt
1 teaspoon honey
1 teaspoon pepper
4 tablespoons cream
2 tablespoons raisins
1 banana, peeled and sliced

Wash the chicken and cut it into pieces. Dry thoroughly with paper towels. Heat margarine in a heavy skillet and brown chicken pieces on all sides. Place chopped onion on top of chicken. Cover and steam until onion is transparent. Pour broth over chicken and simmer for 30 minutes or until chicken is fork tender. Place apples with chicken. Add curry. When well mixed, remove chicken from pan and keep warm.

Remove 2 tablespoons of liquid and stir cornstarch into this to make a smooth paste. Add to liquid in the skillet. Add remaining ingredients in order given, stirring constantly. When the sauce is thickened and hot, pour over the waiting chicken and serve at once.

Grilled Chicken

INDIA	*Yield 4 to 6 servings*

1 2- to 3-pound chicken, halved or quartered, if you prefer
1 tablespoon salt
1 teaspoon curry powder
6 tablespoons butter
4 tablespoons bread crumbs

Wash chicken in cold water and dry with paper towels. Mix salt and curry together and rub mixture into chicken. Melt butter in a skillet. Roll chicken pieces into melted butter and then roll in bread crumbs. Broil in the oven at 500°F for 45 minutes. Baste frequently with remaining butter. Serve at once on a preheated platter.

Curried Chicken Salad

INDIA	*Yield 6 servings*

3 tablespoons instant minced onions
3 tablespoons water
2 tablespoons butter
1¼ teaspoons curry powder
⅓ cup mayonnaise
1 tablespoon lemon juice
½ teaspoon salt
Dash of cayenne pepper
3 cups cooked chicken, diced
1 (1-pound, 4-ounce) can pineapple chunks, drained
½ cup nuts, coarsely chopped

⅓ cup golden raisins
1 red apple, cored, diced
Lettuce
2 tablespoons shredded coconut

Combine onion and water in small bowl; let stand 10 minutes.

Melt butter in small skillet over medium heat; stir in onion and curry powder. Sauté, stirring constantly, 3 to 5 minutes; cool. Combine curry mixture with mayonnaise, lemon juice, salt, and cayenne; blend thoroughly.

Combine chicken, pineapple, nuts, raisins, and apple in large bowl. Add curry dressing; toss gently until mixed. Line salad bowl with lettuce. Add salad; sprinkle with coconut.

Indian Boats

INDIA   *Yield 8 servings*

½ cup flour
2 egg yolks
Generous pinch of salt
4 tablespoons butter
Extra butter for greasing molds
Flour for rolling dough

Filling

1 cup rice, cooked and drained
1 pound cooked, boned chicken meat

Sauce

3 tablespoons butter or margarine
1 small onion, peeled and finely chopped
2 tablespoons curry powder
3 tablespoons flour
2 cups hot chicken broth
Salt and white pepper to taste
Pinch of sugar
Juice of ½ lemon
Pinch of cayenne pepper

1 egg yolk
4 tablespoons cream
Green pepper, seeded and sliced in strips for
  garnish

To make the dough, place flour in a bowl, making a hole in the center. Add egg yolks and salt and cut in butter. Knead into a smooth dough and form into a ball. Refrigerate for 30 minutes.

Grease the boat molds or individual oven dishes. Roll out the dough to ¼ inch thick. Line molds with the dough. Place on a cookie sheet and bake at 300°F for 20 minutes. Remove from oven and invert molds on a rack and allow to cool.

In the meantime, cook and drain the rice. Cook and bone the chicken. Divide the cooked chicken into 8 portions. Set aside.

In a saucepan, heat the butter for the sauce. Add onion and cook until transparent. Dust with curry powder and cook for 2 minutes more. Add flour and cook for another 2 minutes. Gradually stir in the hot chicken broth and boil for 5 minutes. Season to taste with salt, pepper, sugar, lemon juice, and cayenne pepper. In a small bowl, whisk egg yolks and cream together. Gradually add this mixture to the sauce. Mix half the sauce with the cooked rice. Place rice mixture into the bottom of the dough boats. Put a portion of chicken on each and cover with remaining sauce. Garnish with green peppers and serve at once.

Chicken Fritada

PHILIPPINES   *Yield 4 to 6 servings*

1 3-pound chicken, cut into serving pieces
2 tablespoons lard
5 cloves garlic, peeled and crushed
1 large onion, finely sliced
2 ripe tomatoes, diced
1½ teaspoons salt
½ teaspoon black pepper
1½ cups hot chicken stock

1 pound new potatoes, scrubbed
1 red pepper, seeded and cut into strips
1 green pepper, seeded and cut into strips

Make chicken stock, using the neck, back, and wing tips of the chicken.

In a large skillet, heat lard and fry garlic and onion until soft. Gradually add chicken pieces, browning on both sides. Add tomatoes, salt, pepper, and 1½ cups of the stock. Cover and cook on medium heat until chicken is half done. Add potatoes and peppers and continue to cook until potatoes are tender. Serve at once, piping hot.

Chicken with Pork in Peanut Sauce

PHILIPPINES *Yield 6 to 8 servings*

1 3-pound chicken, skinned and boned
1 pound pork, with excess fat removed
4 ounces raw ham, diced
Salt and pepper
Water to cover

Sauce

½ cup uncooked rice
4 tablespoons lard
1 teaspoon annatto seeds
1 clove garlic, peeled and crushed
2 onions, peeled and finely chopped
2 tablespoons pork fat, diced
½ cup peanut butter
Salt to taste

Put chicken and prepared meats in a large saucepan with salt and pepper and water to cover. Bring to a boil; reduce heat and simmer until meat is fork tender.

Use a dry pan to toast rice over low heat until golden. Then grind to a powder with mortar and pestle, electric blender, or food processor. Heat

lard in skillet and fry annatto seeds for 1 minute. (Cover pan to prevent seeds from spattering.) Lift out seeds and discard. The remaining oil will be colored. Fry onions, garlic, and pork fat in this oil until soft.

Use enough stock from the chicken and pork to combine with ground rice and make a smooth cream. Add this plus the peanut butter to the frying pan. Bring sauce to a boil. Add more liquid if necessary. Heat through the chicken and meat in the sauce so that all flavors blend. Serve hot.

Chicken Adobo with Coconut Cream

PHILIPPINES *Yield 4 to 6 servings*

1 3-pound chicken, skinned and cut into serving pieces
¼ cup vinegar
Ground black pepper to taste
2 tablespoons salt
3 cloves garlic, peeled
2 cups coconut cream

In a deep pot, boil the prepared chicken with vinegar, pepper, salt, and garlic until tender. Remove whatever liquid remains in the pot. Add coconut cream and reduce the heat to a low simmer. When the coconut cream thickens into sauce consistency, remove from heat and serve at once.

Chicken Tinola

PHILIPPINES *Yield 4 to 6 servings*

1 3-pound chicken, cut into serving pieces
1 onion, peeled and sliced
2 cloves garlic, peeled and crushed

1 tablespoon fresh ginger, finely grated
1 tablespoon lard
2 cups water
1 green papaya, peeled and sliced
Fish sauce to taste
Pepper to taste

In a heavy saucepan, melt lard and fry onion, garlic, and ginger until tender. Add chicken pieces, stirring until browned on all sides. Put water in, cover pan, and simmer gently until chicken is tender. Add sliced papaya and continue to simmer until papaya is tender. Season with fish sauce and pepper to taste.

Chicken with Dates

CHINA *Yield 4 to 5 servings*

1 chicken, approximately 3 to 3½ pounds
Salt
Pepper
Curry powder
2 tablespoons oil
1 medium onion, chopped
2 green peppers, cut into thin strips
1 cup beef bouillon
½ pound rice
1 teaspoon cornstarch
12 dates, pitted, cut into halves
1 cup yogurt
3 tablespoons sliced almonds, toasted

Divide chicken into 8 pieces. Remove all bones except wing and leg bones. Rub chicken with salt, pepper, and curry powder. Heat oil in heavy skillet. Add chicken; cook until golden on all sides. Add onion; cook until golden. Add green peppers. Pour in bouillon; simmer over low heat 30 minutes.

Chicken curry II

75

Deep-fried sweet-and-sour chicken

Curried chicken salad

Meanwhile, cook rice according to package directions.

Remove chicken from sauce; keep warm. Strain sauce. Blend cornstarch with small amount cold water. Slowly stir into sauce; cook until thick and bubbly. Add dates.

Beat yogurt with fork; stir into sauce. If necessary, correct seasonings. Heat through, but do not boil. Spoon rice into bowl or platter; arrange chicken on top. Pour sauce over chicken; top with almonds.

Deep-Fried Sweet-and-Sour Chicken

CHINA *Yield 4 to 6 servings*

2 tablespoons cornstarch
2 tablespoons soy sauce
1 teaspoon salt
2 eggs
Oil for cooking
1 4-pound cooked chicken, boned, skinned, meat cut into 1-inch cubes

Chicken with date

Sweet-and-sour sauce

¾ cup sugar
2 tablespoons soy sauce
1 tablespoon dry white wine
3 tablespoons wine vinegar
3 tablespoons catsup
2 tablespoons cornstarch
½ cup water

Combine cornstarch and soy sauce; mix well. Combine salt and eggs in mixing bowl; beat with whisk until light. Stir in cornstarch mixture until just mixed.

Heat oil in deep-fryer to 375°F or until small ball of flour mixed with water dropped into oil floats to top immediately. Dip chicken into egg mixture; drain slightly. Drop chicken, several cubes at a time, into oil. Fry until lightly browned; drain on paper toweling. Place chicken in individual serving dishes. Spoon sweet-and-sour sauce over chicken.

To make sauce, combine sugar, soy sauce, wine, vinegar, and catsup in saucepan; bring to boil. Dissolve cornstarch in water; add to sauce. Cook over low heat, stirring, until sauce has thickened. Makes 1 to 1¼ cups.

Chinese Duck

CHINA   *Yield about 4 servings*

2 cups sherry
½ cup honey
2 tablespoons soy sauce
2 tablespoons candied ginger, finely chopped
2 teaspoons powdered mustard
1 teaspoon sesame seeds
1 3-to 4-pound duck

Salt
2 tablespoons margarine

Orange sauce

6 oranges
1 piece of candied ginger, approximately size of a walnut, chopped
2 to 3 tablespoons sugar
¼ cup sherry
1 teaspoon cornstarch
1 11-ounce can mandarin orange sections
1 banana

Garnish

1 orange, sliced
2 maraschino cherries
Parsley sprigs

Blend sherry, honey, soy sauce, finely chopped ginger, mustard, and sesame seeds thoroughly. Pour over duck in large bowl; cover and refrigerate for 3 hours, turning duck occasionally. Remove duck and drain well on paper toweling. Reserve marinade. Salt inside of duck lightly.

Heat margarine in large skillet or Dutch oven. Add duck and brown well on all sides. Place duck in preheated 350°F oven and cook for 1 hour and 10 minutes, basting occasionally with reserved marinade.

To prepare sauce, pare half an orange and cut rind into thin strips. Now squeeze oranges. Blend orange juice, sliced rind, and chopped ginger. Add sugar and half the sherry. Heat mixture in saucepan. Blend rest of sherry with cornstarch, and slowly add to orange sauce, stirring constantly until thick and bubbly. Drain mandarin orange sections and slice banana. Add half of the fruit to sauce. Place duck on preheated platter. Garnish with rest of mandarins, banana and orange slices, cherries, and parsley. Serve sauce separately.

Chicken with Mandarin Oranges and Almonds

CHINA	*Yield 6 servings*

2 ounces seedless raisins
1 jigger Madeira
1 3½- to 4-pound chicken, cut into serving pieces
2 teaspoons paprika
1 teaspoon white pepper
5 tablespoons oil
1 11-ounce can mandarin oranges, drained
1 clove garlic, minced
½ cup hot beef bouillon
1 tablespoon cornstarch
1 tablespoon soy sauce
½ teaspoon powdered ginger
½ cup heavy cream, lightly beaten
1 tablespoon butter
2 tablespoons sliced almonds

Cover raisins with Madeira and soak. Cut chicken into serving pieces. Mix paprika and pepper together, and rub chicken with this mixture. Heat oil in skillet or Dutch oven. Add chicken and fry until golden on all sides, about 10 minutes. Drain mandarin oranges, reserving juice. Measure ½ cup of juice and pour over chicken. Add minced garlic. Pour in beef bouillon, cover, and simmer for 30 minutes. Drain raisins and add them to pot; cook for another 5 minutes.

Remove chicken with slotted spoon; arrange on preheated platter and keep warm. Blend cornstarch with small amount of cold water; add to sauce, stirring constantly until thickened and bubbly. Season with soy sauce and powdered ginger. Add mandarin oranges and lightly beaten heavy cream. Heat through, but do not boil. Heat butter in small skillet. Add sliced almonds and cook until golden. Pour sauce over chicken and top with almonds.

Chicken Salad with Lichees

CHINA	*Yield 5 to 6 servings*

3 cups cooked chicken, diced
2 or 3 stalks celery, chopped
1 green pepper, chopped
Salt and pepper
¾ cup French dressing
Salad greens
1 can litchis
1 small can mandarin oranges

Curry salad dressing

¾ cup mayonnaise
¼ cup sour cream
2 teaspoons curry powder
2 tablespoons grated onions
2 tablespoons chopped parsley

Combine chicken, celery, and green pepper. Add salt, pepper, and French dressing; toss lightly. Chill about ½ hour.

Arrange salad greens around large platter. Pile chicken mixture in center.

Drain lichees and oranges. Place orange segment in each lichee; arrange around edge of platter.

Blend all dressing ingredients together; chill well. Serve dressing separately.

Chicken Livers with Eggs and Noodles

CHINA	*Yield 4 servings*

4 eggs
¼ teaspoon salt
1 tablespoon vegetable oil
½ pound mushrooms, sliced into "T" shapes

2 scallions, sliced
1 pound chicken livers, cubed
2 tablespoons dry sherry
5 tablespoons soy sauce
½ pound thin spaghetti noodles
2 tablespoons parsley, chopped

Combine eggs and salt; pour into oiled skillet. Cook over moderate heat, without stirring, until eggs are set. Cut into ½-inch cubes.

Heat oil in wok. Stir-fry mushrooms and scallions 1 to 2 minutes. Push aside. Stir-fry chicken livers 1 to 2 minutes. Add sherry and 4 tablespoons soy sauce. Combine liver and vegetables; heat through. Add cubed eggs.

Prepare spaghetti according to package directions; drain well. Gently combine with 1 tablespoon soy sauce. Serve noodles on platter with liver mixture. Garnish with chopped parsley.

Chicken Chow Mein

CHINA   *Yield 4 servings*

1 green sweet pepper, cut into slices
1 red sweet pepper, cut into slices
1 cup boiling water
1½ tablespoons butter
1 small onion, chopped
2 stalks celery, sliced
1 tablespoon flour
1 cup chicken broth
2 tablespoons soy sauce
Freshly ground pepper to taste
1 4-ounce can sliced mushrooms, drained
8 ounces cooked chicken breast, cut into bite-size pieces
6 cups water
8 ounces egg noodles
Salt
1 tablespoon butter

Oil for frying
4 ounces sliced almonds, toasted and slightly salted

Cut green and red peppers into slices. Blanch in boiling water for 5 minutes. Remove and drain. Heat 1½ tablespoons butter in saucepan. Add onions and celery and sauté until onions are transparent. Sprinkle with flour, pour in chicken broth, and bring to a boil while stirring constantly. Simmer for 10 minutes. Season with soy sauce and pepper. Add pepper slices, drained mushrooms, and chicken pieces. Cover and simmer for 15 minutes.

Meanwhile, bring 6 cups of slightly salted water to a boil; add noodles and cook for 15 minutes. Drain and rinse with cold water. Set aside ⅓ of the noodles. Place rest of noodles in heated bowl, add 1 tablespoon butter, cover and keep warm.

Heat oil in skillet until very hot. Cut noodles that were set aside into approximately 2-inch-long pieces. Add to hot oil and fry until golden. Drain on paper towels. To serve, spoon chicken mixture over buttered noodles; top with fried noodles and toasted almonds.

Chicken with Chinese Mushrooms

CHINA   *Yield 4 servings*

2 tablespoons soy sauce
1 tablespoon cornstarch
1 small fryer chicken, boned, skinned, and cut into bite-size pieces
1 clove garlic, cut in half lengthwise
3 slices gingerroot, ⅛ inch thick
1 tablespoon vegetable oil
½ pound fresh mushrooms, quartered

4 dried black Chinese mushrooms (soaked in warm water for 30 minutes, drained, and diced)
2 tablespoons hoisin sauce

Combine soy sauce and cornstarch. Pour over chicken; marinate ½ hour.

Brown the garlic and ginger slices in hot oil 2 to 3 minutes. Remove and discard garlic and ginger. Add both types of mushrooms to pan; stir-fry for 1 to 2 minutes. Remove mushrooms; reserve.

Stir-fry chicken 3 to 4 minutes or until done. Add hoisin sauce; return mushrooms to pan. Heat through. Serve over Oriental vegetables.

Chicken with Pineapple

CHINA	Yield 4 servings

1 chicken, approximately 2½ to 3 pounds, boned

Marinade

2 tablespoons cornstarch
3 tablespoons oil
4 tablespoons soy sauce
1 tablespoon sherry
Salt
Pepper

2 tablespoons oil
1 cup pineapple chunks, drained, reserving pineapple juice

Gravy

1 tablespoon oil
1 clove garlic, minced
½ cup pineapple juice
2 tablespoons sherry

Bone chicken and cut meat into bite-size pieces. Combine ingredients for marinade and blend thoroughly. Pour over chicken pieces, cover, and refrigerate for 30 minutes. Heat 2 tablespoons oil in heavy skillet. Drain chicken, reserving marinade. Add chicken to skillet and brown for about 5 minutes, while stirring constantly. Add drained pineapple chunks. Cover skillet and simmer over low heat for 12 minutes.

Remove chicken and pineapple chunks with slotted spoon. Arrange on preheated platter and keep warm. Add additional 1 tablespoon oil to pan drippings. Stir in minced garlic and cook for 5 minutes.

Blend pineapple juice with reserved marinade and sherry. Pour into skillet and heat through. Strain sauce through sieve, spoon over chicken and pineapple, and serve immediately. Delicious over rice.

Chicken with Ginger

INDOCHINA	Yield 4 servings

1½-pound frying chicken, cut into serving pieces
Salt to taste
Oil
Water
1 piece of fresh ginger
1 clove garlic, peeled and minced
1 medium onion, peeled and sliced

Bone the chicken and cut meat into small pieces. Sprinkle liberally with salt. Fry the meat in a small amount of oil until yellow. At the same time, add small amounts of hot water and continue to simmer until meat is tender.

Wash and skin ginger; cut into long pieces. Fry ginger in a small amount of oil until it gives a pleasant aroma. Remove from pan and set aside. In the same pan, fry the garlic and onion until they also give out a pleasant aroma. Remove and add to the ginger.

Place ginger, garlic, and onion in pan with the chicken meat. Add a small amount of hot water and allow all to blend and heat for 10 minutes more. Serve hot.

Chicken with Coconut Milk

INDOCHINA   *Yield 4 to 6 servings*

1 medium onion, peeled and chopped
1 clove garlic, peeled and minced
½ pound ground pork
¼ package fried, cured pork rinds
Red or white pepper to taste
Salt or nam pla to taste
1 cup coconut milk
1 2-pound chicken

Make a stuffing of the onion, garlic, ground pork, pork rinds, pepper, salt, and ¼ cup coconut milk. When this is all mixed and blended, stuff the cavity of the chicken with the mixture. Put the chicken in a deep pan, half filled with coconut milk. (If ¾ of a cup of coconut milk is not enough to half fill the pan, add more.) Cover the pan and cook on low heat until the chicken is fork tender and the coconut milk has thickened, about 30 minutes. Serve when chicken is tender, using the coconut milk as a gravy.

Steamed Chicken with Tomatoes

INDOCHINA   *Yield 4 servings*

1½ pounds breast and thigh pieces of chicken
3 ripe tomatoes, cut in wedges
3 spring onions, finely sliced

3 slices fresh ginger, cut into thin strips
2 tablespoons fish sauce
½ teaspoon salt
½ teaspoon sugar
Ground black pepper to taste
2 teaspoons sesame or vegetable oil

Prepare the chicken by boning and cutting the meat into bite-size pieces. Place chicken in a heat-proof bowl with tomatoes, onions, and ginger. Mix this thoroughly with fish sauce, salt, sugar, pepper, and oil. In order to steam the chicken, place bowl in a pan filled with water halfway up the dish. Cover and steam on the stove for 25 to 30 minutes, or until the meat is fork tender. Add extra fish sauce if desired and serve with a bowl of white rice.

Steamed Chicken with Mushrooms

INDOCHINA   *Yield 4 servings*

6 dried Chinese mushrooms
1 2-pound roasting chicken
1 tablespoon ginger, finely shredded
3 spring onions, sliced diagonally
Ground black pepper, liberally used
2 teaspoons fish sauce
1 small clove garlic, peeled and crushed
¼ teaspoon salt
1 teaspoon sesame oil

Soak mushrooms in hot water for at least 20 minutes. After cutting off and discarding stems, slice caps into thin slices. Divide the chicken in half. Set aside one half to be used at a later meal. Bone the chicken and cut flesh and skin into bite-size pieces. Place in a heat-proof bowl with all remaining ingredients. Mix well.

Bring water to a boil in large saucepan or deep frying pan. Place the bowl with chicken mixture

Chicken chow mein

Chinese duck (see next page)

Chicken salad with litchis

Chicken with Chinese mushrooms

Chicken livers with eggs and noodles

into saucepan; cover and steam for 25 to 30 minutes. If water in saucepan cooks away, add more. When cooked and tender, serve chicken with your favorite rice or noodles.

Braised Chicken with Mushrooms

KOREA *Yield 4 to 6 servings*

10 dried Chinese mushrooms
1 2-pound chicken, cut into small pieces
3 tablespoons light soy sauce
1 tablespoon sesame oil
2 cloves garlic, peeled and crushed
½ teaspoon cayenne powder or chili powder
½ teaspoon ground black pepper
2 tablespoons vegetable oil
1 large onion, cut into 8 wedges and then cut again
2 canned winter bamboo shoots
4 spring onions
2 tablespoons toasted sesame seeds, crushed

Soak mushrooms in boiling water for 20 to 30 minutes. Discard stems and then slice the mushroom caps into thin strips.

Marinate the chicken in a combination of soy sauce, sesame oil, garlic, cayenne pepper, and black pepper. Rub each piece of the chicken with this and allow them to marinate for at least 30 minutes.

Heat vegetable oil in skillet or wok. Over medium heat stir-fry the chicken until golden brown. Add mushroom strips and ½ cup of mushroom liquid. Add remaining marinade and cover. Simmer for 15 to 20 minutes.

Prepare the onion, separating the layers into pieces. Quarter the bamboo shoots and then slice. Cut spring onions into bite-size pieces. Add these to the already-simmering chicken and cook for 2 minutes more. Garnish with sesame seeds.

Chicken in Soy Sauce

KOREA   *Yield 4 servings*

3¾ cups water
1 2½- to 3-pound chicken, cut into serving
  portions
1 medium green pepper, cored, seeded, and
  thinly sliced
2 carrots, peeled and thinly sliced
8 mushrooms, sliced

Sauce

1 cup soy sauce
2 cups water
4 scallions
2 teaspoons garlic, crushed
1 tablespoon sugar
2 teaspoons freshly ground black pepper
1 tablespoon fresh gingerroot, crushed

In a large saucepan, bring water and chicken to a boil. Allow to boil gently for 5 minutes. While this is being done, use another pan to make the sauce. Combine all sauce ingredients, stir well, and allow to come to a boil.

Drain the chicken and add to the sauce; add peppers, carrots, and mushrooms. Return to a boil, then lower heat and simmer for 20 minutes, or until the chicken is tender. Serve at once.

Chicken Stew

KOREA   *Yield 4 to 6 servings*

1 3-pound roasting chicken, cut into small
  serving pieces
¼ cup light soy sauce
2 tablespoons sesame oil
1 tablespoon garlic, finely chopped
½ teaspoon chili powder or cayenne pepper

3 spring onions, finely chopped
¼ teaspoon salt

Place chicken in a heavy pan with all other ingredients in order given. Mix well so that the chicken is covered with the seasonings. Let stand for 2 hours at room temperature. When ready to cook, place on a low heat, cover, and cook 30 minutes or until chicken is fork tender. Delicious with white rice.

Chicken with Vegetables

KOREA   *Yield 4 servings*

1 pound boneless chicken, cut into 1-inch cubes
Vegetable oil for deep frying
2 medium carrots, peeled and sliced
2 medium potatoes, peeled and cubed
½ small red pepper, cored, seeded, and thinly
  sliced
½ small green pepper, cored, seeded, and
  thinly sliced
1 medium onion, peeled and chopped

Batter

1 cup all-purpose flour
2 eggs, well beaten
Approximately 2 tablespoons water

Sauce

2 tablespoons soy sauce
2 tablespoons water
1 tablespoon sugar
2 teaspoons fresh gingerroot, crushed
2 teaspoons garlic, peeled and crushed
2 tablespoons sake
1 tablespoon sesame oil
2 scallions
½ teaspoon salt

After the chicken is cubed and set aside, make the batter. Combine flour and eggs in a bowl. Add the water, stirring constantly until batter is smooth. Coat each piece of the chicken in the batter. Heat the oil in a deep-fat fryer and fry chicken pieces until all are golden brown. Remove from the fat and set aside to drain on paper towels.

Gently blanch the carrots and potatoes in boiling water for 3 minutes. Drain and dry thoroughly. Then deep-fry these vegetables for 5 minutes. Drain on paper towels.

Place all sauce ingredients in a saucepan and bring to a boil. Remove from heat.

Place oil in the bottom of a large skillet. Add chicken, carrots, potatoes, peppers, and onions. Stir-fry for 1 minute very gently. Increase the heat a little and then add the hot sauce. Stir constantly; when sauce has covered all other ingredients, serve at once.

Chicken with Coconut Milk Gravy

MALAYSIA	Yield 6 servings

1 3-pound roasting chicken, cut into serving
   pieces
2½ teaspoons fresh ginger, finely grated
2 medium onions, peeled and chopped
3 stalks lemon grass or rind of 1 lemon
6 fresh red chilies, seeded, or 2 teaspoons
   sambal ulek
1 teaspoon ground turmeric
3 tablespoons oil
3 cups thick coconut milk
3 strips (2 inches) daun pandan or few fresh
   basil leaves
2 teaspoons salt

After the chicken is cut, set aside. Make a paste of the ginger, onions, lemon grass, and chilies, adding a little oil to make the paste. Thoroughly coat the chicken with turmeric.

Heat oil in a heavy saucepan and gently fry the paste for about 15 minutes. Stir constantly. Add chicken and fry for another 10 minutes. Add coconut milk, pandan or basil, and salt. Allow to simmer uncovered for at least 20 minutes or until the chicken is tender. Serve at once.

This is a spicy dish.

Chicken and Bamboo Shoot Curry

MALAYSIA	Yield 6 to 8 servings

1 3-pound roasting fowl, cut into serving pieces
1 can bamboo shoots, drained, quartered, and
   sliced
2 medium onions, finely chopped
4 tablespoons coconut or peanut oil
1½ tablespoons ground coriander
1 teaspoon dried shrimp paste
1 teaspoon laos powder
1 teaspoon chili powder
2 teaspoons salt
2 cups thin coconut milk
1 cup thick coconut milk

Having prepared chicken, bamboo shoots, and onions as directed, heat oil in a large frying pan. Stir onions over medium heat until soft and golden. Add coriander, shrimp paste, laos, chili, and salt, allowing spices to cook until lightly browned. Place chicken pieces in spices and mix well. Add thin coconut milk and allow to simmer for 20 to 25 minutes. Add bamboo shoots and stir thoroughly. Simmer for an additional 20 minutes. When chicken is tender, add thick coconut milk and continue to simmer gently. Adjust salt if needed. Continue to simmer until oil rises to the top. Then serve at once.

Chicken Tarts

MALAYSIA	*Yield 12 tarts*

4 chicken breasts, skinned and boned

Sauce

3 tablespoons butter
1 medium onion, peeled and chopped
1 clove garlic, peeled and crushed
1 tart apple, peeled, cored, and diced
1 teaspoon tomato paste
1 heaping tablespoon flour
1 cup chicken broth
1 tablespoon grated coconut
1 teaspoon curry
Salt to taste

4 tablespoons oil
2 tablespoons mango chutney
12 small shortcake or puff pastry tarts
1 apple, peeled, cored, and cut in 8 slices
1 tablespoon butter
Ginger plums

Cut the chicken into bite-size pieces.

Heat the butter and fry the onion and garlic in it for 5 minutes, until onion is transparent. Add apple, then stir in tomato paste. Sprinkle with flour. Stir and cook for 3 minutes. Gradually stir broth into mixture and simmer gently for 20 minutes. Mix the sauce with coconut and curry and season with added salt if needed.

While the sauce is simmering, heat oil in a skillet and fry the chicken for about 6 minutes, until meat is golden brown. Dice mango chutney. Add this and the chicken to the finished sauce. Set aside and keep warm.

On a baking tin, bake pastry at 350°F for 5 minutes, until hot and crisp. While baking, fry apple slices in butter on each side for 2 minutes, until golden. Cut ginger plums into 8 slices.

Fill the baked tarts with the chicken mixture. Then cover with apple and ginger plum slices. Serve immediately.

Chicken Saté

MALAYSIA	*Yield 4 servings*

Use bamboo skewers, if available, for this saté. The word saté, sometimes spelled satay, refers to the process of grilling or broiling the chicken.

2 pounds chicken, preferably breasts and thighs, boned and skinned
1 tablespoon dark soy sauce
2 shallots, peeled and finely sliced
1 clove garlic, peeled and crushed
Pinch of chili powder, optional
1 tablespoon lemon juice, optional

Cut the chicken meat into 1-inch cubes. In a large bowl, mix remaining ingredients together. Coat each piece of the chicken with this mixture. Marinate for at least 1 hour so flavors are absorbed.

Divide chicken pieces onto skewers. Grill for 5 to 8 minutes, being sure to turn the skewers so that all sides are cooked and crisp. Serve hot with your choice of sauces. Peanut sauce or chili sauce are recommended with this chicken.

Baked Chicken Legs with Fruit

JAPAN	*Yield 6 servings*

1 teaspoon paprika
½ teaspoon ground ginger
1 teaspoon seasoned salt
¼ cup flour
6 chicken legs, disjointed, using thigh and leg
¼ cup shortening
1 29-ounce can or jar fruits-for-salad
3 oranges, peeled and cut into bite-size pieces
1 tablespoon brown sugar

2 teaspoons soy sauce
1 tablespoon cornstarch

Mix together paprika, ginger, seasoned salt, and flour. Place in small paper or double-plastic bag. Drop chicken in bag, one piece at a time, until well coated. Set aside.

Heat shortening in skillet to low-medium heat. Brown chicken on all sides.

Tear 6 pieces of heavy-duty aluminum foil large enough to hold chicken and fruit. On each piece of foil, place 1 thigh and 1 leg. Drain fruits, reserving liquid. Mix the canned fruit with the orange pieces; place 1/6 of fruit on each piece of foil, along with chicken pieces.

Into small saucepan, place 1 cup of fruit syrup, brown sugar, soy sauce, and cornstarch. Mix well; bring to a boil. Simmer for 3 minutes. Spoon sauce over chicken and fruit. Fold foil; seal, by double-folding edges. Place packages in pan; bake at 425°F for 1½ hours or until chicken is tender.

Chicken with Almonds

JAPAN	*Yield 4 servings*

4 ounces almonds, whole, sliced, or slivered
   (blanched)
3 tablespoons oil, peanut or vegetable
¾ cup chopped onion
4 chicken breasts, boned and thinly sliced
2 cans sliced bamboo shoots, drained
1 can water chestnuts, drained and sliced
1 cucumber, unpeeled and thinly sliced
½ cup chicken stock
2 teaspoons sherry
¼ teaspoon ground ginger
1 teaspoon soy sauce
½ teaspoon cornstarch
1 tablespoon cold water
Salt to taste
Freshly ground pepper to taste

Brown almonds in 400°F oven for about 10 minutes. Watch closely.

Pour oil into large frying pan or wok; heat to medium-high heat. Add onion; cook it until limp. Remove onion from pan (or push up the side, if using wok). Add chicken; toss gently for about 1 minute. Add bamboo shoots and water chestnuts; toss gently for 1 minute. Add cucumber; cook for 1 minute.

Combine chicken stock, sherry, ginger, and soy sauce. Add to pan; cook for 1 minute.

Combine cornstarch and water in a small dish. Stir slowly into hot mixture. Season with salt and pepper; cook until liquid is thickened. While it is cooking, return onions to mixture.

Serve chicken with rice and the browned almonds.

Sesame Chicken

JAPAN	*Yield 3 to 4 servings*

1 2½- to 3-pound chicken, cut-up
Flour mixed with salt and pepper
2 eggs, beaten
2 tablespoons milk
1 cup flour mixed with ½ cup sesame seeds, ½
   teaspoon salt, and ¼ teaspoon pepper
Peanut oil for frying

Cream sauce

4 tablespoons butter, melted
4 tablespoons flour
½ cup half-and-half
1 cup chicken stock
½ cup whipping cream
½ teaspoon salt or onion salt, if desired

Wash chicken; pat dry. Dust with seasoned flour. Mix beaten eggs with milk. Dip chicken into this mixture, then roll it in the sesame-seed mixture. Fry in oil until light brown and tender.

To prepare the sauce, blend the flour into the butter over low heat, stirring constantly. Mix

Chicken with pineapple

Chicken with mandarin oranges and almonds

Chicken tarts

together the half-and-half, chicken stock, and whipping cream. Gradually add to the butter and flour, stirring constantly. When smooth, stir in the salt or onion salt. Serve sauce immediately with the chicken.

Chicken Teriyaki

JAPAN   *Yield 4 servings*

This is delicious served with rice that has pan drippings poured over it.

1 2½ - to 3-pound broiler chicken, cut up

Marinade

¾ cup soy sauce
¼ cup sugar
¼ cup sherry or sake
2 teaspoons fresh gingerroot, grated
1 large clove garlic, crushed

Wash chicken; pat dry. Mix together marinade ingredients. Place chicken in marinade. Cover and refrigerate for several hours, turning occasionally.

Drain chicken, reserving marinade. Place skin-side-down in greased baking pan. Bake in 450°F oven for 15 minutes. Turn chicken; bake for another 15 minutes. Reduce oven temperature to 350°F. Pour off and reserve liquid in pan. Continue baking for approximately 30 minutes or until chicken is tender, brushing occasionally with reserved marinade. Broil (if desired) about 6 inches from heat until well browned.

Skewered Chicken Pieces

JAPAN   *Yield 2 servings*

1½ to 2 pounds chicken meat, cut in cubes

Marinade

1 cup soy sauce
1 cup sake (rice wine) or sherry
3 tablespoons sugar, or little less
2 teaspoons freshly ground pepper

Mix together soy sauce, sake or sherry, sugar, and pepper; bring to a boil. Marinate the chicken in the marinade for 30 minutes; put chicken pieces on skewer and broil, or put them on a grill or hibachi. Brush with extra marinade during cooking, turning to brown well on all sides.

Chicken Breasts Teriyaki

JAPAN	*Yield 2 to 3 servings*

2 chicken breasts, halved, boned, and skin
   removed
4 tablespoons oil
4 tablespoons soy sauce
4 tablespoons sugar
½ teaspoon freshly grated ginger or ¼
   teaspoon ground ginger

Parboil chicken breasts for only about 30 seconds. Drain. Heat oil medium high; brown the chicken. Pour off the oil. Add the soy sauce, sugar, and ginger to the pan; cover and simmer until sauce is like syrup. Serve chicken with rice, if desired.

Chicken Patties

JAPAN	*Yield 4 to 6 servings*

¾ cup leftover cooked chicken, chopped
2 cups mashed potatoes
2 eggs
Bread or cracker crumbs
Oil for frying

Combine chicken, potatoes, and eggs. Mix well. Roll in bread or cracker crumbs; fry in hot oil. Dip patties in soy sauce, if desired, before enjoying.

Chicken Sukiyaki

JAPAN	*Yield 2 to 3 servings*

2 cups chicken stock
1 cup sugar
1 cup soy sauce
1 pound chicken meat, cut into bite-size pieces
8 large mushrooms, sliced
3 carrots, sliced diagonally and parboiled
6 scallions, cut into 2-inch lengths

Boil chicken stock that has been mixed with sugar and soy sauce. Add half of the chicken; simmer about 12 minutes. Add remaining ingredients; simmer another 3 minutes. Serve this with rice.

Chicken with Sesame Seeds

JAPAN	*Yield 2 servings*

This may also be made with pork or beef.

12 ounces boned chicken wings or breast meat
2 tablespoons rice wine or sherry
½ teaspoon (scant) salt
½ teaspoon oil
2 teaspoons sesame seeds

Sprinkle chicken with rice wine or sherry and salt. Set aside for 30 minutes. Heat oil in frying pan, brown meat on both sides, and remove to preheated platter. Heat sesame seeds in frying pan; sprinkle on the chicken.

Fried Steak with Chili

INDONESIA   *Yield 4 servings*

1¼ pounds New York sirloin or round steak
2 teaspoons coriander powder
2 tablespoons tamarind water
1 teaspoon brown sugar
1 or more teaspoons salt to taste
Freshly ground black pepper to taste
8 red chilies, seeded and chopped
4 shallots, peeled and chopped
2 cloves garlic, peeled and chopped
6 tablespoons vegetable oil
1 teaspoon lemon juice

Slice the meat into thin strips; then cut into 2-inch squares. Arrange squares on plate singly and sprinkle with coriander, tamarind water, brown sugar, salt, and pepper. Use your fingers to press the spice mixture into the meat. Allow to stand for 2 to 3 hours.

Pound the chilies, shallots, and garlic until just broken into pieces. Set aside.

Heat oil in a skillet; brown the meat evenly on both sides until cooked through. Remove from pan. Add the pounded mixture to the oil and cook for 2 minutes. Return the meat to the skillet and coat with spices. Sprinkle with lemon juice and add more salt if needed. Serve hot at once.

Sliced Beef

INDONESIA   *Yield 4 servings*

1 pound lean steak, rump or round
1 onion, peeled and chopped
4 cloves garlic, peeled
1 teaspoon coarsely ground black pepper
3 tablespoons dark soy sauce

2 tablespoons palm sugar
2 tablespoons peanut oil
2 ripe tomatoes, chopped

Slice the meat thinly and beat with a mallet, being careful not to break the slices.

Make a smooth mixture (electric blender or food processor is good to use here) of onion, garlic, pepper, soy sauce, and sugar. Pour this over the meat slices and allow to marinate at room temperature for at least 1 hour.

Use a skillet or wok and heat oil. Add the drained meat slices and brown on both sides. Pour marinade and tomatoes into skillet and lower heat to medium. Stir frequently while this cooks for about 12 minutes. When meat is fork tender, serve piping hot.

Lamb Stew

INDONESIA   *Yield 6 to 8 servings*

Although very meaty, this is a fairly liquid stew and should be served over rice.

4 kemiri, chopped
1 small onion, peeled and chopped
3 cloves garlic, peeled and chopped
2 teaspoons coriander powder
1 teaspoon ginger powder
½ teaspoon turmeric powder
Pinch of white pepper
Pinch of cayenne pepper
Pinch of chili powder
Pinch of laos powder
2 tablespoons vegetable oil
2 pounds boneless leg or shoulder of lamb,
   cubed small
1 teaspoon brown sugar
¼ cup tamarind water

Salt to taste
1 sereh stalk, bruised
1 small cinnamon stick
3 whole cloves
1 salam leaf, optional
2 cups water
2 cups thick santen (coconut milk)

Make a smooth paste of kemiri, onion, and garlic. Add spices in order given and mix well.

Heat oil in a heavy pan. Stirring constantly, fry the spice paste for 1 minute. Add the lamb and stir-fry for 2 minutes. Stir in brown sugar, tamarind water, and salt to taste. Cover and simmer for 4 minutes.

Add all remaining ingredients except the santen. Simmer, covered, for 20 minutes. Last, pour in the santen, cover, and simmer for 25 minutes more, stirring occasionally. Remove the sereh, cinnamon, cloves, and salam leaf. Pour the stew into a deep serving dish and serve at once.

Spareribs of Beef

INDONESIA	Yield 4 to 6 servings

3 pounds beef spareribs, cut into individual ribs
   and short lengths
3 cloves garlic, peeled and finely chopped
1 teaspoon fresh ginger, finely grated
1 teaspoon salt
3 tablespoons peanut oil
¼ cup dark soy sauce
½ cup water
2 tablespoons dry sherry
½ teaspoon five-spice powder
¼ teaspoon ground black pepper
1 tablespoon palm sugar or honey

Rub prepared ribs with garlic, ginger, and salt. Heat oil in a skillet or wok and stir-fry ribs on high heat until they are browned. Combine remaining ingredients, except the sugar or honey, in a bowl and pour over the ribs. Bring to a boil, then reduce heat to simmer. Cover and cook until meat is tender and liquid absorbed. Then uncover. Stir in sugar or honey and stir until dissolved. Serve hot.

If you prefer ribs with a heavier glaze, place in a moderately hot oven for a few minutes more.

Beef with Hot Salad

THAILAND	Yield 4 servings

1 pound fillet steak
1 large onion, peeled and sliced into rings
2 fresh chilies
2 garlic cloves, peeled and crushed
½ teaspoon sugar
1 teaspoon salt
½ teaspoon soy sauce
Juice of 1 lime or lemon
1 teaspoon chopped mint
Fresh seasonal vegetables (cucumber, tomatoes,
   bok choy, bean sprouts, etc.), chopped

Slice the beef into strips measuring 2½ inches long, 1 inch wide, and ½ inch thick. Set aside.

Place onions and chilies on a skewer and broil until soft; then remove and finely mash them.

Broil the beef; mix cooked beef with onion and chilies. Add all remaining ingredients, except the vegetables, and mix.

Arrange chopped vegetables around the edge of a warm serving dish. Place beef mixture in center and quickly toss vegetables and beef together. Serve at once.

Fried Beef and Horapa

THAILAND	Yield 4 servings

Horapa is a spice used in Thailand. If unavailable, sweet basil may be used as a substitute.

2 tablespoons plus 1 teaspoon vegetable oil
1½ pounds chuck steak, thinly sliced
2 onions, peeled and sliced
3 cloves garlic, peeled and finely chopped
3 tablespoons horapa leaves, freshly chopped
3 fresh chilies, sliced
Nam pla to taste
Chopped scallions for garnish

Heat 1 teaspoon oil in a skillet or wok. Fry the beef until the juices are extracted. Stir twice and cook for about 3 minutes. Remove beef and set aside.

Add remaining oil to skillet and fry onions and garlic until brown. Stir in horapa. Return beef to the pan and add chilies. Stir-fry for 1 minute. Add nam pla to taste. Place meat on a serving dish and garnish with scallions.

Fried Meat Balls

THAILAND   *Yield about 30 small balls*

¼ pound chopped beef
¼ pound chopped pork
¼ teaspoon ground black pepper
½ teaspoon ground nutmeg
2 tablespoons fresh coriander leaves, finely
   chopped
4 cloves garlic, peeled and crushed
½ teaspoon salt
1 spring onion, finely chopped
2 teaspoons fish sauce
1 tablespoon beaten egg
½ cup or more flour
Lard for frying

Mix beef and pork in a bowl. If pork is lean, add 1 tablespoon finely diced pork fat. Mix the meat with all ingredients except the flour and lard. Form into small balls, rolling between your palms. Roll each ball in flour generously. Heat fat on medium heat. Fry meat balls for about 5 minutes or until golden brown and cooked through. Drain on paper towels and serve.

Sweet Pork

THAILAND   *Yield about 4 servings*

While some cooks use sweet pork as an ingredient in other dishes, some serve it by itself with a hot chili sauce and rice.

1 pound loin of pork
3 cups water
½ cup palm sugar
½ cup fish sauce

Cut rind from the pork but save it. Slice the pork into thin slices. In a medium-size saucepan, cook both pork and rind, water, sugar, and fish sauce over medium heat. When mixture comes to a boil, skim off the top. Cover. Reduce heat and cook for 40 minutes. Continue cooking uncovered until the pork is quite tender to the fork. Allow to cool. Use as a main dish or in Pork and Chicken Soup (see Index).

Beef Curry

BURMA   *Yield 4 to 6 servings*

Marinate this beef overnight and then cook very slowly. Cooking time varies according to the tenderness of the meat.

2½ pounds chuck steak, cut into 1-inch cubes
1 tablespoon shrimp-flavored soy sauce
½ teaspoon turmeric powder
1 tablespoon malt or cider vinegar
2 medium onions, peeled and pounded

Skewered lamb

Kabobs

4 garlic cloves, peeled and crushed
1-inch piece of fresh gingerroot, peeled and
   pounded
1 teaspoon chili powder
¼ cup vegetable oil
3 bay leaves
2 pieces of cinnamon stick
5 peppercorns
Salt to taste

Marinate the beef in a bowl with soy sauce, turmeric, and vinegar.

Blend the onions, garlic, ginger, and chili powder. Heat oil in a deep heavy pan and stir-fry the onion mixture for about 10 minutes. When it begins to brown, it is done.

Place beef, bay leaves, cinnamon, peppercorns, and onion mixture in enough boiling water to half cover the beef. Cover and simmer for 45 minutes until meat is tender. Add water if necessary. Adjust seasonings, adding salt if needed at the end of the cooking time. Serve hot with rice or noodles.

99

Meat

Kabobs Kati

Mandarin liver

Dry Pork Curry

BURMA   *Yield 4 servings*

1 pound pork, cut into 2-inch pieces with some
   fat left on meat
1 large onion, peeled and chopped
3 cloves garlic, peeled and crushed
1 teaspoon fresh ginger, finely grated
½ teaspoon chili powder
½ teaspoon ground turmeric
3 tablespoons light sesame oil
1 stalk lemon grass or 2 strips lemon rind
2 tablespoons tamarind liquid
1 tablespoon fish sauce

When meat is prepared, set it aside. Purée and
cook onion, garlic, ginger, chili, and turmeric in
oil over low heat for at least 10 minutes, stirring
with a wooden spoon to prevent sticking to the
pan. Add pork and allow all to simmer until meat

Lamb with saffron rice

Meat platter Szechwan

Chop suey

Beef slices Peking

is tender. Finely chop the lemon grass and add it to the meat along with the tamarind liquid and fish sauce. When the water has evaporated and the oil separates from the gravy, the meat is done. Serve at once.

Beef and Potato Curry

BURMA   *Yield 4 to 6 servings*

1½ pounds beef, cut into large squares
12 ounces potatoes, peeled, cut, and quartered
2 large onions, peeled and chopped
5 large cloves garlic, peeled and crushed
2 teaspoons fresh ginger, chopped
1 teaspoon ground turmeric
1 teaspoon chili powder
8 tablespoons light sesame oil or corn oil
½ teaspoon ground cumin
½ teaspoon ground coriander
1½ teaspoons salt
2 cups water

Purée and cook onions, garlic, ginger, turmeric, and chili powder in oil over low heat for at least 10 minutes. Stir with a wooden spoon to prevent sticking. Add the meat, cumin, and coriander and stir-fry for 5 minutes. Add salt, water, and potatoes. Reduce heat and simmer slowly until meat and potatoes are both fork tender. Serve from a warmed serving platter or in individual portions.

Red Pork

BURMA   *Yield 4 to 6 servings*

This dish takes its name from the color of the chili powder and is very rich and flavorful.

2 pounds boneless pork, cubed into 1-inch pieces

3 tablespoons soy sauce
1 teaspoon freshly ground black pepper
2-inch piece of fresh gingerroot, peeled
3 medium onions, peeled and pounded
3 garlic cloves, peeled and crushed
1 cup boiling water
1 teaspoon chili powder
⅓ cup vegetable oil

Mix the pork with 2 tablespoons soy sauce and pepper. Set aside.

Pound half the ginger and mix with onions and garlic. Stir in all but 1 tablespoon of the boiling water. Strain and save both the liquid and the ingredients.

Stir chili powder into reserved boiling water. Slice remaining ginger into strips. Heat oil in large skillet and fry ginger until just sizzling. Add pork and stir-fry until brown. Pour in reserved liquid, cover the pan, and simmer for 10 minutes, until liquid has been absorbed. Add chili water, remaining soy sauce, and reserved mixture. Reduce heat and cook for 40 minutes covered, stirring occasionally. If needed, add a small amount of extra water during cooking time to prevent sticking.

Spiced Beef in Yogurt

INDIA   *Yield 4 servings*

1 pound beef, thinly sliced
1 teaspoon salt
1¼ cups unflavored yogurt
¾ cup ghee
1 large onion, peeled and sliced
3 cloves garlic, peeled and sliced
1½ teaspoons ginger powder
2 teaspoons coriander powder
2 teaspoons chili powder
½ teaspoon cumin powder
1½ teaspoons turmeric powder
1 teaspoon garam masala

Tenderize beef slices with a mallet; rub with salt and place in a bowl. Cover with yogurt and allow to marinate overnight.

Melt ghee in a heavy skillet. Fry onion and garlic gently until soft. Add spices and stir-fry for 3 minutes. Add beef and marinade to pan. Stir to blend and cover. Reduce heat and simmer for 1½ hours or until meat is tender. Serve at once.

Skewered Lamb

INDIA	*Yield 6 servings*

2 pounds lamb, preferably from the leg, cubed
1 teaspoon ground caraway
1 teaspoon salt
White pepper to taste
Pinch of saffron
½ teaspoon ground ginger
1 clove garlic, peeled and crushed
½ bunch parsley, chopped
6 onions, peeled
2 cups sour cream
¼ pound bacon
1 tablespoon ground caraway
1 tablespoon ground black pepper

In a bowl, put 1 teaspoon caraway, salt, pepper, saffron, ginger, garlic and parsley. Finely chop 1 onion and add to the spices with the sour cream. Mix well. Add the meat and cover. Refrigerate for at least 2 hours.

Quarter remaining onions and cut bacon into ½-inch pieces. Set aside.

When ready to cook, remove meat from marinade, reserving the liquid. Place meat on skewers, alternating with onion pieces and bacon. Grill for 45 minutes, turning frequently and basting with marinade. Dish on a preheated platter and sprinkle with caraway and pepper.

Kabobs

INDIA	*Yield 4 to 6 servings*

2 quarts salted water
1 pound lamb, ground
2 small potatoes, cooked in jackets, peeled and mashed
1 onion, peeled and grated
1 small green pepper pod, finely chopped
½ bunch parsley, chopped
1 teaspoon mustard
1 teaspoon curry
1 teaspoon salt
4 tablespoons rice flour
Oil for frying

When salted water has come to a boil, place ground lamb in a kitchen strainer and submerge the meat in the water for 2 minutes. Drain and place in a mixing bowl.

Add mashed potatoes to meat with onion, pepper, and parsley. Season with mustard, curry, and salt. Mix well.

Run cold water over your hands and then roll the meat mixture into small balls. Put each ball into rice flour, then fry in heated oil for 5 to 7 minutes. Remove from the pan and drain on paper towels, then serve.

Kabobs Kati

INDIA	*Yield 4 to 6 servings*

Marinade

2 cups yogurt
Juice of 1 lemon
2 onions, peeled and grated
1 clove garlic, peeled and finely chopped
Salt to taste
2 fresh pepper pods, finely chopped

1 teaspoon curry
½ teaspoon ground ginger
1 pound beef fillet
1 pound lamb
3 tablespoons oil
Parsley for garnish

Mix yogurt and lemon juice in a large bowl. Add onion, garlic, salt, and pepper pods. Stir in the curry and ginger and mix well.

Notch the meat deeply — but do not cut through — into cubes. Place meat in yogurt mixture, cover and let stand for 1 hour. Remove meat and allow to drain. Cut into cubes. Place on four skewers and brush with oil. Put skewers into rotating mechanism or place them on grill so that handles can be turned to brown meat on all sides. Grill for 30 minutes. Place meat on platter. Garnish with parsley and serve.

Tasty Kabobs

INDIA *Yield 4 to 6 servings*

Marinade

2 medium onions, peeled and grated
2 tablespoons currant jelly
10 pimiento corns, crushed
Generous dash of ground ginger

1½ pounds pork fillet, cubed
4 tablespoons butter
2 tablespoons water
2 tablespoons peanut butter
½ teaspoon ground cinnamon
Pinch of ground cloves
2 teaspoons cornstarch
3 tablespoons yogurt

In a large bowl, mix onions with currant jelly. Add pimientoes and ginger to onion mixture. Place meat cubes in this and allow to stand for 2 hours. Stir from time to time. Remove meat and scrape off any remnant of the marinade with a knife. Put cubes on skewers.

Heat butter and water in a pot. Stir in peanut butter until a creamy mass forms. Season with cinnamon and cloves. In a cup, mix cornstarch with yogurt, then add to bowl. Mix well. Place skewers of meat on rotating mechanism of grill. Brush with peanut butter mixture. Grill meat for 50 minutes, turning and brushing several times. Serve hot.

Lamb with Saffron Rice

INDIA *Yield 4 to 6 servings*

4 cups water
1 cup long-grain rice
1 teaspoon salt
3 tablespoons boiling water
¼ teaspoon saffron threads
6 tablespoons oil
2 onions, peeled and finely chopped
½ teaspoon chopped caraway
¼ teaspoon yellow ginger
1 pound lean ground lamb
Salt to taste
1 bunch parsley, chopped
¼ teaspoon fennel seed
1 cup chicken broth

Bring water to a boil. Add salt and stir in rice. Boil uncovered for 10 minutes. Drain.

Meanwhile, pour 3 tablespoons boiling water over saffron threads in a cup. Let sit for 10 minutes.

Heat 3 tablespoons oil in a skillet. Fry onions for 3 minutes. Sprinkle with caraway and ginger. Stir for 1 minute more. Add ground lamb and season with salt. Fry for 10 minutes, stirring to prevent sticking. Remove from the range. Mix chopped parsley into it.

Heat remaining oil in a fire-proof casserole. Stir in fennel and drained rice. Cook for 2 minutes. Add saffron threads with their liquid and mix well. Remove from heat.

Remove ⅔ of saffron rice mixture from casserole. Spread the remaining evenly on the bottom. Cover with half the ground lamb. Add a layer of rice, the remaining meat, and then the remaining rice. Carefully pour chicken broth over all. Return to stove and allow to come to a boil. Then remove and cover casserole. Place in a 350°F oven for 25 minutes. When rice is soft and liquid absorbed, remove from oven. Fluff the surface with a fork and serve at once.

Ground Beef with Fresh Peas

INDIA	Yield 4 to 6 servings

2 tablespoons ghee
1 large onion, peeled and finely sliced
2 cloves garlic, peeled and crushed
½ teaspoon fresh ginger, finely grated
1 teaspoon ground turmeric
½ teaspoon chili powder
1 pound ground meat
½ cup yogurt
1 cup fresh green peas
1 teaspoon garam masala
1½ teaspoons salt
2 tablespoons fresh coriander leaves, finely chopped
1 fresh, red chili, finely sliced

Fry onions in heated ghee until soft. Add garlic and ginger and continue to fry until onions are golden brown. Add turmeric and chili powder, stir briefly, and add meat.

Continue to stir meat, breaking up large lumps, until it is browned. Then add yogurt and peas and lower the heat. Cover and cook for 15 minutes. Stir in garam masala and continue cooking until meat and peas are tender. Garnish with coriander leaves and chili.

Pork Vindaloo

INDIA	Yield 4 to 6 servings

Vindaloo mixtures can be purchased in many specialty food stores. Use only if you prefer a hot curry. Vindaloo is used dry or mixed into a paste with vinegar, according to the needs of the recipe.

3 tablespoons onions, peeled and chopped
½ teaspoon garlic, peeled and chopped
½ cup butter or fat
3 tablespoons vindaloo, made into paste with vinegar
2 pounds pork, cut into cubes
1 teaspoon salt

In a large heavy skillet, heat butter and sauté onions and garlic until onions are golden. Add the vindaloo mixture and cook, stirring constantly, for 3 minutes, using low heat. Add pork and salt. Cover and simmer over low heat until pork is tender and cooked through. Add water if needed to make a thick gravy. Stir frequently, as this dish can burn quickly. Serve hot.

Beef and Pork Balls

PHILIPPINES	Yield 4 servings

½ pound ground pork
½ pound ground beef
1 teaspoon salt
¼ teaspoon pepper
1 small egg, beaten
1½ tablespoons oil

Ginger beef

Chinese stir-fried beef and mushrooms

Pork with peppers and cashews

Meat

Tasty fondue

Teriyaki meatballs

Pork and peas

108

2 cloves garlic, peeled and finely chopped
1 medium onion, peeled and finely chopped
2 ripe tomatoes, diced
4 cups broth
2 teaspoons soy sauce

Mix meats, salt, pepper, and egg in a bowl. Roll into small balls about 1½ inches in diameter.

In a deep pan, heat oil and fry garlic and onion until golden. Add tomatoes and stir-fry until soft. Add broth and bring to a boil. Put in meatballs one at a time and let them simmer slowly until cooked through. Add soy sauce and serve at once.

Pork Adobo

PHILIPPINES	*Yield 6 servings*

6 pork loin chops or leg chops, about 2 pounds
8 to 10 cloves garlic, peeled
1 cup white vinegar
1 cup water
1½ teaspoons salt
2 bay leaves
½ teaspoon ground black pepper
Lard or oil for frying

Cut chops into serving pieces. In a deep sauce-pan, marinate the meat in all the listed ingredients except the lard. Allow to stand for 1 hour. Bring this to a boil, then reduce the heat and simmer until pork is tender—40 minutes to 1 hour. Lift the meat out of the pan.

Allow the liquid to boil by itself until it is reduced and thickened. Strain this into a small bowl. Allow to stand until fat rises to the top. Take off the fat and put it in a frying pan. Add enough fat to cover the bottom of the pan. Fry the pork until it is crisp and brown on both sides. Arrange on a serving platter and pour gravy over all. Serve with white rice.

Sweet-and-sour pork

Stuffed Rolled Beef

PHILIPPINES	*Yield 6 to 8 servings*

1 3-pound flank steak, in 1 piece
1 ½ teaspoons salt
½ teaspoon ground black pepper
2 tablespoons lemon juice
2 cloves garlic, peeled and crushed
2 sweet gherkin pickles
2 chorizo sausages
2 thick slices cooked ham
2 hard-boiled eggs, cut into quarters
2 tablespoons lard
2 tablespoons vinegar
3 ripe tomatoes, peeled and chopped
2 cups water

Begin at the thickest edge of the steak and make cuts in the meat, being careful not to cut all the way through. This will flatten the meat and almost double the size. Season this with salt, pepper, and lemon juice, and rub crushed garlic into the meat.

Picadillo

PHILIPPINES	*Yield 6 servings*

1 tablespoon lard
4 cloves garlic, peeled and finely chopped
1 medium onion, peeled and finely chopped
1 pound lean ground beef
2 tomatoes, peeled and chopped
2 cups beef stock
1 teaspoon salt
¼ teaspoon ground black pepper
1 pound potatoes, peeled and cubed

Cook garlic and onions in lard until both are soft and golden. Add beef and stir until meat is browned. Put in tomatoes and cook until soft. Add stock, salt, and pepper and bring to a boil. Reduce heat to medium, cover the pot, and cook for 20 minutes. Add the potatoes and cook 25 minutes more or until potatoes are done. Serve at once.

Marinated steak

Slice pickles and chorizos the long way and slice the ham into strips. Arrange all of these ingredients plus the quartered eggs on top of the meat. Roll the meat around the ingredients and tie with a string.

In a large frying pan, heat the lard. Brown the meat on all of its outer surfaces, turning with tongs. If there is excess fat, drain. Add remaining ingredients and bring to a boil. Cover the pan, reduce heat, and simmer for 1¼ hours, until meat is tender. Lift out meat and place on a cutting board. Thicken sauce by bringing it to a rapid boil. Remove string from meat and slice into serving pieces. Serve with its own gravy.

Meat Platter Szechwan

CHINA	*Yield 4 servings*

7 tablespoons oil
6 ounces fresh mushrooms, sliced
½ pound tomatoes, peeled, sliced
½ pound green peppers, cut in half, seeds removed, cut into julienne strips
1 ½ pounds lean pork, cut into 2-inch-long julienne strips
Salt
¼ teaspoon ground ginger
½ pound onions, minced
1 clove garlic, minced
2 tablespoons sherry
1 cup hot beef broth (made from cubes)
1 tablespoon soy sauce
2 tablespoons cornstarch
4 tablespoons water

Heat 4 tablespoons oil in skillet. Add mushrooms, tomatoes, and green peppers. Cook 5 minutes; set aside.

Heat 3 tablespoons oil in another skillet. Add meat strips. Season to taste with salt and ginger, stirring constantly. Brown 10 minutes. Add onions and garlic; cook 5 minutes. Pour in sherry. After 1 minute, pour in broth and soy sauce. Add vegetable mixture. Cover; cook over medium heat 25 minutes.

Blend cornstarch with water; stir in. Cook until thickened and bubbly. Serve immediately on preheated platter.

Chop Suey

CHINA	*Yield about 3 servings*

1 pound lean pork, cut into thin slices
2 tablespoons sherry
2 tablespoons soy sauce
Salt to taste
Freshly ground pepper to taste
Pinch of powdered ginger
2 ounces transparent noodles, broken into small pieces
1 stalk celery, cut into thin slices
4 tablespoons dried Chinese mushrooms, soaked in water for 30 minutes
8 tablespoons oil
2 medium onions, thinly sliced
¼ cup bamboo shoots, thinly sliced
1 cup fresh bean sprouts
½ pound fresh mushrooms, sliced
3 tablespoons soy sauce
1 teaspoon sugar
1 tablespoon cornstarch
2 jiggers sherry
Cooked rice

Cut pork into thin slices and mix with 2 tablespoons sherry, 2 tablespoons soy sauce, salt, pepper, and ginger. Place in glass or ceramic bowl. Press down meat and cover. Let marinate for 1 hour.

Break noodles into small pieces and boil in salted water for 5 minutes. Drain and set aside. Cut celery in thin slices; blanch for 5 minutes. Drain and set aside. Slice Chinese mushrooms into bite-size pieces.

111

Heat oil in skillet until very hot. Add marinated pork and fry for 2 minutes. Remove and keep warm. Add onions, bamboo shoots, bean sprouts, and fresh mushrooms. Simmer for 3 minutes. Fold in meat, celery, and noodles. Season with 3 tablespoons soy sauce and sugar. Stirring carefully, cook for an additional 3 minutes. Blend cornstarch with 2 jiggers sherry and slowly stir it into the sauce until sauce is thick and bubbly. Correct seasonings if necessary and serve immediately with rice.

Mandarin Liver

CHINA   *Yield 4 servings*

1 pound liver (pork, baby beef, or calves)
2½ tablespoons flour
5 tablespoons safflower oil
Salt to taste
Pepper to taste
3 tablespoons soy sauce
2 tablespoons Chinese rice wine or sherry
2 large onions, thinly sliced
1 cup beef bouillon (from cubes)
1 red pepper, cut into strips
1 green pepper, cut into strips
½ pound savoy cabbage, cut into strips
6 ounces fresh bean sprouts
1 small can bamboo shoots (approximately 6 ounces)

Pat liver dry with paper towels; cut into thin slices. Coat with flour. Heat oil in a heavy skillet. Add liver; brown on all sides; remove. Season to taste with salt and pepper. Set aside; keep warm.

Add soy sauce, wine, and onions to pan drippings; simmer 5 minutes. Pour in beef bouillon. Add red and green peppers and cabbage; simmer 10 minutes. Vegetables should still be crisp. Add bean sprouts, bamboo shoots, and liver; heat through. Serve immediately.

Beef Slices Peking

CHINA   *Yield 2 servings*

Marinade

3 tablespoons soy sauce
1 tablespoon sherry

1 pound lean beef, sliced paper thin
1 cup oil
2 tablespoons flour
2 leeks, thinly sliced
2 cloves garlic, minced
½ teaspoon powdered ginger
2 tablespoons soy sauce
⅛ teaspoon ground anise
½ cup beef broth
1 teaspoon cornstarch

In a deep bowl, blend soy sauce and sherry. Add beef slices, coat well, cover, and let stand for 1 hour. Heat oil in a large skillet. Thoroughly drain beef slices on paper toweling. Sprinkle with flour, add to hot oil, and deep-fry for 3 minutes. Remove meat slices with slotted spoon and drain; set aside and keep warm.

Take 4 tablespoons of hot oil and pour into another skillet. Throw away rest of frying oil. Reheat oil; add leeks and garlic. Cook for 5 minutes while stirring. Add meat slices. Season with powdered ginger, soy sauce, and anise. Pour in beef broth. Cover and simmer over very low heat for 1 hour.

At end of cooking time, bring to a quick boil. Blend cornstarch with small amount of cold water; add it to skillet, stirring constantly until sauce is slightly thickened and bubbly. Correct seasoning, if necessary, and serve immediately.

Ginger Beef

CHINA	*Yield 6 to 8 servings*

1 cup onions, minced
2 cloves garlic, pressed
2 teaspoons turmeric
2 teaspoons ginger
1 teaspoon chili powder
1 teaspoon salt
3 pounds of lean beef, cut into cubes
8 fresh tomatoes, peeled and cut into large
    pieces
½ cup peanut oil
4 cups beef bouillon
Boiled rice
Strips of red sweet pepper for garnish

Combine onions, garlic, turmeric, ginger, chili powder, and salt in a bowl. Mix well. Prepare the beef and place in a shallow dish. Sprinkle with the onion-garlic mixture and refrigerate for 3 hours, stirring occasionally. Prepare the tomatoes.

In a large skillet, heat the oil. Stir-fry the beef until browned on all sides. Place beef in a casserole and add skillet drippings, tomatoes, and bouillon. Bake, covered, in a 325°F oven for about 2 hours or until the beef is tender. Serve with boiled rice and garnish with strips of red sweet pepper.

Chinese Stir-Fried Beef and Mushrooms

CHINA	*Yield 6 to 8 servings*

½ pound dried Chinese mushrooms
3 pounds lean steak, cut into thin strips
¼ cup flour
1 tablespoon sugar
½ cup sherry
½ cup soy sauce

¾ cup oil, divided
1 2-inch slice fresh gingerroot, minced
1 cup onions, chopped
2 cups beef bouillon
Salt to taste

Soak the mushrooms in water for 30 minutes. Drain well and set aside. Cut the steak into strips. In a bowl, combine flour, sugar, sherry, and soy sauce. Add the beef and marinate for 30 minutes, stirring frequently.

Heat ½ cup of the oil in a wok. Stir-fry the gingerroot for 1 minute. Add the beef with the marinade and stir-fry until the beef changes color. Remove the beef from the wok. Add the remaining oil to wok. Add the onions and stir-fry until almost tender. Add the mushrooms and stir-fry until soft. Place the beef in the wok and stir-fry for about 2 minutes. Add the bouillon, bring to a boil, and reduce heat. Add salt, cover, and cook for 2 minutes.

Pork with Peppers and Cashews

CHINA	*Yield 4 servings*

1 pound pork, cut into ¾-inch cubes
2 tablespoons soy sauce
½ teaspoon sugar
2 tablespoons vegetable oil
1 small onion, cut into ¾-inch cubes
1 large green pepper, cut into ¾-inch cubes
1 large red (vine-ripened green) pepper, cut into
    ¾-inch cubes
1 tablespoon soy sauce
1 tablespoon cornstarch in ½ cup cold water or
    chicken broth
4 ounces cashews

Combine pork, 1 tablespoon soy sauce, and sugar; let sit while vegetables are prepared.

Heat oil in wok; stir-fry pork mixture 4 to 5 minutes, until pork is well done. Push aside. Stir-fry onion 1 to 2 minutes; add green peppers. Stir-fry for 2 to 3 minutes. Return pork; add combined 1 tablespoon soy sauce and cornstarch mixture. Heat and stir gently until sauce is thickened and clear. Add cashews; allow to heat through. Serve at once with rice.

Sweet-and-Sour Pork

CHINA *Yield 4 servings*

1½ pounds lean pork, cut into 1-inch cubes
3 tablespoons dry white wine
3 tablespoons soy sauce
2 medium carrots, in julienne strips
1 large red sweet pepper, cut into rings
4 tablespoons olive oil
1 slice ginger, minced
1 medium onion, chopped
¼ pound fresh mushrooms, sliced
½ cup beef broth
Salt to taste
1 cup your favorite sweet-and-sour sauce

Place pork in shallow dish. Combine wine and soy sauce; pour over pork, turning to coat all sides. Marinate at least 15 minutes, stirring frequently. Prepare carrots and pepper.

Heat 2 tablespoons oil to medium heat; stir in ginger. Add pork; stir-fry about 5 minutes. Remove pork; set aside.

Add remaining oil to pan. Add carrots, pepper, onion, and mushrooms. Stir-fry for 5 minutes. When carrots and pepper are crisp-tender, add pork; stir-fry for 5 minutes more. Add broth and salt; mix well. Stir in sweet-and-sour sauce, and bring to boil. Reduce heat; cover pan. Cook for 2 minutes more. Serve pork with rice.

Beef and Pork with Bean Sprouts

CHINA *Yield 4 servings*

½ pound beef (chuck or round), finely chopped
½ pound pork (butt or shoulder), finely chopped
2 tablespoons soy sauce
1 tablespoon vinegar
1 clove garlic, peeled and grated
1 teaspoon gingerroot, grated
2 tablespoons vegetable oil
¼ to ½ cup green beans, cut into 1-inch pieces
¼ pound mushrooms, sliced into "T" shapes
1 cup bean sprouts
½ tablespoon cornstarch in ½ cup chicken or beef broth

Marinate beef and pork in combined soy sauce, vinegar, garlic, and gingerroot for 20 to 30 minutes.

Heat oil in wok or skillet. Stir-fry beans 2 to 3 minutes; push up to sides. Stir-fry mushrooms 2 to 3 minutes; push up to sides. Additional vegetable oil may be needed. Stir-fry sprouts 1 to 2 minutes; push up to sides. Stir-fry beef and pork 3 to 4 minutes, until well done. Return vegetables to center of the pan with the meat. Add cornstarch mixture; heat until the sauce is thickened and clear. Serve at once with rice.

Pork Cooked with Sugar

INDOCHINA *Yield 6 to 8 servings*

2 to 2½ pounds fresh pork or loin, cubed
2 tablespoons oil
3 spring onions, finely chopped

2 teaspoons sugar
½ teaspoon salt
¼ teaspoon ground black pepper
4 cups water
2 tablespoons fish sauce

When cubing pork, let fat remain. Set aside meat. Use a large saucepan to heat oil. Fry spring onions until golden. Add pork and fry until meat loses its pink color. Stir constantly. Add sugar, salt, and pepper, continuing to stir until meat is brown. Add water and allow to simmer uncovered for 1 hour. Stir occasionally as liquid will become absorbed.

Add fish sauce and stir. This dish is done when meat is almost dry. Serve with plain white rice.

Beef with Sesame Sauce

INDOCHINA   *Yield 3 to 4 servings*

½ pound round steak, shredded into thin strips
½ teaspoon salt
¼ teaspoon baking soda
2 tablespoons hot water
1 tablespoon soy sauce
1 clove garlic, peeled and crushed
3 tablespoons peanut oil
½ cup beef stock
3 teaspoons cornstarch
2 tablespoons cold water
2 teaspoons sesame paste
1 to 2 teaspoons Chinese chili sauce

Set shredded meat aside. Mix salt and baking soda with hot water and soy sauce. Pour over meat and squeeze meat with hands until liquid is absorbed. Allow to stand for 2 hours or refrigerate overnight.

Heat peanut oil in a wok or skillet. Stir-fry garlic and meat until meat is browned, about 2 minutes. Add stock and bring to a boil. Mix cornstarch with cold water and add to the boiling liquid. Stir until liquid has thickened. Turn off heat. Stir in sesame paste and chili sauce and serve at once.

Beef with Bamboo Shoots

INDOCHINA   *Yield 3 to 4 servings*

¾ pound sirloin steak
2 tablespoons peanut oil
Extra 2 tablespoons peanut oil
1 large can bamboo shoots, sliced
6 spring onions, sliced
1 tablespoon fish sauce
½ teaspoon salt
1 clove garlic, peeled and crushed
4 tablespoons sesame seeds, toasted and crushed

Slice beef very thinly into 2-inch strips. Use a wok or heavy skillet to heat peanut oil and stir-fry beef for 1 minute. Remove meat while it is still pink. Set aside. Heat extra oil in pan and stir-fry bamboo shoots and onions for 2 minutes. Add fish sauce and salt and continue frying for 5 minutes more. Add crushed garlic for 1 more minute. Return meat and stir-fry for 1 minute. Add sesame seeds. When well mixed, serve at once. (Do not double this recipe for a larger quantity. Rather, make it in 2 separate batches for best flavor and texture.)

Pork Loaf

INDOCHINA   *Yield 4 to 6 servings*

8 to 10 dried Chinese mushrooms
1½ pound ground pork
6 spring onions, finely chopped
4 eggs, beaten
1 tablespoon fish sauce
½ teaspoon salt
¼ teaspoon ground black pepper

Prepare mushrooms by soaking in hot water for 30 minutes. Squeeze out moisture. Cut off and dis-

Sukiyaki

card stems and finely chop the caps. Use a mixing bowl to blend pork, mushrooms, and spring onions.

In another bowl, mix eggs, fish sauce, and salt and pepper. Add this to the pork mixture and mix well. Place mixture in a well-greased loaf tin, 9 x 5 x 2 inches. Cover with foil. Allow to steam over high heat for 1 hour or longer. (Pork must always be well cooked.)

When meat is done, allow it to cool in loaf pan slightly. Turn out and slice; put on serving platter.

Barbecued Spareribs

INDOCHINA   *Yield 4 servings*

5 shallots, peeled
2 cloves garlic, peeled
2 tablespoons sugar
¼ cup fish sauce
¼ teaspoon freshly ground black pepper
1½ pounds pork spareribs

Use a mortar and pestle to pound the shallots, garlic, and sugar together. When a paste has formed, add fish sauce and pepper and stir well. Put spareribs in a roasting pan and pour mixture over them, turning the ribs to coat both sides. Allow ribs to marinate for at least 1 hour.

Preheat oven to 350°F. Roast spareribs for 45 minutes until they are well browned. Cut ribs into separate pieces and serve hot with a dish of Nuoc Cham (see Index) beside them.

Boiled Pork

KOREA   *Yield 4 to 6 servings*

2 pounds pork
3½ cups boiling water

2 teaspoons salt
¼ cup soy sauce

Vinegar soy sauce

½ cup soy sauce
1 tablespoon sugar
3 tablespoons vinegar

Place pork and salt in a pot with boiling water. Simmer until almost tender, at least 1 hour. Add the soy sauce and simmer for another 20 minutes. Remove pork from broth and allow to cool. Then slice thin and serve with vinegar soy sauce.

To make the sauce, combine ingredients listed above in a bowl, stirring until all sugar has dissolved. Adjust sugar and vinegar to your personal taste.

Fried Cucumbers with Beef

KOREA   *Yield 4 servings*

½ pound lean sirloin
2 teaspoons sesame oil
1 tablespoon light soy sauce
½ teaspoon salt
½ teaspoon sugar
¼ teaspoon cayenne pepper
2 large green cucumbers
1 tablespoon vegetable oil
2 tablespoons toasted, crushed sesame seeds

Cut beef into paper thin slices, 2 inches long. (It's easier to slice thin if it is partially frozen.) Place beef in a bowl with sesame oil, soy sauce, salt, sugar, and cayenne. Mix well to be sure the flavors penetrate the meat.

Peel cucumbers, leaving strips of green at intervals. Cut in half the long way and scoop out seeds. Cut the cucumbers crossways into medium slices.

Cover the bottom of a skillet or wok with oil, and heat. Stir-fry beef on high heat for 1 minute. Add the cucumbers, tossing lightly to blend flavors. Reduce heat and allow to simmer a few minutes until cucumber is tender but still crisp. Place in a serving bowl and garnish with sesame seeds.

Sliced Beef in Sweet Sauce

KOREA *Yield 4 servings*

This is made in a special pan in Korea, but it works quite well in a heavy skillet. It's quick and easy to make, especially if the beef is partially frozen when sliced.

1½ pounds beef top round, sliced thin into 2-inch squares
1 small apple, peeled, cored, and grated
1 small hard pear, peeled, cored, and grated
2 tablespoons onions, chopped
¼ cup scallions, thinly sliced
¼ cup soy sauce
2 tablespoons sake
½ cup water
1 tablespoon garlic, chopped
2 tablespoons sesame-seed oil
2 teaspoons sesame seeds
1 teaspoon freshly ground black pepper
2 tablespoons sugar

Place thinly sliced meat in a large bowl. In another bowl, mix all the remaining ingredients, which will be used as a marinade. Pour this over the beef and allow to marinate for at least 3 hours. Overnight is even better.

Heat skillet until moderately hot. Add beef and marinade and stir-fry for 5 minutes, until beef is tender. Serve piping hot with pickled Chinese cabbage.

Braised Meat with Onions

KOREA *Yield 4 to 6 servings*

1½ pounds lean round steak
24 spring onions, using only the white part, sliced
3 tablespoons toasted sesame seeds
1 clove garlic, peeled and quartered
½ teaspoon fresh ginger, finely chopped
¼ cup light soy sauce
½ teaspoon chili powder or cayenne pepper
2 tablespoons vegetable oil
6 dried mushrooms, soaked and sliced

Slice and cut meat into bite-size pieces. Then beat the meat with a mallet until very thin. Slice onions and set aside. In a large bowl, combine sesame seeds, garlic, ginger, soy sauce, and chili powder with the beef. Use your hand to rub seasonings into beef.

Heat oil in a skillet and stir-fry beef and mushrooms, using high heat, until beef is done. Remove beef and mushrooms with a slotted spoon and set aside. Add just enough oil needed to stir-fry the onions. Spoon onions over waiting meat and serve at once with white rice.

Beef Saté

MALAYSIA *Yield 6 servings*

1½ pounds steak
2 teaspoons ground turmeric
2 teaspoons ground cumin
2 teaspoons ground fennel
Finely grated rind of half a lemon
1½ teaspoons salt
1 tablespoon sugar
4 tablespoons thick coconut milk

Cube beef into 1-inch cubes, leaving a thin layer of fat where possible. Combine remaining ingredients in a bowl and stir until sugar is dissolved. Add beef and cover thoroughly with marinade. Let stand for at least 1 hour. The longer it marinates, the better the meat flavor.

Thread meat on skewers, about 5 pieces per skewer. Grill either on hot coals or in the broiler until meat is crisp, brown, and well done. Remove from skewers and serve at once with peanut sauce.

Spiced Braised Liver

MALAYSIA	*Yield 4 servings*

1 pound calves' liver
3 tablespoons oil
1 medium onion, peeled and finely sliced
2 cloves garlic, peeled and finely chopped
1 teaspoon fresh ginger, finely grated
1½ teaspoons ground coriander
½ teaspoon ground cumin
½ teaspoon salt
¼ teaspoon ground black pepper
2 tablespoons dark soy sauce
⅓ cup water

Use a sharp knife to slice the liver very thin. Drain on paper towels and set aside.

Using a heavy skillet, heat the oil. Fry the onion, garlic, and ginger on medium heat for 5 minutes, until golden. Add liver slices in single layers. Sprinkle with coriander, cumin, salt, and pepper. Fry each side of liver for 2 minutes. Last, add soy sauce and water and simmer for about 5 minutes, until liver is cooked but not hard. Remove to heated platter and serve at once.

Pork in Soy Sauce

MALAYSIA	*Yield 4 servings*

4 garlic cloves, peeled and crushed
2 tablespoons all-purpose flour
1 tablespoon light soy sauce
1½ pounds pork loin, cubed
3 ounces dried Chinese mushrooms, soaked in warm water for 30 minutes or 1 cup button mushrooms, sliced
7 tablespoons vegetable oil or melted pork fat
1 teaspoon ginger powder
5 scallions, thinly sliced
Freshly ground black pepper to taste
3 tablespoons dark soy sauce
1 teaspoon white vinegar
2 tablespoons rice wine

Mix 2 cloves garlic, flour, and light soy sauce and use this to thoroughly coat the pieces of pork. Allow to stand for 30 minutes. If using Chinese mushrooms, discard the stalks and cut the caps into 4 pieces.

Heat the oil in a skillet or wok and fry half of the meat for 6 to 8 minutes, turning frequently; remove meat and drain on paper towels. Repeat process for the remaining meat.

Reduce fat in skillet to 3 tablespoons. Fry mushrooms in this for 3 minutes. Add remaining garlic to pan with ginger. Stirring to mix, add meat, scallions, dark soy sauce, and vinegar. Stir-fry for 2 minutes; add rice wine at the end. Serve piping hot.

Marinated Steak

JAPAN	*Yield about 4 servings*

1 to 1½ pounds filet mignon or round steak

Marinade

4 tablespoons sherry
4 tablespoons soy sauce

1 ½ heaping tablespoons cornstarch
Salt
Pinch of sugar
Pinch of white pepper

4 tablespoons oil

Cut filet mignon into thin slices.

Prepare marinade by stirring sherry, soy sauce, cornstarch, a little salt, and a pinch each of sugar and white pepper thoroughly until well blended. Pour marinade over meat slices; marinate for 1 hour.

Heat oil in heavy skillet until very hot. Add meat, including marinade; cook for 5 minutes, stirring constantly. Serve steak immediately.

Pork and Peas

JAPAN	*Yield about 4 servings*

12 ounces lean pork or tenderloin

Marinade

2 tablespoons soy sauce
2 teaspoons rice wine or sherry
1 egg white
1 teaspoon cornstarch
Salt
White pepper

4 ounces frozen peas
8 tablespoons oil
½ cup hot beef broth
Salt
Sugar
1 leek
1 clove garlic
1 sugared or candied ginger
4 ounces canned sliced mushrooms
4 ounces canned bamboo shoots
1 tablespoon rice wine or sherry

1 tablespoon cornstarch
2 tablespoons oyster sauce
2 teaspoons soy sauce
White pepper
Pinch of ground ginger

Cut pork or tenderloin crosswise into thin strips. Prepare marinade by stirring soy sauce, rice wine (or sherry), egg white, and cornstarch together until well blended. Season to taste with salt and white pepper. Pour marinade over meat, cover, and refrigerate for 30 minutes.

In the meantime, let peas thaw for 5 minutes. Heat 2 tablespoons of the oil in a small saucepan. Add peas. Pour in beef broth; season to taste with salt and sugar. Cook for 5 minutes. Drain peas, reserving cooking liquid. Set peas aside; keep them warm.

Thoroughly clean the leek; cut it into long, thin strips. Mince the garlic. Cut sugared ginger into slices. Drain mushrooms and bamboo shoots. Heat 3 tablespoons of the oil in a large saucepan. Add all the vegetables and garlic; cook for 5 minutes, stirring constantly. Set aside; keep them warm.

Heat remaining oil (3 tablespoons) in skillet. Add meat strips and marinade; cook for 3 minutes, stirring constantly. Add meat and reserved peas to vegetables. Pour in rice wine (or sherry) and cooking liquid from peas. Bring to a boil.

Blend together cornstarch, oyster sauce, and soy sauce. Pour into meat-vegetable mixture; stir until smooth and bubbly. Correct seasoning, if necessary, with salt, pepper, ground ginger, and sugar. Serve immediately.

Tasty Fondue

JAPAN	*Yield 4 servings*

Bouillon

6 cups chicken bouillon
2 carrots
1 leek

1 stalk celery
2 tablespoons parsley, coarsely chopped

Sauce tartare

5 tablespoons mayonnaise
2 tablespoons capers
2 tablespoons chives, finely chopped
2 dill pickles, finely chopped
2 teaspoons lemon juice
2 tablespoons evaporated milk
Salt
Pinch of sugar
White pepper

Catsup sauce

5 tablespoons mayonnaise
2 tablespoons tomato catsup
1 teaspoon Worcestershire sauce
1 teaspoon (or less) curry powder
Pinch of sugar
Salt

2 to 2½ pounds very lean beef
2 cups boiling water

Bring chicken bouillon to a boil either in pot placed on the burner or in fondue pot. Chop carrots, leek, and celery; add to broth together with chopped parsley. Cook for 20 minutes.

To prepare sauces, stir listed ingredients together until well blended. Season to taste.

Thoroughly dry meat with paper towels. Cut into thin strips.

Place chicken-vegetable broth on top of burner; make sure it continues to simmer (or leave in fondue pot over low heat). Since the liquid will evaporate, it is necessary to add some of the hot water from time to time.

Each person places a piece of meat on a fondue fork, puts it in simmering broth for 1 to 2 minutes, and dunks it in sauce. Each person should have a separate bowl for each of the sauces. Serve with rice.

Grilled Steaks

JAPAN	*Yield 4 servings*

Marinade

½ cup soy sauce
4 tablespoons onions, minced
2 cloves garlic, minced
1 tablespoon (or less) sugar
1 tablespoon minced fresh gingerroot
¼ cup rice wine, or dry white wine

4 small steaks of your choice, boneless
Cherry tomatoes for garnish

Mix marinade ingredients together. Pour marinade over steaks. Refrigerate overnight or let sit at room temperature for 3 to 4 hours. Broil steaks in the oven or on a grill or hibachi. Baste steaks with marinade while they are grilling. When steaks are almost done, grill tomatoes and use for garnish.

Teriyaki Meatballs

JAPAN	*Yield 4 servings*

1 pound lean ground beef
2 tablespoons parsley, chopped
2 tablespoons chives, chopped
Leaves from 2 stalks of celery, finely chopped
1 egg
3 tablespoons bread crumbs
Salt
White pepper
Butter or margarine for frying

Sauce

½ cup soy sauce
Salt
White pepper
Sugar
⅛ teaspoon allspice

Grilled steaks

Teriyaki steak

Ground ginger
1 sugared ginger

Mix ground beef thoroughly with chopped parsley, chives, and celery leaves. Stir in egg and bread crumbs. Season to taste with salt and pepper. Shape into balls about 1½ to 2 inches in diameter. Heat butter or margarine in heavy skillet. Add meatballs; fry for about 5 minutes or until browned on all sides.

While meatballs are frying, prepare the sauce. In a small saucepan, heat soy sauce over low heat. Season with salt, pepper, sugar, allspice, and ground ginger. Dice sugared ginger; add to sauce. Pour hot sauce over meatballs; let stand for 5 minutes, so flavors can blend.

Serve meatballs in preheated bowl.

Teriyaki Steak

JAPAN	*Yield 4 servings*

4 boneless steaks, about ½ pound each

Marinade

1 clove garlic, finely minced
1 sugared or candied ginger, finely minced
1 tablespoon brown sugar
Salt
Pepper, freshly ground
½ cup rice wine or sherry
6 tablespoons soy sauce
½ cup white wine
Juice of half a lemon

Stuffed-tomato garnish

4 medium tomatoes
Salt
White pepper

Tokyo steak

4 tablespoons bean sprouts, canned or fresh (if using fresh bean sprouts, blanch, then rinse them with cold water before using)
1 tablespoon tomato catsup

Combine marinade ingredients in shallow dish large enough to hold the steaks. Stir until well blended. Add steaks to marinade; coat well. Marinate for 12 hours, turning steaks frequently.

Drain steaks; arrange on broiler pan. Place under preheated broiler. Broil 4 minutes on each side.

Meanwhile, remove stems from tomatoes; cut off approximately ½-inch slices from bottoms. Scoop out seeds; discard. Sprinkle insides of tomatoes with salt and pepper. Place bean sprouts and catsup into a small skillet. Heat for 5 minutes. Spoon into tomatoes.

Arrange steaks on preheated serving platter. Garnish with stuffed tomatoes.

Sukiyaki

JAPAN	*Yield 4 servings*

1 pound rice
1½ to 2 pounds beef tenderloin
2 tablespoons bacon drippings
½ pound transparent or silver noodles
8 dried mushrooms
4 small onions
4 leeks
¼ head white cabbage (about ½ pound)
½ pound fresh spinach
1 pound canned bamboo shoots
½ pound bean sprouts

Sauce

1 cup soy sauce
6 tablespoons rice wine or sherry
2 teaspoons sugar

4 egg yolks

Cook rice according to directions; keep it warm.

Beef tenderloin must be cut into paper-thin slices. To achieve this, place meat in freezer for about 2 hours, or until partially frozen. You will then be easily able to slice it thin. Or, have the butcher slice it for you. Arrange meat slices on round platter, slightly overlapping. Place 2 tablespoons of bacon drippings (unmelted) into the middle, cover with aluminum foil, and refrigerate.

Place noodles and mushrooms into separate bowls. Cover with boiling water; soak for 20 minutes. Repeat procedure two more times. Drain; arrange in separate bowls.

Cut onions and leeks into thin slices. Place in separate bowls. Core cabbage, separate into individual leaves, and tear into bite-size pieces. Clean spinach; remove stems from leaves. Drain bamboo shoots, reserving liquid. Drain bean sprouts, if canned. If fresh, blanch, then rinse with cold water, and drain them.

To prepare sauce, bring soy sauce, rice wine or sherry, and sugar to a boil. Pour into sauce dish.

Place electric wok (or use frying pan on top of burner) in the middle of your table. Spoon rice into 4 individual bowls. Place slightly beaten egg yolks into 4 other small bowls. Now arrange all ingredients around the wok. Prepare the meal in portions; place one-fourth of bacon drippings into wok and heat, add one-fourth of meat slices and brown quickly. Push aside and pour some of the sauce over the meat. Add one-fourth of each of the vegetables and noodles and simmer for 3 minutes, while stirring constantly.

Each guest is given part of the cooked ingredients and starts eating while the second portion is being prepared. Cooked vegetables are dipped into raw egg yolk before being placed on plates. Sukiyaki is seasoned with sauce according to each individual's taste.

Oriental Meatballs

JAPAN   *Yield 6 servings*

2 pounds lean ground beef
2½ teaspoons salt
⅛ teaspoon freshly ground black pepper
1 egg, beaten
2 tablespoons flour
Small amount freshly ground black pepper
½ cup oil
12 ounces canned chicken broth
3 tablespoons cornstarch
2 to 3 teaspoons soy sauce
½ cup vinegar
½ cup light corn syrup
5 medium green peppers, cut in sixths
8 slices canned pineapple, quartered or cut into chunks
10 maraschino cherries, optional

Combine beef, 1 teaspoon of the salt, and ⅛ teaspoon pepper. Shape into small meatballs. Combine egg, flour, ½ teaspoon salt, and a small amount of pepper. Beat until smooth. Heat oil and remaining 1 teaspoon salt in large frying pan.

Gently place meatballs in batter, 1 or 2 at a time, and fry in the hot oil, browning well on all sides. Remove meatballs from pan. Drain off remaining oil.

Blend ½ cup of the chicken broth with cornstarch. Add remaining chicken broth, soy sauce, vinegar, and corn syrup; cook over medium heat, stirring constantly, until thick and clear. Add green peppers, pineapple, and cherries. Lower heat; cook slowly for about 10 minutes. Pour over meatballs. Serve with rice.

Tokyo Steak

JAPAN   *Yield 4 servings*

Delicious with rice and stir-fried bean sprouts.

Salt
Ground ginger to taste
Pepper to taste, freshly ground
2 tablespoons rice wine or sherry
4 filet mignon steaks, about 6 ounces each
1½ tablespoons butter

1 11-ounce can mandarin oranges
1 tablespoon capers
1 tablespoon butter, cut into small pieces

Combine salt, ginger, pepper, and rice wine (or sherry); blend well. Rub mixture onto steaks.

Heat 1½ tablespoons butter in heavy skillet. Add steaks; sauté 2 minutes on each side. Arrange mandarin oranges and capers on top of steaks; dot with remaining 1 tablespoon butter. Place skillet under preheated broiler; broil for 3 minutes. Serve steaks immediately on preheated plates.

Skewered Pork

JAPAN	Yield 2 to 3 servings

1 pound pork, cut into bite-size pieces, ½ inch thick
1 small eggplant, cut into bite-size cubes
4 or 5 scallions, cut into 1½-inch lengths
2 green peppers, cut into chunks
Flour for dredging
Oil for frying

Skewer pork, eggplant, scallions, and peppers on skewers. Dredge in flour; fry in oil for about 4 minutes, or until browned. Remove from oil and, if desired, brush with soy sauce. Serve with rice.

Beef Stew

JAPAN	Yield about 6 servings

8 cups beef stock
3 pounds beef stew meat, cut into bite-size pieces
4 turnips, quartered
2 carrots, cut into bite-size pieces
2 cans water chestnuts, sliced if desired
10 small potatoes, peeled and left whole

Salt to taste
Freshly ground black pepper to taste
2 tablespoons soy sauce
4 stalks celery, cut into 1-inch pieces
10 small white onions
4 scallions, cut into ½-inch pieces

Bring beef stock to a boil; add all ingredients except celery, white onions, and scallions. Simmer for 30 minutes, add celery and onions, and continue simmering until meat is tender. Add scallions; simmer for 2 minutes more. Serve stew with rice, if desired.

Pepper Steak

JAPAN	Yield 4 servings

1 pound round steak
¼ cup oil
½ teaspoon salt
Pepper to taste
½ cup scallion, chopped
2 cloves garlic, finely chopped
4 green peppers, cut into bite-size pieces
1 cup celery, sliced
1½ cups beef bouillon
2 tablespoons cornstarch
¼ cup cold water
1 tablespoon soy sauce
Cooked rice

Cut steak into thin slices, then into 2-inch pieces. To make slicing easier, partially freeze the meat. Heat oil in large skillet. Add salt and pepper. Cook meat over medium to high heat until brown, stirring frequently. Add scallion and garlic. Add green peppers and celery; stir. Add bouillon; cover and cook until vegetables are tender but still crisp. Do not overcook.

Meanwhile, combine cornstarch and water. Blend in soy sauce until it makes a smooth paste. Slowly add paste to meat mixture, stirring constantly until liquid is thickened. Serve with rice.

Watercress in Sweet Gravy

INDONESIA	Yield 6 servings

The Indonesian vegetable used for this is called kangkung, a dark green leaf. Substitutes for this are watercress, spinach, or chicory.

1 pound kangkung or substitute
½ cup hot water
4 tablespoons dehydrated shrimp
1½ cups coconut milk
1 large onion, peeled and finely chopped
1 small clove garlic, peeled and crushed
1 teaspoon salt
1 teaspoon fresh ginger, finely grated
1 fresh red chili, seeded and sliced
2 tablespoons palm sugar
½ teaspoon laos powder

Wash greens 3 times in cold water and drain; then slice coarsely. Soak shrimp for 5 minutes in hot water. If brown dried shrimp are used, they will need to soak for 25 minutes.

Place coconut milk and all other ingredients in a large saucepan. Bring to a boil, uncovered. Add shrimp, plus the water in which they soaked, and green vegetables. Cover pan and simmer for 20 minutes or until greens are tender. Serve hot.

Djakarta Salad

INDONESIA	Yield 4 to 6 servings

4 cups water
1 teaspoon salt
½ cup long-grain rice
1½ pounds cooked chicken, boned and diced

1 red and 1 green pepper pod, cut into thin strips
2 bananas, peeled and sliced
1 cup yogurt
3 tablespoons mayonnaise
2 tablespoons ketchup
1 tablespoon curry
¾ teaspoon ground ginger
Salt
White pepper
Cayenne pepper
Pinch of sugar

Bring water with salt to a boil. Add rice and cook on medium heat for 15 minutes. Drain well; rinse with cold water and allow to cool.

Add chicken and pepper pods to rice. Mix well. Gently stir in bananas.

In a separate bowl, combine yogurt, mayonnaise, ketchup, curry, and ginger until well blended. Add remaining seasonings to taste. Pour this over the rice mixture. Cover and allow to marinate in refrigerator for at least 1 hour. Mound on a large platter when ready to serve.

Spiced Cabbage in Coconut Milk

INDONESIA	Yield 6 or more servings

1 pound cabbage, coarsely shredded
2 onions, peeled and chopped
2 cloves garlic, peeled and chopped
2 fresh red chilies, seeded and chopped, or 1 teaspoon chili powder
1 teaspoon dried shrimp paste (trasi)
1 daun salam or 3 curry leaves
2 tablespoons peanut oil

2 strips lemon rind
1 ½ cups thick coconut milk
1 teaspoon salt
3 tablespoons tamarind liquid

After shredding the cabbage, blend onions, garlic, and chilies into a fine paste. Use either electric blender, food processor, or mortar and pestle. Wrap the dried shrimp paste in foil and broil for 5 minutes, turning once.

In a large saucepan or wok, fry the curry leaves in hot oil for 1 minute. Add the onion paste mixture and the dried shrimp paste and stir-fry until mixture darkens in color. Add lemon rind, coconut milk, and salt and reduce heat to a simmer. At this point, put in the cabbage and simmer uncovered for about 3 minutes or until cabbage is cooked but still crisp. Last, stir in the tamarind liquid; then serve.

Carrots and Cauliflower

INDONESIA   *Yield 4 servings*

6 carrots, peeled and sliced diagonally
3 large cauliflower florets
Boiling water
2 tablespoons vegetable oil or melted butter
1 clove garlic, peeled and crushed
1 slice dried shrimp paste (trasi), crushed,
   optional
4 scallions, cut into ½-inch lengths
1 tablespoon light soy sauce
Pinch of chili powder
Pinch of ginger powder
Salt to taste

Boil the carrots and cauliflower in a saucepan for 3 minutes. Drain.

Use a wok or deep frying pan to heat the oil or butter. Fry the garlic and trasi for just a few sec-

onds. Stir in scallions and soy sauce; then stir in the carrots and cauliflower. Add chili and ginger powders and salt to taste. Stir constantly for 2 minutes. Serve at once.

Spiced French Beans

INDONESIA   *Yield 4 servings*

2 tablespoons vegetable oil
3 shallots, peeled and finely sliced
1 garlic clove, peeled and crushed, optional
1 teaspoon ginger powder
Pinch of chili powder
Pinch of grated nutmeg
1 pound string beans, topped, tailed, and cut in
   half
Salt
Freshly ground black pepper
6 tablespoons strong-flavored chicken stock

Heat oil in deep frying pan and fry shallots and garlic gently for 1 minute. Stir in remaining ingredients, except for the chicken stock. Stir-fry this for 2 minutes.

Gradually stir in chicken stock and cover the pan. Simmer gently for 5 minutes. Cook uncovered 2 minutes more, stirring constantly. Adjust seasonings if needed and serve hot.

Cooked Salad with Coconut Dressing

INDONESIA   *Yield 4 servings*

Use any combination of fresh vegetables that you choose but be careful not to overcook them. They should be crisp when served.

129

1 slice dried shrimp paste (trasi), broiled in foil
   for 5 minutes
2 cloves garlic, peeled and chopped
1 shallot, peeled and chopped
½ teaspoon chili powder
1 teaspoon brown sugar
1 tablespoon tamarind water
Salt to taste
2 cups white coconut flesh, grated
1½ cups cabbage
¼ pound string beans, topped and tailed
2 medium carrots, peeled and sliced
2 cups bean sprouts
Boiling water
Watercress for garnish
Cucumber slices for garnish

Pound shrimp paste, garlic, and shallots to a very thin paste. Add chili powder, sugar, tamarind water, and salt and mix very well. Put in the coconut and mix some more.

Cook vegetables separately in boiling water for just 3 minutes, so that they remain crisp. Drain.

When ready to serve, toss vegetables with coconut mixture until all are well coated. Put in serving bowl and garnish with watercress and cucumber slices.

Apple Salad

THAILAND   *Yield 6 servings*

3 tart, green cooking apples, peeled, and thinly
   sliced
1 teaspoon salt
1 tablespoon peanut oil
4 cloves garlic, peeled and thinly sliced
6 spring onions, sliced
½ pound pork, finely shredded
1 tablespoon dried shrimp powder
1 tablespoon fish sauce

2 tablespoons roasted peanuts, crushed
1 teaspoon palm sugar
Pepper to taste
Red chili, finely chopped, for garnish

Sprinkle prepared apples with salt in a large bowl.

Heat oil and fry garlic. Remove from pan and fry spring onions. Set aside. In the same pan, stir-fry pork. When cooked, add shrimp powder, fish sauce, peanuts, and sugar. Remove from heat.

When ready to serve, mix everything together and season with pepper to taste. Garnish with chilies and serve.

Cucumber Salad

THAILAND   *Yield 4 servings*

2 green cucumbers
1 small onion
2 tablespoons dried shrimp powder
1 or 2 fresh red chilies, seeded and chopped
2 tablespoons fish sauce
Lemon juice to taste

Peel, seed, and grate cucumbers coarsely. Peel and grate the onion. Mix all ingredients in a bowl until well blended, adding lemon juice at the end to taste. Serve slightly chilled.

Pork Skin Salad

THAILAND   *Yield 4 servings*

½ cup boiled pork skin, finely sliced
½ cup boiled lean pork, finely chopped
1 cup fresh mint leaves
½ teaspoon lemon rind, grated
3 tablespoons dried shrimp powder

1 tablespoon fresh coriander leaves, chopped
1 tablespoon spring onions, chopped
2 to 3 tablespoons coconut cream
1 tablespoon nam prik (shrimp sauce)
1 tablespoon lime juice
1 tablespoon fish sauce
1 to 2 teaspoons sugar
Greens for garnish

Slice the fat away from the boiled pork skin, leaving only the jelly-like skin.

Mix all the rest of the ingredients together just before serving. Toss with pork and pork skin. Garnish with your choice of greens.

Water Chestnut Salad

THAILAND *Yield 4 to 6 servings*

8 ounces fresh water chestnuts or 1 small can, drained
1 tablespoon lard or oil
1 small onion, peeled and finely chopped
2 teaspoons garlic, peeled and finely chopped
2 tablespoons fish sauce
2 tablespoons lemon juice
1 tablespoon sugar
¼ cup cooked pork, diced
¼ cup cooked shrimp, chopped
¼ cup crab meat, flaked
2 tablespoons fresh coriander leaves, chopped
3 or 4 tender citrus leaves, chopped
2 fresh red chilies, seeded and chopped

Wash and peel water chestnuts; slice and cut into strips. (If using canned, drain and cut the same way.)

Heat fat and stir-fry onion and garlic over medium heat for 2 minutes. In a bowl, make a dressing of the fish sauce, lemon juice, sugar, and onions and garlic. In a larger bowl, combine chestnuts, pork, shrimp, and crab meat. Pour the dressing over this mixture and toss gently. Garnish with citrus leaves and chilies.

Fried Eggplant

BURMA *Yield 4 servings*

1 large eggplant
2 tablespoons vegetable oil
1 medium onion, peeled and sliced
1 garlic clove, peeled and crushed
½-inch piece fresh gingerroot, peeled and pounded
½ teaspoon salt
2 scallions, including greens, chopped for garnish

Djakarta salad

131

Bake eggplant on lightly oiled sheet at 425 °F for about 1 hour or until soft to the touch. Remove from oven and allow to cool.

Heat oil in a skillet and fry onion and garlic gently until lightly browned. Peel skin from eggplant. Scoop out flesh and mash with a fork. Add this to the skillet with ginger and salt, and stir-fry for 5 to 10 minutes. Transfer to a warmed serving dish and garnish with spring onions. This may be served hot or cold.

Vegetable Curry

BURMA	Yield 4 servings

The vegetables suggested here can be changed, depending on what is available seasonally.

3 medium potatoes, peeled and cut into 1-inch
    cubes
1 medium eggplant, cut into 1-inch slices
4 carrots, peeled and diced
1 medium cauliflower, divided into florets
½ pound okra, cut into 1-inch lengths
¼ cup vegetable oil
1 medium onion, peeled and pounded
3 garlic cloves, peeled and crushed
½-inch piece fresh gingerroot, peeled and
    pounded
1 teaspoon chili powder
½ teaspoon turmeric powder
3 tomatoes, roughly chopped
3 tablespoons coriander leaves

Place potatoes, eggplant, carrots, cauliflower, and okra in a bowl. Cover with cold water and set aside.

Heat oil in deep-fat fryer or wok. Stir-fry onion, garlic, ginger, chili powder, and turmeric until quite fragrant. Stir in 1 tomato and the coriander. Add potatoes and enough water to cover. Bring to a boil; reduce heat and simmer for 10 minutes.

Add eggplant and carrots and simmer for 5 minutes more. Add cauliflower and a little more water if needed. Bring back to a boil. Put in remaining tomatoes and simmer 5 minutes. Add okra and simmer for 5 minutes more. Most of the liquid will be absorbed. Serve piping hot.

Split Pea Fritters

BURMA	Yield 4 to 6 servings

1 cup split peas, soaked in water overnight
2 medium onions, peeled and finely chopped
2 fresh red chilies, finely chopped, or ¼
    teaspoon chili powder
½ teaspoon ground turmeric
½ teaspoon salt
Oil for deep frying
Sliced onion and lemon wedges for garnish

Drain the soaked peas and grind them to a paste, using either a blender, food processor, or a mortar and pestle. Mix in all of the ingredients, except for the oil. Roll into small balls about 1 inch in diameter and then flatten with the palm of your hand to ½ inch thick.

Heat oil in heavy skillet. Fry fritters, dropping into the oil one at a time. Do not crowd the skillet. When fritters are golden brown, remove and drain on paper towels. Garnish with raw onion and lemon wedges.

Tomato Salad

BURMA	Yield 4 servings

The flavor of the salad will be improved if you use tomatoes that are not fully ripe.

¼ cup vegetable oil
1 medium onion, peeled and sliced

4 tomatoes, thinly sliced
1 tablespoon pounded, roasted, shelled peanuts
3 tablespoons coriander leaves, chopped
1 teaspoon shrimp-flavored soy sauce
Juice of ½ lemon
Coriander leaves for garnish

In a small skillet, heat 3 tablespoons of the oil. Fry the onion until crisp and golden. Use a slotted spoon and remove from pan. Drain on paper towels.

Place tomatoes in a bowl with peanuts, coriander, soy sauce, and remaining oil. Toss lightly. Spoon the tomato mixture onto a serving plate. Sprinkle with lemon juice and then put onions on top. Garnish with coriander and chill before serving.

Assorted Vegetable Salad

BURMA	*Yield 6 to 8 servings*

Although the vegetables in this salad are cooked, the cooking time is short so that they do not lose their crispness. The vegetables can be cooked ahead.

4 carrots, scraped
Saltwater, boiling
1½ cups string beans, topped and tailed
1 cup okra
2 cups fresh bean sprouts
2 large cauliflower florets
1 cup bamboo shoots, optional
5 tablespoons sesame seeds
2 tablespoons vegetable oil
1 medium onion, peeled and sliced

Cook carrots in boiling saltwater for 7 minutes. Remove and allow to cool. Cook the remaining vegetables separately in the same saltwater, for 3 minutes each. Allow to cool.

Use a small skillet and fry sesame seeds over dry heat until golden brown, shaking pan constantly. Remove and set aside. Add oil to pan. When hot, fry onion until golden. Remove and drain on paper towels. Reserve 1 tablespoon of oil, adding a pinch of salt.

Slice carrots into thin strips. Slice beans and okra into ½-inch pieces, diagonally. Arrange vegetables in separate piles on serving dish. Sprinkle oil over vegetables, followed by sesame seeds and onions. Chill and serve.

Medley of vegetables

Medley of Vegetables

INDIA	*Yield 4 to 6 servings*

2 tablespoons butter or margarine
2 large onions, peeled and diced
4 cups hot water
½ head cabbage, sliced into thin strips
1 small cauliflower, cut in small florets
2 leeks, sliced
2 carrots, diced
1 bay leaf
2 teaspoons caraway seeds

4 teaspoons curry powder
2 cloves garlic, peeled and finely chopped
2 tomatoes, diced
2 small eggplants, peeled and sliced
½ cup frozen green beans
½ cup frozen peas
Salt to taste
Sambal ulek to taste
Tabasco sauce to taste

Heat butter or margarine in a large saucepan and cook onions until transparent. Add water and bring to a boil. Place cabbage, cauliflower, leeks, and carrots in the boiling liquid. Add bay leaf, caraway, curry, and garlic; cook at medium heat for 15 minutes. Add remaining vegetables and cook for 5 minutes more. Last, add seasonings to taste and serve.

Spicy Fried Beans

INDIA	*Yield 4 to 6 servings*

1 pound tender green beans, topped and tailed
    and cut into bite-size pieces
1 tablespoon ghee
1 medium onion, peeled and finely chopped
½ teaspoon ginger, finely grated
1 teaspoon ground turmeric
1 teaspoon garam masala
½ teaspoon chili powder, optional
2 teaspoons salt
2 ripe tomatoes, chopped
1 or more teaspoons lemon juice to taste

Heat ghee in a saucepan. Using medium heat, fry onion and ginger until onion is golden. Add spices and stir-fry for 2 minutes. Put in tomatoes and continue stirring until tomatoes are cooked through and most of the liquid is evaporated. Add the beans and stir well. Partially cover the pan and allow beans to steam until just tender. Stir in lemon juice and serve at once.

Fried Cabbage

INDIA	*Yield 6 servings*

Half a large head cabbage, shredded coarsely
4 tablespoons oil
1 large onion, peeled and finely sliced
2 or 3 fresh green or red chilies, seeded and
    sliced
2 cloves garlic, peeled and finely grated
1 teaspoon fresh ginger, finely grated
1 teaspoon ground turmeric
1½ teaspoons salt
2 tablespoons desiccated (dehydrated) coconut

Using a large saucepan, heat the oil. Fry onions and chilies until soft. Add garlic and ginger and stir until golden. Last, put in turmeric and cabbage, stirring until all of the ingredients are well blended. Cover and cook over low heat for 10 minutes. Cabbage should be tender but not mushy. Sprinkle with salt and coconut and mix well. Uncover and continue cooking over medium heat until all liquid is absorbed. Serve hot.

Braised Okra

INDIA	*Yield 4 servings*

¼ cup ghee
1 large onion, peeled and sliced
3 cloves garlic, peeled and sliced
1-inch piece of fresh gingerroot, finely chopped
2 green chilies, finely chopped
½ teaspoon chili powder
1 pound okra, topped and tailed
1 cup water
Salt
2 teaspoons coconut, shredded

Using a heavy pan, melt the ghee. Gently fry the onion, garlic, ginger, chilies, and chili powder for

5 minutes, until soft. Stir occasionally. Put in okra, water, and salt to taste and bring to a boil. Reduce heat, cover, and simmer for 5 to 10 minutes until the okra is tender. Just before serving, stir in the coconut.

Fried Onions or Leeks

INDIA   *Yield 4 to 6 servings*

5 or 6 large leeks or 3 large onions
2 tablespoons ghee
1 teaspoon cumin seeds
1 teaspoon ground turmeric
1 teaspoon fresh ginger, finely grated
1 teaspoon garam masala
1 teaspoon salt

Wash leeks well at least twice or peel the onions. Cut them into fairly thick slices. Heat ghee in large saucepan and stir-fry the cumin for 2 minutes. Add turmeric and ginger and fry for 1 minute more. Add leeks or onions and stir well to cover with the seasonings. Fry for 5 minutes. Sprinkle with garam masala and salt, and cover. Cook until vegetables are tender, stirring occasionally.

Spiced Potatoes and Cauliflower

INDIA   *Yield 4 servings*

¾ cup ghee
2 pounds potatoes, peeled and cut into 1-inch pieces
2 large onions, peeled and sliced
4 cloves garlic, peeled and sliced
2 teaspoons chili powder
1 teaspoon turmeric powder

1 teaspoon coriander powder
2 teaspoons salt
½ teaspoon freshly ground black pepper
5 cups water
8 large cauliflower florets
2 teaspoons garam masala

Using a large saucepan, melt the ghee. Stir-fry the potatoes for about 1 minute. Remove them from the pan and set aside.

Put the onions and garlic in remaining ghee and fry gently until soft. Add chili powder, turmeric, coriander, salt, and pepper and stir-fry for 3 minutes more. Return potatoes to the pan along with the water. Bring to a boil; then lower the heat to simmer for 10 minutes. Place cauliflower in with potatoes and continue to simmer for 15 minutes. The dish is done when vegetables are tender and sauce has thickened. Add garam masala. Mix well and serve hot.

Chicken and Shrimp Salad

INDIA   *Yield 4 to 6 servings*

½ pound dark meat of chicken, cooked and diced
½ cup cooked rice
1 leek, cut in half lengthwise and finely chopped
¼ pound shrimp, cooked, deveined, and cut in half
1 small onion, peeled and finely chopped

Marinade

2 tablespoons each of mango chutney, oil, and lemon juice
1 teaspoon vinegar
½ teaspoon Worcestershire sauce

Pinch of curry
Salt and white pepper to taste

Garnish

Lettuce leaves, washed and drained dry
1 banana, peeled and sliced

Prepare chicken and rice. Add the chopped leek to the rice during the last 5 minutes of cooking. When the rice has cooled, put chicken, shrimp, and onion in a bowl with the rice. Mix well.

In a small bowl, mix ingredients for the marinade and stir well or blend with a whisk. Pour this mixture over the salad and toss all together gently. Line serving dish with lettuce leaves. Make a mound of the salad and garnish with slices of bananas. Allow to chill for 30 minutes before serving.

Yogurt Salad with Cucumber and Tomato

INDIA *Yield 4 to 6 servings*

1 large cucumber, peeled
4 shallots, peeled and finely chopped
1 teaspoon salt
2 tomatoes, cut in quarters, seeded, then diced
1 bunch parsley, chopped
4 cups yogurt
1 teaspoon ground caraway
Salt to taste
White pepper to taste
1 bunch dill, for garnish

Cut the peeled cucumber in half, lengthwise and crosswise. Scrape out and discard the seeds; cut the cucumber into strips and then into 1-inch pieces. Mix in a bowl with tomatoes, shallots, and salt. Let stand for 15 minutes.

Mix parsley with cucumber mixture. Beat yogurt with a whisk until it is light. Pour over the vegetables. Add salt, caraway, and pepper to taste.

Refrigerate for 1 hour. Garnish with dill and serve at once.

Stuffed Eggplant

PHILIPPINES *Yield 4 servings*

2 medium eggplants, peeled and halved
** lengthwise**
Lightly salted water
1 tablespoon oil
3 cloves garlic, peeled and finely chopped
1 medium onion, peeled and finely chopped
½ pound ground pork
1 large ripe tomato, chopped
1 teaspoon salt
½ teaspoon black pepper
1 cup soft, fresh breadcrumbs
1 egg, beaten
Dry breadcrumbs for coating
Oil for frying

Place eggplants in lightly salted boiling water and cook for 5 minutes. Remove from water and drain, cut side down. Scoop out a thin layer of the pulp, being sure to leave a firm shell.

Using a large skillet, heat the oil. Fry the garlic and onion until golden; then add the pork and fry until it browns all through. Add tomato, salt, and pepper and lower heat for 15 minutes, stirring from time to time. Chop pulp taken from the eggplant and add it to the skillet, cooking until most of the moisture has disappeared. Remove from heat. Mix in the soft breadcrumbs and add extra seasoning if needed.

Divide the mixture and spoon it into eggplant halves. Brush the top with beaten eggs and coat with dried breadcrumbs.

Heat oil in a skillet and fry the eggplant halves, first on one side, then on the other. When golden brown, serve at once. (If preferred, eliminate the last frying by putting eggplants into a 400°F oven for 15 minutes, until tops of eggplants are golden brown.)

Papaya Salad

PHILIPPINES	*Yield 6 servings*

1 medium, firm papaya (pawpaw), peeled
1 small ripe pineapple, peeled and diced
2 spring onions, finely sliced
1 cooking apple, peeled and diced
½ cup celery, thinly sliced
½ cup prepared salad dressing or mayonnaise
Salt and pepper to taste

Cut the papaya in half and scoop out the seeds. Dice the fruit into a serving bowl. Add all of the other ingredients in the order given and toss gently. Cover the bowl and chill the salad for at least 1 hour before serving.

Vegetables with Pork

CHINA	*Yield 6 servings*

4 tablespoons butter
4 cups celery, sliced diagonally
1 green pepper, sliced
1 red pepper, sliced
½ pound fresh mushrooms, sliced
½ cup onions, sliced
2 cups cooked pork, cubed
1 ¼ cups beef bouillon
1 tablespoon cornstarch
3 tablespoons soy sauce
½ teaspoon ginger
¼ teaspoon salt
Freshly ground pepper to taste
Boiled rice

Melt the butter in a wok or large skillet. Add celery; stir-fry for 5 minutes. Stir in green and red peppers, mushrooms, and onions; stir-fry for another 5 minutes. Add pork and bouillon; bring to boil. Reduce heat; simmer for 5 minutes.

Blend cornstarch with soy sauce, ginger, salt, and pepper. Stir into pork mixture. Cook, stirring constantly, just until heated through and thickened. Serve vegetables and pork on a bed of rice.

Fried Vegetables

CHINA	*Yield 2 servings*

Oil for cooking
½ cup celery, sliced diagonally
4 ounces bamboo shoots
4 ounces water chestnuts, sliced
3 scallions, sliced into 1-inch pieces
½ cup fresh mushrooms
1 cup bean sprouts, fresh or canned
Soy sauce to taste

Heat the oil in a skillet or wok. Add celery, bamboo shoots, and water chestnuts. Stir-fry for 2 minutes. Add scallions, mushrooms, and bean sprouts and stir-fry for 1 minute or until heated through. Sprinkle with soy sauce to taste and serve immediately.

Pea-pod Casserole

CHINA	*Yield 4 servings*

1 package frozen pea pods, boiled
1 can water chestnuts, sliced
2 cups fresh bean sprouts, or 1 can bean sprouts
1 can cream of mushroom soup
1 can onion rings, optional

Boil pea pods for 2 minutes. Drain and place in casserole dish. Place sliced water chestnuts on top of pea pods.

Next, add a layer of bean sprouts. If fresh sprouts are used, first blanch, then rinse with cold water and drain well. If canned bean sprouts are used, drain, rinse with cold water, and drain well.

Cover with cream of mushroom soup. Bake for 15 minutes at 350°F. Place onion rings on top and heat again for about 2 or 3 minutes.

Bean Sprouts with Celery and Mushrooms

CHINA *Yield 4 servings*

2 tablespoons oil
3 stalks celery, sliced diagonally
1 onion, chopped
¼ pound fresh mushrooms, sliced
½ cup chicken stock
1 tablespoon soy sauce
1 pound fresh bean sprouts
1 tablespoon cornstarch mixed with ¼ cup cold
   water

Add oil to a preheated pan. Sauté celery, onion, and mushrooms until onion is soft. Add chicken stock and soy sauce. Bring to a boil and add bean sprouts. Stir-fry only for about 30 seconds. Cover and simmer 3 seconds.

Thicken with the cornstarch mixture, adding it a little at a time. Serve immediately.

Spinach with Mushrooms and Bamboo Shoots

CHINA *Yield 2 servings*

1 pound fresh spinach, washed and cut into 2-
   inch pieces
2 tablespoons oil

Salt to taste
1 small can bamboo shoots
8 fresh mushrooms, sliced
¼ cup chicken broth

Wash and cut the spinach into pieces. Heat the oil in a wok or skillet. Add salt and spinach and stir-fry for 2 minutes. Add bamboo shoots, mushrooms, and chicken broth. Mix; cover and simmer for about 2 minutes, or until heated through.

Sweet-and-Sour Yams and Pineapple

CHINA *Yield about 8 servings*

1 20-ounce can sliced pineapple
1 tablespoon cornstarch
¼ teaspoon salt
3 tablespoons fresh lemon juice
2 1-pound cans of yams, drained
Oil
4 scallions, sliced
1 small green pepper, cut into small chunks
½ cup celery, sliced diagonally

Drain pineapple; reserve syrup. In a saucepan, combine the reserved syrup, cornstarch, and salt. Blend well. Bring to a boil over medium heat. Cook until thickened, stirring constantly. Stir in the lemon juice.

Arrange the pineapple and yams in a casserole and pour the sauce over them. Bake, covered, in a 350°F oven for about 30 minutes or until hot.

In a small amount of oil in a skillet, sauté the scallions, green pepper chunks, and celery until just tender, but still crisp. Stir carefully into yam mixture. Serve immediately.

Mandarin-Orange Gelatin

CHINA   *Yield 6 servings*

1 11-ounce can mandarin oranges, drained;
    reserve ½ cup liquid
3 tablespoons sauterne
2 3-ounce packages orange-flavored gelatin
1 envelope unflavored gelatin
2 cups hot water
1 cup cold water

Combine oranges with 2 tablespoons sauterne.
Combine orange-flavored and unflavored gela-
tins in a large bowl; mix well. Add hot water; stir
until gelatin is dissolved. Stir in 1 tablespoon sauterne, reserved mandarin-orange liquid, and cold
water. Chill until gelatin is thick and syrupy.

Yogurt salad with cucumbers and tomatoes

Indian salad

Vegetables with pork

Pour about ½ cup gelatin into 1½-quart mold rinsed in cold water. Arrange orange segments petal-fashion in gelatin. Chill until set. Spoon about a 1-inch layer of thickened gelatin over the oranges. Arrange a layer of orange segments around edge of mold. Chill until set. Spoon another layer of gelatin over the oranges. Repeat layers. Chill until set.

Asparagus Salad

CHINA	*Yield about 4 to 5 servings*

1 tablespoon soy sauce
½ teaspoon red-wine vinegar
2 teaspoons sesame oil
1 teaspoon sugar
1 pound asparagus, tough ends broken off,
   sliced into 2-inch lengths

Combine soy sauce, vinegar, oil, and sugar; stir until sugar dissolves. Bring pot of water to boil. Drop asparagus into water; cook 1 minute. Drain; rinse with cold water. Toss asparagus with soy-sauce mixture; chill.

Sweet-and-sour yams and pineapple

Mixed Vegetables Chinese-style

CHINA	*Yield 2 servings*

5 large dried Chinese mushrooms
1 cup lukewarm water
5 ounces green cabbage
4 ounces carrots
4 ounces cucumbers
5 ounces canned bamboo shoots
4 tablespoons sesame-seed oil
2 ounces frozen peas

½ cup hot chicken broth
2 tablespoons soy sauce
Salt
Pinch of sugar

Soak the mushrooms in water for 30 minutes. Shred the cabbage. Cut the carrots, cucumber, and bamboo shoots into julienne strips. Cube the mushrooms.

Heat oil in a skillet. Add cabbage; cook 2 minutes. Add mushrooms, cucumber, carrots, bamboo shoots, and peas. Pour in broth. Season with soy sauce, salt, and sugar. Simmer over low heat for 15 minutes. Serve at once.

Fried Bean Curd Peking-style

CHINA   *Yield about 4 servings*

1 cup peanut oil
2 bean curds, each cut into 8 pieces
¼ cup soy sauce

Mixed vegetables Chinese-style

Mandarin-orange gelatin

2 tablespoons red-wine vinegar
1 tablespoon white vinegar
4 tablespoons scallions, chopped
1½ teaspoons hot oil

Heat peanut oil to 350°F. Cook bean curds until golden brown.

Mix together soy sauce, red-wine vinegar, white vinegar, scallions, and hot oil in bowl. Serve sauce with bean curds.

Vegetable Platter

INDOCHINA   *Yield 4 servings*

1 head lettuce, washed and leaves separated
Mint leaves
Coriander leaves

Fruit salad

2 cucumbers, partially peeled and halved, cut into half-moon shapes

Mound the lettuce leaves in center of serving platter. Surround the center with piles of the mint leaves, coriander leaves, and prepared cucumbers. Any arrangement that is pleasing to the eye will do. Serve chilled with your favorite dressing.

Stir-Fried Mixed Vegetables

INDOCHINA   *Yield 4 servings*

6 dried Chinese mushrooms, soaked in hot water for 30 minutes
½ cup water
1 tablespoon dark soy sauce
1 teaspoon sesame oil
2 teaspoons sugar
3 stalks celery, sliced diagonally

¼ medium cabbage or white Chinese cabbage
Few leaves mustard cabbage, if available
1 small head lettuce
3 spring onions, cut into 1-inch pieces
1 tablespoon oil
1 clove garlic, peeled and finely grated
½ teaspoon fresh ginger, finely grated
1½ tablespoons light soy sauce
¼ cup water
1 teaspoon cornstarch

Cut off and discard the mushroom stems. Slice tops thin and simmer in ½ cup water with dark soy sauce, sesame oil, and sugar until the liquid is absorbed. Prepare celery and cut greens into bite-size pieces.

In a wok or skillet, heat the oil and fry the garlic and ginger for 30 seconds or less. Add vegetables and stir-fry for 2 minutes on high heat. Add the light soy sauce and prepared mushrooms and mix well. Add ¼ cup of water. Allow it to come to a boil, add cornstarch blended with 1 tablespoon cold water, and stir until it thickens. Serve at once.

Leeks in egg shirts

142

Leeks in Egg Shirts

KOREA	*Yield 4 servings*

8 thin leeks
1 quart water
1 teaspoon salt
1 tablespoon oil
Ground nutmeg
4 tablespoons flour
1 egg, beaten
6 tablespoons oil

Sauce

2 tablespoons soy sauce
1 tablespoon lemon juice
Salt and white pepper to taste
Pinch of sugar

Clean the leeks, removing dark green leaves. Cut the leeks diagonally into 2-inch-long pieces. In a pot, bring water, salt, and 1 tablespoon of oil to a boil. Add leeks. Cover and cook over medium heat for 10 minutes. Remove and drain leeks. Then sprinkle with nutmeg.

Place the flour on one plate, the egg on a second plate. Roll the leeks first in flour and then in egg. Immediately, put them in hot oil and fry for 2 minutes until golden brown and crisp. Drain on paper towels and keep warm.

Combine remaining ingredients for dip sauce and serve with the fried leeks.

White Radish Salad

KOREA	*Yield 4 servings*

2 giant white radishes, peeled and cut into matchstick strips
1 or 2 crisp cooking apples, peeled, cored, and cut into thin strips
Juice of half lemon

3 spring onions, including green tops, very finely sliced

Dressing

3 tablespoons light soy sauce
1 tablespoon salad oil
2 teaspoons sesame oil
3 tablespoons mild vinegar
3 teaspoons sugar
1 teaspoon salt
1 tablespoon toasted, crushed sesame seeds
1 fresh, hot red chili, seeded and finely chopped

Prepare radishes and set aside. Prepare apples and soak in cold water with lemon juice to prevent discoloration. Slice onions as directed.

Mix ingredients for the dressing in the order given. Drain the apples and combine with radishes, onions, and dressing in a large bowl. Be sure vegetables are well coated with the dressing. Serve chilled.

Green Beans with Shrimp

KOREA	*Yield 4 to 6 servings*

1 pound small shrimp, shelled and deveined
1 pound tender green beans, topped and tailed
2 tablespoons vegetable oil
1 tablespoon sesame oil
1 medium onion, peeled and thinly sliced
3 tablespoons light soy sauce
1 teaspoon sugar
3 teaspoons toasted, crushed sesame seeds

Chop shrimp and set aside. Prepare beans and cut into thin diagonal slices.

Heat vegetable and sesame oil in a wok or skillet. Fry the onions and shrimp together for 2 minutes. Add beans and stir-fry for 3 minutes more. Put in seasonings and mix well; cover and simmer on low heat for 5 to 8 minutes. When beans are tender, serve at once.

Fruit Salad

KOREA   *Yield 4 to 6 servings*

½ cup water
6 tablespoons sugar
1 tablespoon white wine
2 oranges
2 pears
2 peaches
1 cup morello cherries
3 tablespoons lime juice
2 tablespoons peeled pistachio nuts

In a pot, bring water, sugar, and wine to a boil. Allow to cool.

Peel, seed, and dice the oranges. Peel, core, and halve the pears. Peel, seed, and dice the peaches. Remove seeds from cherries. Place all fruit in a serving bowl. Add lime juice to the cooled liquid and pour over the fruit. Cover and refrigerate at least 30 minutes. When ready to serve, mix fruit with slotted spoon. Sprinkle nuts on top and serve.

Sweet Spinach with Garlic

KOREA   *Yield 4 servings*

1½ pounds fresh, young spinach leaves
Boiling water
3 tablespoons soy sauce
1 tablespoon sesame seeds
1 tablespoon sesame-seed oil
1 tablespoon peeled, crushed garlic

2 tablespoons scallions, chopped
2 teaspoons sugar
Salt to taste
Carrot, boo, and parsley for garnish

Wash spinach twice and remove and discard stalks. To a large pan of boiling water, add spinach and cook for 3 minutes. Drain and then chop the spinach.

Place hot spinach on a serving platter and sprinkle with the remaining ingredients. Garnish as desired and serve at once.

Pickled Chinese Cabbage

KOREA   *Yield 4 to 6 servings*

1 head bok choy, chopped
3 tablespoons salt
2 teaspoons hot chili powder
2 teaspoons crushed garlic
4 scallions, finely chopped
1 tablespoon sugar
1 hard pear, peeled, cored, and grated

Use a large bowl to hold the bok choy. Sprinkle with salt and stir well. Allow to stand overnight.

When ready to prepare, rinse the cabbage under cold running water. Drain and pat dry with paper towels. Put it in a large jar. Mix the remaining ingredients together and add to the cabbage. Stir well. Cover with a heavy weight, such as a heavy can. Allow the spices to mingle this way for 1 or 2 days before using.

This may be stored refrigerated for as long as 3 weeks.

Corn Fritters

MALAYSIA	*Yield 4 servings*

This is really an all-purpose dish—it may be served hot or cold, for a vegetable with a meal, or as a between-meal snack.

6 ears corn-on-the-cob, or 1 12-ounce can corn,
   drained
2 medium shrimp, shelled, optional
4 shallots, peeled
2 garlic cloves, peeled, optional
½ teaspoon chili powder
1 teaspoon coriander powder
1 teaspoon or more salt to taste
1 large egg, beaten
Vegetable oil

Cut corn kernels from the cob. Grind shrimp, shallots, and garlic. Mix with corn. Add chili powder, coriander, and salt. Last, put in a beaten egg and mix thoroughly.

Heat enough oil in a skillet to cover the bottom of the pan. Drop batter by heaping tablespoons into skillet. Flatten fritters with a spatula. Cook about 5 at a time. Fry about 2 minutes on one side, and then turn to brown the other side. Remove and drain on paper towels. Add oil to pan if needed and continue to fry fritters until all the batter is used. Serve hot or cold.

Bean Curd and Bean Sprouts

MALAYSIA	*Yield 4 to 6 servings*

2 squares yellow bean curd, cut in slices
½ pound fresh bean sprouts, washed, drained,
   and tails pinched off
2 cloves garlic, peeled and crushed
2 tablespoons oil

Salt and pepper to taste
Soy sauce to taste

Prepare bean curd and sprouts as directed above. Heat oil in a skillet and fry the crushed garlic until it turns golden. Add bean curd and bean sprouts and stir-fry for 3 to 4 minutes. Add seasonings to taste and serve at once.

Chili-Fried Cauliflower

MALAYSIA	*Yield 6 servings*

3 tablespoons peanut oil
4 fresh red chilies, finely chopped, or 2
   teaspoons sambal ulek
1 large onion, peeled and finely chopped
2 cloves garlic, peeled and finely chopped
1 teaspoon dried shrimp paste
1 teaspoon salt
1 pound cauliflower, washed and sliced
2 tablespoons hot water

Using a wok or skillet, heat the oil. On low heat, fry chilies, onion, and garlic until onion is soft, stirring constantly. Add shrimp paste and crush with back of spoon. Fry for 1 minute. Add salt and cauliflower and stir constantly, coating the vegetable with the fried onion and chili mixture. Sprinkle with hot water; cover and cook for 10 minutes. Serve at once.

Vegetable Curry

MALAYSIA	*Yield 4 servings*

Fiddlehead ferns are used for this dish in Malaysia. A good substitute for the fern is curly kale.

6 kemiri, chopped
6 shallots, peeled and chopped
3 cloves garlic, peeled and chopped
2 red chilies, seeded and chopped, or ½
    teaspoon chili powder
2 teaspoons ginger powder
1 teaspoon turmeric powder
Pinch of laos powder
Pinch of sereh powder
Salt to taste
2 cups thick coconut milk
¼ cup tamarind water
3 sprigs mint
1 ¼ pounds fiddlehead ferns or kale, cut into
    2-inch lengths

Make a smooth paste of the kemiri, shallots, garlic, and chilies. Add the spices, salt, coconut milk, tamarind water, and mint and mix well.

In a saucepan, bring the mixture to a boil for 5 minutes. Add the kale and cover. Reduce the heat to a simmer and cook for 10 minutes. Bring back to a boil just long enough to reduce the sauce. Adjust seasonings and serve hot.

Stuffed Eggplant

JAPAN	*Yield 4 to 6 servings*

6 eggplants, small size

Stuffing

½ onion, chopped
Oil, butter, or margarine
8 ounces ground chicken
½ to ¾ cup bread crumbs
½ teaspoon salt
1 tablespoon water (a little more, if necessary)
4 tablespoons grated cheese

Cornstarch
Oil for frying

Grated gingerroot
Soy sauce for dipping

Remove stem part of eggplants. Make a cut lengthwise in half, but not all the way through. Soak eggplants in salted water.

Saute onion in a small amount of oil, butter, or margarine just until soft. Combine with chicken, bread crumbs, salt, and water. Gently mix in cheese. Divide into 6 parts.

Wipe eggplants dry. Sprinkle cut surfaces with cornstarch. Place a layer of meat mixture inside the eggplant. Sprinkle a small amount of cornstarch on the meat.

Heat oil in a deep frying pan; cook over medium heat until meat is well done. Serve with grated ginger and soy sauce.

Mixed Salad

JAPAN	*Yield 6 servings*

1 large cucumber
2 carrots
1 large white radish
Salt
½ pound fresh mushrooms
10 ounces fresh shrimp
2 tablespoons parsley, chopped
1 tablespoon fresh dill, chopped

Salad dressing

2 eggs
Salt
Pinch of sugar
3 tablespoons melted butter
2 tablespoons wine vinegar
1 teaspoon paprika

Garnish

1 peach, sliced
1 mandarin orange or 1 tangerine, sectioned
½ orange, sliced

Grate unpeeled cucumber, carrots, and radish. Sprinkle with salt; let stand for 30 minutes. Drain off as much liquid as possible. Thinly slice mushrooms; mix with vegetables. Add shrimp and chopped fresh herbs. Toss; set aside for 15 minutes.

Meanwhile, prepare the dressing by placing eggs, salt, sugar, and melted butter in top of double boiler. Beat over hot water until creamy. Remove from heat. Gradually add vinegar, beating constantly until dressing has cooled off. Season to taste with paprika.

Pour dressing over salad. Garnish with peach slices, mandarin orange or tangerine sections, and orange slices.

Rice Salad

JAPAN *Yield 4 servings*

2 cups water
Salt
4 ounces long-grain rice
1 ounce dried mushrooms
8 ounces bean sprouts, canned or fresh
8 ounces canned bamboo shoots
4 ounces cooked ham
1 medium cucumber
4 tablespoons rice wine or brandy

Salad dressing

5 tablespoons oil
5 tablespoons lemon juice
3 tablespoons rice wine or sherry
2 tablespoons soy sauce
Salt

Garnish

1 small head Boston lettuce
1 lemon
Salt

Bring salted water to a boil. Add rice; cook for 15 minutes (or use your own method). Place rice in sieve. Pour cold water over it; drain thoroughly.

Chop mushrooms; place in small bowl. Cover with boiling water; let soak for 20 minutes. Drain bean sprouts, if canned. If using fresh bean sprouts, blanch, rinse with cold water, and drain them. Drain the bamboo shoots. Cut bamboo shoots into ¼-inch-wide strips. Cut ham into ¼-inch-wide, 2-inch-long strips. Cut unpeeled cucumber in half, then into thin slices lengthwise, and finally into 2-inch-long thin strips. Drain the mushrooms.

To prepare the salad dressing, combine oil, lemon juice, rice wine or sherry, soy sauce, and salt to taste; stir until well blended. Add rice, bean sprouts, bamboo shoots, ham, cucumber, and mushrooms to dressing; toss thoroughly. Cover; refrigerate for 30 minutes to let flavors blend.

Meanwhile, wash the lettuce and pat it dry. Tear it into large pieces and line a serving platter with it. Arrange rice salad on top.

Cut off both ends of a lemon until pulp is visible. Place on platter. Sprinkle top of lemon with salt. Heat rice wine or brandy; pour it over the lemon and ignite. Serve immediately. (Lemon is only a garnish, it is not eaten).

Cauliflower Salad

JAPAN *Yield 4 servings*

1 small cauliflower
3 tablespoons peanut butter
Water
Pinch of salt
Chopped peanuts

Boil cauliflower; separate into florets. Mix peanut butter with water until thin. Season with salt. Mix in with the cauliflower. Sprinkle a little chopped peanuts over the top.

Cauliflower with Water Chestnuts and Mushrooms

JAPAN   *Yield 4 servings*

1 small cauliflower
2 tablespoons oil
8 mushrooms, sliced
1 cup hot chicken broth
¼ cup water chestnuts, sliced
2 tablespoons soy sauce
Salt to taste
1 tablespoon cornstarch mixed with cold water

Trim and wash cauliflower. Break into florets. If florets are large, slice them.

Heat oil in pan; gently sauté cauliflower. Add sliced mushrooms; sauté for about 30 seconds. Add chicken broth, sliced water chestnuts, soy sauce, and seasonings. Bring mixture to a boil, cover, and simmer until cauliflower is just tender, i.e., still crunchy.

Mix cornstarch with enough cold water to make a smooth paste; slowly add to cauliflower mixture, stirring constantly until thickened.

Marinated Bean Sprouts

JAPAN   *Yield 4 servings*

This is an excellent salad to serve with meat or fish. It has a unique flavor.

1 pound fresh bean sprouts

Marinade

3 tablespoons chopped scallion (use green and white parts)
2 tablespoons sesame-seed oil
2 tablespoons soy sauce
1 tablespoon vodka
1 tablespoon vinegar

Place bean sprouts in colander; blanch. Immediately rinse them with cold water; drain well. Combine remaining ingredients in a large bowl. Add bean sprouts and marinate at room temperature for 1 hour. Refrigerate for at least 3 hours before serving.

Pancakes with chicken and fruit filling

Eggs in Fried Chili Sauce

INDONESIA   *Yield 4 servings*

1 medium onion, peeled and sliced
½ cup oil
1 tablespoon ground chili
2 tomatoes, peeled and chopped
1 chicken stock cube

1 or more teaspoons salt
6 hard-boiled eggs, shelled

In a skillet, fry onions until they change color. Reduce heat. Add chili, tomatoes, crumbled chicken cube, and salt. Simmer for 5 minutes, stirring constantly. Add the shelled eggs and simmer for 5 minutes more.

Remove from heat and remove eggs from pan. Cut each egg in half and arrange on a prepared platter. Pour the sauce over eggs and serve at once.

149

Marbled Eggs

INDONESIA   *Yield 6 or more servings*

10 eggs
3 tablespoons loose tea or 6 tea bags
2 stalks parsley
2 stalks shallots
2-inch piece fresh green ginger, thinly sliced
½ tablespoon salt
2 chicken cubes
2 tablespoons soy sauce

Make enough strong tea to cover 10 eggs. Allow to stand for 10 minutes. Strain into a large saucepan. Place all ingredients except the eggs in the tea solution. Allow to come to a boil. Lower the heat and add eggs one by one. Simmer for 30 minutes.

Take the eggs out and rinse. Very gently, crack the egg shells all over but do not remove the shells. Strain the liquid and return to pan. Return eggs to the pan and continue to simmer for 20 minutes more. Turn off the heat but let eggs remain in the liquid for at least 3 hours, and up to 24 hours. When the eggs are peeled, the marbled effect will show where the shell was cracked. Serve hot or cold.

These may be made ahead and refrigerated for several days.

Shredded Omelet

INDONESIA   *Yield 2 servings*

3 eggs
½ teaspoon salt
Dash of pepper
3 tablespoons butter or margarine
¼ cup onion, peeled and chopped

Beat the eggs in a bowl, together with the salt and pepper. Melt, but do not brown, the butter in a medium-size skillet. Sauté the chopped onions for 2 minutes—just until they are transparent.

Pour the eggs into the pan so that they cover the onions and are spread evenly over the bottom of the skillet. When set and firm, turn with a spatula to brown the top side. Remove from the pan and cut into thin slices. Serve at once.

Stuffed Savory Pancakes

INDONESIA   *Yield 6 to 8 servings*

These delicacies are eaten as snacks at Indonesian open-air market stalls. If you don't want to make your own dough, substitute wonton skins from your Oriental grocery store.

Dough

2½ cups all-purpose flour
1 teaspoon salt
2 eggs
Water to mix

Filling

1 tablespoon olive oil
2 large onions, peeled and finely sliced
2 garlic cloves, peeled and crushed
1 teaspoon coriander powder
½ teaspoon cumin powder
½ teaspoon ginger powder
½ teaspoon chili powder
½ teaspoon turmeric powder
1 teaspoon sereh (lemon grass) powder
Salt to taste
1 pound cooked lamb or beef, ground

To complete the pancake

2 to 3 eggs
5 medium scallions, chopped
¾ cup chopped coriander leaves
Vegetable oil for shallow frying

To make the dough, place the flour, salt, and eggs in a bowl. Add enough water to make a smooth, firm dough. Sprinkle a board with cornstarch and place the ball of dough on the board. Roll out as thin as possible and cut into 3-inch squares. Refrigerate squares until you are ready to use them.

To make the filling, heat the olive oil in a deep frying pan or wok. Fry onions and garlic until soft. Add spices and salt and stir-fry for 30 seconds more. Stir-fry the meat for 1 or 2 minutes until browned. Set aside to cool for 1 hour.

To complete the pancake, break eggs into the cooled filling mixture. Add scallions and coriander and mix well.

Take 1 square of dough. On it, place 1 heaping tablespoon of filling. Top with another square and then seal all edges. Heat about 5 tablespoons oil in a frying pan, add the square, and press down flat with a spatula. Fry for just 1 minute on each side. Remove from pan and drain on paper towels. Add more oil if needed during cooking.

These may be served either hot or cold. They may also be cut into triangles.

Fried Stuffed Eggs

THAILAND   *Yield 6 to 8 servings*

4 large eggs, boiled slowly, shelled and halved
    lengthwise
½ cup raw prawns or shrimp, chopped
½ cup cooked crab meat
½ cup cooked pork, chopped
1 teaspoon fresh coriander leaves, chopped
Hearty dash of ground black pepper
½ teaspoon salt
1 tablespoon fish sauce
1 to 2 tablespoons thick coconut milk

Batter

½ cup flour
½ cup tepid water

2 teaspoons oil
¼ teaspoon salt
Oil for deep frying

After eggs are prepared, scoop out the egg yolks into a bowl. Add all ingredients except the coconut milk. When well mixed, add enough of the coconut milk to make the mixture hold together without getting too moist. Divide this yolk mixture into 8 portions and stuff each egg.

Mix the batter in order given. Dip each egg into the batter, then drop it stuffed-side-down into heated oil for quick deep fry. When golden brown, remove and drain on paper towels. This can be served hot or cold.

Stuffed Pancakes

THAILAND   *Yield 4 servings*

1 cup ground pork
2 tablespoons tung chai
1 teaspoon sugar
2 tablespoons soy sauce
2 onions, peeled and finely chopped
2 tablespoons vegetable oil
6 eggs, beaten well
Coriander leaves for garnish

In a large bowl, mix pork, tung chai, sugar, soy sauce, and onions until well blended. Heat 1 tablespoon oil in a wok or frying pan. Stir-fry the pork mixture for 3 minutes and then remove from pan. Wipe off the surface of the pan with paper towels.

Add remaining oil to the wok and allow to heat until slightly smoking. Pour in half the beaten eggs. Spoon ½ the pork mixture into the center of the eggs. Fold over the already firm edges to cover. Turn the omelet once until cooked through and lightly browned. Remove to a heated platter. Proceed the same way with remaining eggs and filling. Arrange on the heated platter and garnish with coriander. Slice to serve.

Son-in-Law Eggs

THAILAND	*Yield 4 servings*

2 tablespoons vegetable oil
5 shallots, peeled and finely chopped
4 hard-cooked eggs, shelled and quartered
2 tablespoons tamarind water
1 tablespoon water
2 teaspoons brown sugar
Nam pla to taste

Using a wok or deep skillet, heat oil. Fry shallots until brown. Remove from pan.

Add eggs and fry until crisp on the outside. Remove from pan with slotted spoon and set aside.

Place remaining ingredients in skillet; cook for 5 minutes, stirring constantly. Return eggs to pan and cook gently for 2 minutes more. Arrange egg mixture on a warm platter and garnish with the shallots. Serve at once.

Eggs in Coconut Milk Gravy

INDIA	*Yield 4 to 6 servings*

6 hard-boiled eggs, shelled, halved, and set
   aside
1½ cups thick coconut milk
2 cups thin coconut milk
2 tablespoons ghee or oil
1 large onion, peeled and finely sliced
3 cloves garlic, peeled and finely chopped
2 teaspoons fresh ginger, finely grated
3 fresh green chilies, seeded and sliced
6 curry leaves
1 teaspoon ground turmeric
1 teaspoon salt
2 tablespoons lemon juice

Prepare coconut milk, keeping the thick milk separate from the thin.

Fry onions, garlic, ginger, chilies, and curry leaves in heated ghee. Cook only until onions are soft. Add turmeric and stir for 1 minute. Add thin coconut milk and simmer gently for 10 minutes. Add thick coconut milk and salt and stir constantly. When mixture has come to a soft simmer, put in egg halves and simmer for 6 or 7 minutes more. Remove from heat. Add lemon juice to taste and serve at once.

Curried Eggs with Mushrooms

INDIA	*Yield 3 or 4 servings*

6 hard-cooked eggs, cut in half lengthwise
8 ounces mushrooms
1 large onion, peeled and finely chopped
2 tablespoons margarine or butter
1 teaspoon ground coriander
1 teaspoon salt
½ teaspoon ground turmeric
½ teaspoon ground ginger
½ teaspoon ground cumin
3 medium tomatoes, cut into wedges
¼ cup chicken broth
1 teaspoon lemon juice
3 cups hot cooked rice

In a medium-size skillet, stir mushrooms and onions in margarine for 5 minutes. Add coriander, salt, turmeric, ginger, and cumin. Stir-fry together for 1 minute. Put in tomatoes and chicken broth and bring to a boil. Then reduce heat to a simmer, cooking uncovered for 5 minutes.

Place eggs gently in skillet and spoon the sauce over them. Simmer again without stirring, for 5 minutes. Sprinkle with lemon juice and serve eggs with sauce over rice.

Egg Curry

INDIA *Yield 4 to 6 servings*

6 hard-boiled eggs, cooled, shelled, halved, and
   set aside
2 tablespoons ghee or oil
2 medium onions, peeled and finely chopped
3 cloves garlic, peeled and finely chopped
2 teaspoons fresh ginger, finely grated
3 teaspoons ground coriander
2 teaspoons ground cumin
1 teaspoon ground turmeric
½ teaspoon chili powder
2 to 3 ripe tomatoes, diced
1 teaspoon salt
½ cup hot water
½ teaspoon garam masala

After the eggs are prepared and set aside, heat
ghee in skillet. Stir-fry onions, garlic, and ginger
until soft and light brown. Add coriander, cumin,
turmeric, and chili and stir for a few seconds. Put
in tomatoes and salt and cook until tomatoes are
pulpy. Add hot water and then cover and simmer
until gravy has thickened. Last, stir in garam
masala and the egg halves, and mix well until all is
hot and spicy. Serve at once with rice.

Scrambled Eggs

INDIA *Yield 4 to 6 servings*

6 to 8 eggs, well beaten
4 tablespoons milk
¾ teaspoon salt
¼ teaspoon ground black pepper
2 tablespoons ghee
6 spring onions, finely chopped
2 to 3 fresh red or green chilies, seeded and
   chopped
1 teaspoon fresh ginger, finely grated

Dash of ground turmeric
2 tablespoons fresh coriander leaves, chopped
1 ripe tomato, diced, optional
½ teaspoon ground cumin
Tomato wedges to garnish
Fresh coriander leaves to garnish

When eggs are well beaten, add milk, salt, and
pepper. In a large skillet, heat ghee and cook
onions, chilies, and ginger until soft. After you add
turmeric, coriander leaves, and tomato, fry for 1
minute.

Stir in egg mixture with ground cumin. Cook
over low heat. Stir the eggs as they start to set. The
eggs are finished when they are of a creamy consistency, not dry. Place on a serving plate and garnish
with tomato wedges and coriander.

Pancakes with Chicken and Fruit Filling

INDIA *Yield 4 to 6 servings*

3 eggs
4 cups water
1 teaspoon salt
1 cup flour
2 teaspoons curry powder
¼ cup coconut oil
Oil for frying pancakes

Filling

1 cup boned chicken, cut in strips
3 tablespoons butter
2 teaspoons curry powder
¼ cup canned royal cherries
¼ cup canned green gage plums
¼ cup canned Mandarin orange slices
1 large banana
Lemon juice

153

¼ cup canned sliced pineapple
4 tablespoons slivered almonds

For the pancake, mix eggs, water, and salt in a bowl. Gradually blend in the flour. Last, add coconut oil very slowly. When all are blended into a fairly smooth batter, fry pancakes in oil on a hot griddle. Keep warm.

To make the filling, put butter in deep skillet and fry chicken pieces. Add 1 teaspoon curry powder. Then stir in cherries, plums, and orange slices. Lower heat so fruit does not burn. Peel and slice banana and sprinkle with lemon juice. Add banana and pineapple to other fruits. Add remaining curry powder to taste.

Fill each pancake with some of the meat and fruit mixture and roll up loosely. Sprinkle with almonds and serve at once.

Dosas (Pancakes)

INDIA *Yield 12 to 15 servings*

These are particularly popular in southern India as breakfast snacks.

1 cup urhad dal (or lentils)
¼ cup rice
2½ cups water
½ teaspoon baking soda
1 teaspoon chili powder
½ teaspoon salt
Vegetable oil for shallow frying

Wash and drain dal and rice. Put them in a bowl with the water and allow to soak overnight. The next day, put this mixture in an electric blender or food processor and mix until smooth. Put in soda, chili powder, and salt and stir well.

Prepare a heavy frying pan or skillet with a light coating of oil. Pour in enough batter to cover the bottom of the pan. Fry until golden and then turn once. Remove from pan and roll up like a crepe. These can be filled if you prefer, but are good as they are. Continue frying and rolling until all batter is used.

Rice Pancakes

INDIA *Yield 25 to 30 pancakes*

2 tablespoons shredded coconut
1 cup water
1 cup rice
½ teaspoon baking soda
½ teaspoon salt
2 tablespoons butter

Allow the coconut to soak in water for at least 4 hours. Meanwhile, with a mortar and pestle, blender, or food processor, grind the rice.

Strain the coconut water into the ground rice with baking soda and salt. Continue beating this until a smooth batter forms. Allow the rice to absorb the liquid by letting mixture stand for at least 12 hours. When ready to cook, beat the batter again to stir in air.

Use a hot frying pan greased lightly with butter. Pour in a little batter, tilting the pan to spread it all over the pan. Cook for just 30 seconds or until the center of the pancake is solid. Place on a warm platter. (Do not turn. Only 1 side is cooked.) Continue in the same way until all batter has been used, adding butter if needed.

Crepes

CHINA *Yield 4 servings*

8 ounces lean pork or ham
1 tablespoon water
1 tablespoon dry vermouth
½ teaspoon curry
½ teaspoon paprika
2 scallions, minced
1 green pepper, chopped
1 red pepper, chopped
1 can bean sprouts, drained and heated
8 ounces small shrimp, peeled and deveined

2 tablespoons soy sauce
2 tablespoons white wine (optional)
8 warm crepes
2 tablespoons grated Parmesan cheese
1 tablespoon polyunsaturated margarine

Cut meat into thin strips. Over high heat, cook meat slightly in water and vermouth. Sprinkle with curry and paprika. Add scallions and peppers; cook for 2 minutes longer. Add heated bean sprouts and shrimp. Season with soy sauce, and wine if desired.

Spread filling on crepes. Roll up; place seam-side-down on greased baking dish. Sprinkle with grated cheese, if desired, and dot with a few pats of margarine. Bake in preheated 400°F oven 10 to 15 minutes.

Egg Foo Yong

CHINA   *Yield 2 to 4 servings*

Oil to cover bottom of skillet
½ pound fresh mushrooms, sliced
½ cup celery, chopped
½ cup scallions, diced
1 cup fresh bean sprouts, rinsed and drained
1 cup leftover cooked chicken, beef, or shrimp, cut into small pieces
4 eggs
Salt and pepper to taste

Sauté mushrooms, celery, and scallions for 5 minutes. Cool. Add bean sprouts and chicken, beef, or shrimp to sautéed mixture. In large bowl, beat eggs well with salt and pepper. Combine other ingredients with eggs.

Drop by spoonfuls into greased skillet. Cook over medium-high heat until browned on both sides. You may use a wok, and drop mixture by spoonfuls just to cover bottom of wok.

Shrimp Egg Foo Yong

CHINA   *Yield 4 servings*

1 cup chopped fresh bean sprouts
¼ cup chopped white onions
¼ cup chopped fresh mushrooms
¼ cup cooked shrimp, finely chopped
1 teaspoon soy sauce
Pinch of salt
4 eggs
¼ cup crisp noodles
Oil for frying

Mix together sprouts, onions, mushrooms, shrimp, soy sauce, and salt. Add eggs; mix. Mix in noodles. Shape mixture into hamburger-size patties. Heat oil (small amount) in frying pan. Cook each patty about 2 minutes on each side. Can be served with sweet-and-sour sauce (see Index).

Simple Egg Foo Yong

CHINA   *Yield 2 to 4 servings*

These are simple and delicious. Leftover chicken, beef, shrimp, etc., may also be added to rest of ingredients.

Oil for cooking
½ cup celery, thinly sliced diagonally
½ cup scallions, diced
½ cup fresh mushrooms, sliced
4 eggs
Salt and pepper to taste
1 cup fresh bean sprouts

Heat oil in skillet (or wok, preferably) and sauté celery for 2 minutes. Add scallions and mushrooms and sauté another minute. Remove vegetables from skillet. Beat eggs in bowl with seasonings and add sautéed vegetables and bean sprouts. Add more oil to skillet or wok, if necessary; add egg mixture to skillet by spoonfuls, or, if cooking in wok, add enough egg mixture just to cover bottom of wok. Cook over medium-high heat until brown, turn and brown other side. Serve with duck sauce.

Unusual Scrambled Eggs

CHINA	Yield 2 servings

4 eggs
½ teaspoon salt
Freshly ground black pepper to taste
½ cup green pepper, finely chopped
Oil for cooking, enough to cover bottom of pan

Beat eggs with salt and pepper. Add green pepper. Heat oil in skillet and cook mixture over medium-high heat until desired doneness. (Don't cook until dry.)

Scrambled Eggs with Shrimp

CHINA	Yield 3 to 4 servings

½ pound shrimp, cooked
1 teaspoon rice wine or sherry
½ teaspoon cornstarch
Salt (about ½ teaspoon)
2 tablespoons oil
6 eggs, beaten lightly
Salt to taste

Marinate shrimp in mixture of wine or sherry, cornstarch, and salt for 15 minutes. Heat oil in large skillet and sauté shrimp over medium-high heat for approximately 2 minutes. Remove from

skillet. Add salt to taste to beaten eggs and add shrimp to egg mixture. Add more oil if necessary to skillet, heat to medium-high. Pour in egg-shrimp mixture and cook and stir until done to taste.

Crab Omelet

INDOCHINA	Yield 3 to 4 servings

4 eggs
½ teaspoon salt
¼ teaspoon black pepper
4 ounces crab meat, fresh, frozen, or canned
2 spring onions, chopped
1 fresh red chili, optional
1 teaspoon fish sauce
Oil for frying

Put eggs in a small bowl; beat slightly and season with salt and pepper. Pick over crabmeat for bits of shell.

In a frying pan, sauté onions and chili in oil for 1 minute. Add crabmeat and stir for another minute. Sprinkle mixture with fish sauce and remove to a small plate.

Add 1 teaspoon oil to frying pan if needed and pour in seasoned, beaten eggs. Draw the eggs from the sides of the pan until they are set on the bottom. Spoon the crab mixture in center of omelet and fold in half. Cook for 1 minute more. Lift with a spatula to a warm serving plate.

Bean Pancakes

KOREA	Yield 20 pancakes

1 cup mung beans or dried split peas
1 cup water
2 eggs, beaten
4 ounces ground pork
1 small onion, peeled and finely chopped

1 spring onion, finely chopped
2 cloves garlic, peeled and crushed
1 teaspoon salt
¼ teaspoon ground black pepper
1 teaspoon fresh ginger, finely grated
½ cup fresh bean sprouts, chopped
½ cup kim chi or shredded white Chinese
   cabbage
2 tablespoons sesame oil

Wash beans and soak overnight in cold water. Drain well and then grind to a paste with 1 cup of water. (This is easiest done in a blender or food processor). When smooth, pour into a bowl large enough to hold all ingredients. Add remaining ingredients and mix well.

Use a griddle or heavy frying pan. Heat well and grease lightly. Drop the pancake mixture by spoonfuls onto the griddle. When bottom is lightly browned, turn and brown the other side. Remove to a waiting heated platter and continue cooking in this manner until all batter is used. These pancakes are frequently served cold as well as hot.

Crepes (China)

Bintatok

KOREA	Yield 4 servings

This pancake would be delicious for a light supper or an evening snack.

1⅓ cups mung beans
¼ cup vegetable oil
1 large onion, peeled and finely chopped
4 scallions, greens only, finely chopped
1 carrot, peeled and finely chopped
1 small red pepper, cored, seeded, and thinly
   sliced
¼ cup ground beef
Salt and fresh ground pepper to taste
Korean soy sauce

Cover beans with warm water and allow to soak overnight. Work beans with their liquid to a smooth batter using either mortar and pestle, blender, or food processor.

Use a small 6-inch omelet pan to heat ¼ of oil. Add a quarter of the batter and tilt pan to spread batter evenly. Sprinkle with ¼ of all remaining ingredients. When edges begin to curl, lift the pancake and turn once. It should cook about 3 minutes a side. Lift out and place on a warmed platter. Repeat process until all batter is used.

Lacy Pancakes

MALAYSIA	Yield about 12 pancakes

2 eggs
2¾ cups coconut milk or fresh milk

2 cups plain flour
½ teaspoon salt
2 tablespoons oil for frying

Beat eggs and milk together until well mixed and frothy. Place flour and salt into a large bowl. Make a well in the middle of the flour, adding liquid fairly rapidly. Stir with a wooden spoon; beat well until batter is smooth.

Lightly grease and heat a heavy skillet. Pour batter into pan. Use your ladle to make holes in the batter and give a lacy effect. Cook until both sides are pale and golden. Proceed in this way until all the batter is used.

If batter thickens on standing, add enough water to give needed consistency.

Coconut Pancakes

MALAYSIA	Yield 4 to 8 servings

Filling

1 cup brown palm sugar
1¼ cups water
4 cups white coconut flesh, freshly grated
Pinch of ground cinnamon
Pinch of grated nutmeg
Pinch of salt
2 teaspoons lemon juice

Crepes

1 cup flour
1 egg, beaten
1¼ cups milk
Oil for shallow frying

Melt the brown palm sugar in water. Place in a small saucepan and heat slowly until sugar has dissolved. Add remaining ingredients except lemon juice and stir. Simmer for just a few minutes, until coconut has absorbed all the water.

Sift flour into a bowl. Stir in beaten eggs and gradually add milk until batter is very smooth and even. Lightly grease a small frying pan and put on moderate heat. Pour in enough batter to coat the bottom of the pan. Tilt pan to spread batter. Cook for 1 minute on each side.

When all crepes are cooked, add lemon juice to the filling. Divide the filling between the crepes, roll up, and serve warm.

Chicken and Mushrooms in Eggs

JAPAN	Yield 4 servings

¼ pound chicken meat
¼ pound fresh mushrooms
2 onions

Sauce

½ cup chicken stock
4 tablespoons soy sauce
4 tablespoons rice wine or sherry

4 eggs
4 cups rice

Thinly slice chicken meat, mushrooms, and onions. Combine the chicken stock, soy sauce, and rice wine or sherry. Bring to boil. Add chicken, mushrooms, and onions to sauce. Cook this mixture slowly for about 15 minutes.

Place ¼ of the cooked mixture in a small frying pan. Pour a lightly beaten egg over this; cook until almost firm. Remove from pan and serve over rice. This is repeated 3 more times.

Zucchini and Mushroom Omelet

JAPAN	*Yield about 4 servings*

1 zucchini, sliced thin
12 fresh mushrooms, sliced
¼ cup chopped onions
Butter or oil
Salt
Pepper
6 eggs, beaten

Slice zucchini; set it aside. Slice mushrooms; set them aside. Chop onions; combine with zucchini. Heat butter or oil in skillet; sauté the zucchini and onions until just tender. Add the mushrooms; cook for about 30 seconds more. Add salt and pepper to season.

Add beaten eggs to mixture in skillet. Cook on medium heat until bottom is browned. Carefully turn omelet, cover, and cook until browned on other side.

Fish Omelet

JAPAN	*Yield 4 servings*

4 ounces white fish meat, finely minced
2½ tablespoons flour
½ teaspoon salt
6 eggs, beaten
3 tablespoons sugar
Oil for frying

Mix fish, flour, and salt together. Add beaten eggs; mix well. When thoroughly blended, add sugar.

Heat oil in pan; when hot, pour in egg mixture. Cover; simmer for 15 minutes or until bottom is browned. Turn; cook other side. If desired, sprinkle with finely chopped scallion.

Scrambled Eggs

JAPAN	*Yield 2 servings*

4 fresh mushrooms, sliced
2 scallions, cut into ½-inch pieces
Butter or oil
4 eggs, lightly beaten
Few sprinkles of soy sauce

Slice mushrooms and scallions; sauté in butter or oil for 2 minutes.

Beat eggs, add a few sprinkles of soy sauce, and scramble in skillet with mushrooms and scallions until sufficiently cooked. If desired, add ½ teaspoon sherry to the eggs before cooking.

Rolled Fish Omelet

JAPAN	*Yield 4 to 5 servings*

6 ounces white fish, such as sole, flounder, etc.
6 eggs, lightly beaten
3 tablespoons soy sauce
3 tablespoons sugar
3 tablespoons water
3 tablespoons mirin or sherry
Salt
Dash freshly ground pepper
Oil

Chop fish finely; mix with eggs, soy sauce, sugar, water, mirin (if sherry is substituted, add 1½ tablespoons more sugar), salt to taste, and pepper. Cook half of this mixture in pan on medium heat, turning to cook both sides. Remove from pan; roll it up like a jelly roll. Serve omelet hot.

Fried Rice (Nasi Goreng)

INDONESIA   *Yield 8 servings*

Side dishes—such as spiced pickles, fried banana slices, soy sauce, relishes, and roasted peanuts—can be served in bowls on the table for each person to dip into as he prefers.

1 2-pound chicken from a can
4 cups water
Pinch of salt
3 cups long-grain rice
6 tablespoons oil
4 medium onions, peeled and chopped
3 cloves garlic, peeled and chopped
1 red pepper pod, seeded and cut into strips
1 pound canned shrimp, drained
½ pound crab meat
½ pound cooked ham, cut into strips
2 tablespoons oil
3 eggs
1 teaspoon sambal ulek
White pepper
Curry
Ground ginger
Ground caraway
Coriander
Ground nutmeg
Saffron
Parsley for garnish

Remove chicken from can. Skin and loosen meat from bones. Cut into small pieces. Set aside. Place the juice and fat from the can in a big pot. Add water and salt. Bring to a boil. Place rice in boiling broth and reduce heat. Simmer for 12 minutes. Drain rice and set aside.

Heat 6 tablespoons oil in a large pot. Cook onions, garlic, and pepper pod for 5 minutes. Add the rice. Steam for 10 minutes and stir often. Mix shrimp, crab meat, ham, and chicken into rice. Stir to mix well.

Heat 2 tablespoons oil in a skillet. Whisk eggs until frothy and then scramble until firm. Mix your choice of spices with 1 tablespoon water in a cup. Add this to the rice along with the scrambled eggs. Allow to blend for 10 minutes. Then dish rice mixture on a platter. Garnish with parsley and serve with your choice of side dishes.

Rice Salad

INDONESIA   *Yield 4 to 6 servings*

2 cups water
1 teaspoon salt
½ cup long-grain rice
1 cup cooked chicken, cubed
1 apple, peeled, seeded, and quartered
1 orange, peeled, seeded, and quartered
1 banana, peeled and sliced
½ fennel bulb, coarsely chopped
1 red paprika pod, seeded and chopped
1 pepperoni, preserved in vinegar, seeded, and chopped
1 ginger plum from a jar, chopped
2 tablespoons oil
1 onion, peeled and chopped
2 heaping teaspoons curry powder

Marinade

Juice of 1 lemon
4 tablespoons ketchup
1 to 2 teaspoons anise spirits
4 tablespoons mayonnaise
2 tablespoons sour cream

Garnish

¼ cup almond slices
1 orange, sliced
8 maraschino cherries

Bring water to a boil. Add salt. Stir in the rice and cook for 20 minutes. Strain; rinse with cold water and drain well. Prepare fruits, fennel, paprika, pepperoni, and ginger plum as directed.

Heat oil in a skillet and fry onion for 5 minutes. Remove from heat. Stir curry powder into rice and put in serving dish. Prepare the marinade by stirring lemon juice, ketchup, anise spirits, mayonnaise, and sour cream together.

Mix chicken, fruit, vegetables, and marinade in a bowl. Allow to absorb flavors by setting aside for 1 hour. Taste and add more seasoning if needed.

Dry-roast almonds for 5 minutes in a skillet, stirring constantly.

Mix meat and vegetable mixture into rice, stirring gently. Garnish with almonds, orange slices, and cherries and serve at once. This refreshing cold salad is particularly good on a hot summer's day.

Rice in Coconut Milk

INDONESIA   *Yield 6 servings*

1 pound long-grain rice, washed and drained
4½ cups coconut milk
2½ teaspoons salt
1 onion, peeled and finely chopped
2 cloves garlic, peeled and chopped
1 teaspoon ground turmeric
1 teaspoon ground cumin
2 teaspoons ground coriander
½ teaspoon dried shrimp paste (trasi)
1 teaspoon lemon rind, finely chopped, or 1 stem of lemon grass

Place all ingredients except rice in a saucepan with a tight-fitting lid. Uncovered, bring the mixture slowly to a boil, stirring at intervals.

Add rice; stir and bring back to a boil. Cover the pan tightly, reduce heat to its lowest possible point, and steam for 20 minutes. Uncover. Use a fork to stir rice from sides of the pan, mixing in any liquid not yet absorbed. Replace lid and steam for 5 minutes more.

Fried Noodles

INDONESIA   *Yield 4 servings*

8 ounces fine egg noodles
1 large pork chop, diced
8 ounces shrimp, raw or cooked, shelled and deveined
4 tablespoons peanut oil
1 onion, peeled and finely chopped
3 cloves garlic, peeled and finely chopped
1 fresh red chili, seeded and sliced
½ teaspoon dried shrimp paste
2 stalks celery, finely sliced
Small wedge of cabbage, finely shredded
1 teaspoon salt
½ teaspoon pepper
1 to 2 tablespoons light soy sauce
4 spring onions for garnish, chopped greens and all
Thinly sliced cucumber for garnish

Put a large saucepan of water on the heat to boil. While water is coming to a boil, soak the noodles in hot water. Drain and drop into the boiling water. Cook for 1 to 3 minutes, testing so that noodles do not overcook. They should be tender but firm. Drain and run cold water over them until they are cool. Set aside. Prepare pork and shrimp and set aside.

Heat oil in a wok or large skillet. Fry onion, garlic, and chili until onion is soft and golden. Add shrimp paste, pork, and shrimp and stir-fry until all are cooked through. Add celery, cabbage, salt, and pepper and stir-fry for 1 minute more. Put in the noodles and stir until noodles are hot. Season with soy sauce.

Put in a serving dish. Garnish with spring onions on top and arrange cucumber slices around the edges.

Savory Yellow Rice

INDONESIA   *Yield 4 to 6 servings*

1 ½ cups long-grain rice
2 tablespoons vegetable oil
1 teaspoon turmeric powder
2 ½ cups chicken stock
1 teaspoon coriander powder
½ teaspoon cumin powder
1 cinnamon stick
1 whole clove
1 salam leaf or 2 bay leaves

Soak the rice for 1 hour in cold water. Then wash it under cold running water and drain thoroughly.

Heat oil in a saucepan and fry the rice for 2 minutes, stirring constantly. Add turmeric and stir for 2 minutes more. Add remaining ingredients in the order given and bring mixture to a boil. Allow to boil gently until the rice has absorbed the liquid. Stir the rice and reduce heat. Cover pan tightly and cook for 10 minutes more. Serve at once.

Apple Rice

INDONESIA   *Yield 4 to 6 servings*

1 small onion, peeled and chopped
2 apples, peeled, cored, and diced
2 tablespoons oil

3 tablespoons raisins
2 tablespoons almonds, blanched and slivered
2 tablespoons fresh mushrooms, sliced
2 tablespoons black olives, halved
1 teaspoon salt
1 tablespoon sugar, or more to taste
Curry powder to taste
½ pound cooked rice

Place onions and apples in oil and cook together for 3 minutes. Add raisins, almonds, mushrooms, and olives and stir until all are tender but not overcooked. Add salt, sugar, and curry to taste. Adjust seasonings if needed.

Last, stir in cooked rice with a fork to keep it fluffy and mix gently until blended and hot. Transfer to a serving bowl and serve at once.

Rice Banquet

INDONESIA   *Yield 10 servings*

A typical Indonesian rice banquet consists of 9 or 10 dishes attractively set up on the table. Each guest assembles the food he wants on his own plate.

Roast grated coconut

½ cup grated coconut
4 tablespoons shelled raw peanuts
1 teaspoon sugar
1 teaspoon salt

Mix ingredients together in the order given. Brown in a hot dry frypan for 5 minutes, stirring constantly. Divide into small dishes.

Roast peanuts

1 cup shelled raw peanuts
1 tablespoon oil
Salt to taste

Heat oil and fry peanuts for 10 minutes on moderate flame. Salt while cooking. When nuts are

Nasi goreng

Rice banquet

a golden brown, remove from heat and divide into serving bowls.

Shrimp bread

Oil for deep fat frying
1 package shrimp bread

Shrimp bread, made from shrimp and tapioca meal, can be bought at an Oriental grocery store. The thin pieces become double in size when cooked. So prepare just a few at a time.

Heat oil in deep-fat fryer. Cook shrimp bread one or two pieces at a time until the pieces swell. Do not let them brown. Dish up on a platter and set aside.

2 or 3 kinds of sambal

2 dishes small pickled cucumbers
2 dishes marinated beets
2 dishes pearl onions
2 dishes sweet-and-sour ginger
Hard-boiled eggs, cut into halves, 1 per person
2 dishes boiled, diced chicken

These may be made in your own home or purchased ready-made at your Oriental store.

The above are just some of the choices you can offer your banquet guests.

Curry soup

3 red and 3 green pepper pods, seeded and
  finely chopped
3 tablespoons oil
5 shallots, chopped
½ teaspoon ground coriander
1 teaspoon caraway seeds
Salt to taste
1 clove garlic, peeled and chopped
1 teaspoon ground ginger
1 teaspoon laos powder
1 2- to 3-pound chicken, boned and diced
4 tablespoons butter
3 pieces bleached celery (canned), finely
  chopped
1 bay leaf

Rice salad

6 cups hot water
Juice of 1 lemon

Heat oil in soup pot. Steam pepper pods, shallots, coriander, caraway seeds, salt, and garlic, stirring constantly. Add ginger and laos and brown for 15 minutes. Grind the above in a blender and return to pot.

In a large skillet, melt butter and brown chicken for 15 minutes, stirring occasionally. Add celery.

Place chicken and celery in soup pot and add bay leaf and seasoning mixture. Put in hot water and cook for 30 minutes. Add lemon juice and adjust salt if needed. Remove bay leaf and keep warm.

Meat dumplings

1 pound ground beef
1 teaspoon ginger powder
2 tablespoons bread crumbs
5 tablespoons cold water
1 teaspoon crushed coriander
1 teaspoon caraway seeds
Pinch of dried mint
1 onion, peeled and chopped
2 teaspoons salt
1 clove garlic, peeled and chopped
4 tablespoons oil
1 cup hot beef broth
1 teaspoon curry powder
2 teaspoons cornstarch
¼ cup cold water

In a pot, mix ground beef, ginger, bread crumbs, and cold water into a thick mass. Place on medium heat and cook, stirring constantly, for 5 minutes. Remove from heat. Add coriander, caraway, mint, onion, salt, and garlic. Knead this mixture to mix well. Add extra salt if needed.

Rinse your hands under cold water and roll meat into small dumplings. Heat fat in a skillet and fry dumplings for 10 minutes until brown. Remove from pan and keep warm.

Make a gravy by adding hot broth to skillet. Add curry powder. Mix cornstarch with ¼ cup cold water and add. Bring this to a boil and, when slightly thickened, pour over the meat dumplings.

Baked shrimp

1 pound frozen shrimp
2 egg yolks
4 tablespoons bread crumbs
5 tablespoons oil

Flatten the thawed shrimp with spatula. Dip in beaten egg yolks, then roll in bread crumbs. Heat oil in skillet and fry shrimp for 10 minutes until brown in color. Set aside and keep warm.

In addition to the dishes above, serve 1 large bowl of grainy cooked rice. Another nice accompaniment would be bananas fried in butter.

Steamed Rice

THAILAND	*Yield 6 to 8 servings*

1 pound long-grain rice
3 cups water

Wash rice thoroughly and allow to drain. Then put it in a large saucepan with the water. Bring water to a boil and lower heat. Cook uncovered. When water is absorbed and holes appear on the surface of the rice, the texture is right.

Remove from heat and place in a steamer. Steam over water, which is at a rolling boil, for 25 minutes or until the grains are firm and separate. Serve at once or use in any recipe that calls for steamed rice.

Fried Rice

THAILAND	*Yield 4 servings*

4 cups cold steamed rice
3 tablespoons peanut oil
2 medium onions, peeled and finely chopped
1 large pork chop, diced
½ pound raw shrimp, shelled and deveined

1 6-ounce can crab meat
3 eggs, beaten
Salt and pepper to taste
2 tablespoons fish sauce
1 tablespoon chili sauce, optional
2 tablespoons tomato paste
1 cup spring onions, chopped, tops included
3 tablespoons fresh coriander leaves, chopped

Spread out the cooked, steamed rice and allow it to cool. Heat oil in a wok or skillet. Using medium-low heat, fry the onions until soft and transparent. Increase heat to high. Add pork, shrimp and crab meat and fry, stirring constantly, for 3 minutes. Season eggs with salt and pepper and pour into center of pan. Stir until egg mixture begins to set. Add rice and continue to stir.

When rice is heated, sprinkle with fish sauce; add chili sauce and tomato paste and toss well so that rice is red in color. Remove from heat. Stir in spring onions, mixing well. Place on serving platter and sprinkle coriander leaves over all. Serve at once.

Rice Vermicelli with Sauce

THAILAND	*Yield 4 servings*

Vegetable oil for deep frying
6 ounces rice noodles, broken into pieces

Sauce

1 tablespoon vegetable oil
1 onion, peeled and finely chopped
2 garlic cloves, peeled and finely chopped
½ pound shrimp, shelled and deveined
½ cup crab meat
2 teaspoons brown sugar
2 tablespoons tamarind water
1 teaspoon salt

168

1 tablespoon soy sauce
2 teaspoons orange rind, grated, for garnish
2 red chilies, shredded, for garnish
2 cups fresh bean sprouts

Use a deep-fat fryer or wok to fry rice noodles, a few at a time, for about 30 seconds per batch. The noodles will swell and float. When done, remove from fat, drain on paper towels, and set aside.

Heat 1 tablespoon oil in a wok or deep skillet; add onion and garlic and stir until lightly brown. Then add shrimp and crab and cook until they turn pink. Stir in remaining ingredients except for garnishes. Add noodles and mix well. Adjust seasonings if needed. When heated through, place on a serving dish. Surround vermicelli with bean sprouts and sprinkle all with orange rind and chilies.

Oil Rice

BURMA	Yield 4 to 6 servings

2 cups glutinous rice, washed, drained, and
   allowed to dry
3 large onions, peeled and thinly sliced
1½ teaspoons turmeric
6 tablespoons oil
4 cups hot water
2 teaspoons salt
4 tablespoons toasted sesame seeds mixed with
   a little salt

Prepare rice and onions as directed. Sprinkle onions with turmeric, mixing lightly. Heat oil in saucepan and brown the onions. Remove two-thirds of the onions and set them aside for garnish.

Add rice to the pan and mix well with the remaining onions and oil. Add water and salt and stir well. Bring to a boil; lower heat and simmer, covered tightly, for about 20 minutes. Water will be absorbed. If you prefer slightly crusty rice, leave on simmer for about 5 minutes more. Garnish the cooked rice with onion and sprinkle with lightly salted sesame seeds. Serve at once.

Cellophane Noodles

BURMA	Yield 6 to 8 servings

Since cellophane noodles are fairly bland in taste, they are usually served with a spicy accompaniment, which can be anything from roasted chick peas to soup or curry.

12 ounces cellophane noodles
Boiling salted water

Cut noodles into short lengths, 1 to 2 inches long. Bring salted water to boil in a large saucepan. Put in noodles and cook for 20 minutes, uncovered. Drain and serve in a large bowl. Allow diners to dish separate bowls of the noodles topped with the accompaniment of their choice.

Rice Mixed with Fingers

BURMA	Yield 6 servings

1 cup long-grain rice, cooked dry and fluffy
2 fresh red chilies or 1 teaspoon chili powder
2 tablespoons oil
2 tablespoons water
4 ounces rice vermicelli
2 ounces cellophane noodles
4 ounces fine egg noodles
3 large potatoes
8 ounces bean sprouts

Accompaniments

3 eggs
10 medium onions, peeled
20 cloves garlic, peeled
1 cup oil
1 cup powdered dried shrimp
1 cup roasted chick-pea powder

2 tablespoons chili powder
½ cup fish sauce
½ cup dried tamarind pulp

Make a paste of the chilies and cook with oil and water over low heat until it smells cooked. Mix with the cooked rice and set aside.

Boil rice vermicelli for 2 minutes or until tender. Drain and set aside. Boil cellophane noodles; drain and set aside. Boil egg noodles until tender; drain and rinse with cold water. Boil potatoes, then peel and slice. Pour boiling water over bean sprouts and let stand for 10 minutes. Drain. Since all of these are served cold, arrange them on a platter in separate mounds. The accompaniments will be served in separate bowls.

To prepare the accompaniments, first fry the eggs as for an omelette. When firm and cooked, cut into shreds and set aside. Thinly slice half of the onions and put them into an individual bowl. Slice the remaining onions and half of the garlic. Fry them in oil until both are light brown. Put in a serving bowl, oil included. Peel remaining garlic and put the raw garlic into a small bowl. Place shrimp, chick-pea powder, and chili powder in individual bowls. Make tamarind liquid by soaking pulp in 1½ cups hot water. When cool, squeeze to dissolve the pulp and strain, keeping the water and discarding seeds and fibers.

Coconut Rice

BURMA *Yield 4 to 6 servings*

2¼ cups long-grain rice, washed and drained
4½ cups water
6 tablespoons thick coconut milk
1 medium onion, peeled and quartered
½ teaspoon salt
1 teaspoon vegetable oil

Place rice and water in a large saucepan. Add the rest of the ingredients in the order given. Bring this to a boil over high heat. Reduce heat, cover pan tightly, and simmer for about 20 minutes.

Remove the lid and stir lightly with a fork. Rice is finished cooking when liquid is absorbed and grains are fluffy.

Rice Platter

INDIA *Yield 8 servings*

2 cups long-grain rice
2 teaspoons salt
2 quarts water
4 tablespoons butter or margarine
½ cup sultana raisins

Curry sauce

6 tablespoons butter or margarine
½ cup flour
2 cups hot beef broth
Salt and white pepper to taste
2 heaping tablespoons curry
Pinch of sugar
½ cup white wine
2 tablespoons cream

For the entrées

1 pound pork fillets
Salt and pepper to taste
4 tablespoons oil
½ pound fillet of sole
Juice of 1 lemon
½ pound shrimp, canned or frozen
6 tablespoons butter
1 small can pineapple slices, cut into bite-size
    pieces
1 small jar red marinated paprika pods
½ cup black olives, seeded and sliced
½ pound fresh mushrooms, washed and
    quartered
2 teaspoons lemon juice
6 bananas, halved lengthwise and sliced

Rice platter

½ **cup sliced almonds, toasted in 2 tablespoons butter**

Place rice in boiling salted water and allow to boil for 10 minutes. Drain and rinse with cold water. Drain again. Use half the butter to grease baking dish and spread rice out evenly. Dot with remaining butter and bake at 350°F for 15 minutes.

Meanwhile, soak raisins in water and prepare curry sauce.

Heat butter or margarine in saucepan. Stir in the flour and hot beef broth until very smooth. Season lightly with salt and pepper. Add curry, sugar, and wine. Bring to a boil and remove from heat. Stir in the cream. Keep sauce warm.

Cut pork fillets into even strips. Season with salt and pepper. Heat 2 tablespoons oil in a frying pan. Add pork and stir constantly for 5 minutes. When meat is browned all over, set aside and keep warm.

Wash and dry the fish with paper towels. Sprinkle with lemon juice. In a different skillet, heat 2 tablespoons oil. Fry the fish for 5 minutes on each side. Add the shrimp and cook until it is hot through.

Heat 3 tablespoons of butter in a saucepan. Add raisins, pineapple, paprika pods, and olives. Stir until all are hot. Set aside and keep warm.

Heat remaining 3 tablespoons butter and fry mushrooms for 10 minutes. Season with lemon juice. Keep warm.

171

Apple rice

Finally, heat remaining 2 tablespoons butter in a skillet and fry the bananas to a golden brown, about 10 minutes. Keep turning bananas as they cook.

To serve, spread rice on a large platter. Alternately add meat, sole-shrimp mixture, raisins, pineapple, paprika and olives, mushrooms and bananas. Garnish with almonds. Offer the curry sauce separately.

Rice with Vegetables

INDIA	*Yield 4 to 6 servings*

2 tablespoons ghee
2 tablespoons oil
2 medium onions, peeled and finely sliced
1 clove garlic, peeled and finely chopped
2 cups long-grain rice
4 cups hot water

172

Soft-fried noodles with mushrooms
Deep-fried crispy noodles

2 teaspoons salt
1 teaspoon garam masala
2 carrots, cut into matchstick pieces
12 green beans, thinly sliced
½ cup diced red or green chili
1 small potato, peeled and cubed
½ cup fresh or frozen peas
1 teaspoon salt

Heat ghee and oil in a heavy saucepan with a tight-fitting lid. Cook onions slowly for about 10 minutes. Add garlic and cook for 2 minutes more. Add rice and increase heat to medium. Stir-fry for 2 minutes. Add hot water, salt, and garam masala. Bring to a boil and then reduce heat to lowest possible simmer. Cover and cook for 10 minutes.

Place vegetables on top of rice; do not stir. Sprinkle with a teaspoon of salt. Replace lid and cook for 12 minutes more. Uncover pan and allow steam to escape. Then use a fork to fluff up the rice and stir vegetables through. Transfer to a serving platter, using a slotted spoon to dish the rice.

Fried rice with mushrooms

Rice with Fresh Green Peas

INDIA   *Yield 4 to 6 servings*

1 tablespoon ghee or oil
4 whole cloves
1 small cinnamon stick
2 cardamom pods
1 teaspoon cumin seeds
½ teaspoon ground turmeric, optional
1¼ cups long-grain rice, washed and drained
1¼ cups shelled green peas
2 teaspoons salt
2½ cups hot water

Using a heavy saucepan, heat the ghee. Fry cloves, cinnamon, cardamom, and cumin on medium heat for 1 minute, stirring well. Add turmeric and rice and stir-fry for 2 more minutes. Put in peas, salt, and water and bring to a boil. Reduce heat to a simmer, cover the pan, and cook for 25 minutes. Do not lift the lid or stir during cooking time. Remove spices and use a fork to fluff the rice with the peas. Serve at once.

Rice and Lentils

INDIA   *Yield 4 to 6 servings*

1 cup long-grain rice
1 cup red lentils
2½ tablespoons ghee
2 medium onions, peeled and finely sliced
5 cups hot water
2½ teaspoons salt
1½ teaspoons garam masala

Wash rice and drain well. Wash lentils and drain well also. Heat ghee in a large saucepan and fry the onions until they are golden brown. Remove half the onions and set aside for garnish.

Put rice and lentils in pan with the remaining onions, stirring well to mix. Stir for about 3 minutes. Add hot water, salt, and garam masala. Bring this to a boil and cover the pan tightly. Reduce heat and simmer for 25 minutes. Do not lift the lid until cooking time is over. Rice and lentils will be the consistency of porridge. Garnish with reserved onions and serve hot.

Saffron Rice

INDIA   *Yield 4 servings*

¾ cup ghee
2 large onions, peeled and sliced
1½ cups rice, washed thoroughly and drained
1 teaspoon whole cloves
4 whole cardamoms
1 teaspoon salt
1 teaspoon freshly ground black pepper
½ teaspoon saffron threads, soaked in 1
   tablespoon boiling water for 30 minutes
3 cups water
Varak to garnish

Melt ghee in a large saucepan. Fry onions gently until soft. Add drained rice to the pan with spices and seasonings and stir-fry for 3 minutes.

Add saffron and the liquid it has soaked in, and mix well. Put in water and allow to come to a boil. Reduce and simmer for 15 to 20 minutes. Drain rice well. Transfer to a serving bowl and garnish with varak. Serve very hot.

Spiced Rice

INDIA   *Yield 4 to 6 servings*

2½ cups long-grain rice, washed, and drained
   dry
½ teaspoon saffron strands, soaked in 2

tablespoons boiling water for 10 minutes
2 tablespoons ghee
4 cardamom pods, bruised
1 small cinnamon stick
4 whole cloves
10 black peppercorns
4 cups hot water
2½ teaspoons salt
Rind of 1 orange, finely grated
2 tablespoons raisins
2 tablespoons sliced almonds
2 tablespoons pistachios, halved

After rice and saffron are prepared, heat oil in a heavy saucepan. Gently stir-fry cardamom, cinnamon, cloves, and peppercorns for 2 minutes. Add the rice and continue to stir for 3 minutes more. Put in hot water, salt, saffron and the liquid it has been soaking in, and orange rind. Bring quickly to a boil; then reduce heat, cover, and cook for 20 minutes. Lift lid long enough to scatter raisins on top of rice. Replace lid and simmer for 5 minutes more. Then garnish with almonds and pistachios and serve at once.

Fried Noodles with Mixed Meats

PHILIPPINES　　　*Yield 6 to 8 servings*

This is a meal in itself, with noodles as the very filling base.

1 pound raw shrimp
1½ cups lightly salted water
1 pound thin egg noodles
3 to 4 tablespoons lard or oil
5 cloves garlic, peeled and crushed
2 onions, peeled and finely sliced
1 cup cooked chicken, diced
1 cup cooked pork, cut in thin strips
½ cup ham, cut in thin strips
1 cup cabbage, shredded
3 tablespoons light soy sauce
Salt and pepper to taste
Lemon wedges for garnish

Cook shrimp in water until it just turns pink. Allow to cool; then shell, devein, and cut into pieces. Reserve 1 cup of stock.

Soak noodles in warm water. While they are soaking, bring a large pan of water to a boil. Drain noodles and put in boiling water. Cook for 2 minutes only. Drain and spread on a large pan lined with paper towels. Sprinkle with oil and allow to dry for at least 30 minutes.

Put 1 tablespoon lard into a large wok or skillet. Fry the noodles, a few at a time, until golden on both sides. Add more lard if needed and continue until all noodles are fried. Set aside.

Add more lard or oil to the pan. Separately, fry garlic, onion, shrimp, chicken, pork, and ham. Use ¼ of each of these for garnish. Return remainder to pan along with cabbage, soy sauce, shrimp stock, salt, and pepper. Cook uncovered until most of the juices have disappeared. Return the noodles to pan and mix well. When good and hot, arrange on a serving platter surrounded with reserved ingredients and wedges of lemon.

Noodles with Meat and Vegetables

PHILIPPINES　　　*Yield 4 to 6 servings*

½ pound wide egg noodles
¼ cup vegetable oil
1 clove garlic, peeled and ground
1 cup lean pork, thinly sliced
1 cup chicken breast meat, thinly sliced
1 cup fresh shrimp, shelled, deveined, and diced
1 medium onion, peeled and thinly sliced

1 cup shredded cabbage
2 tablespoons fish sauce
¾ cup chicken stock
Pinch of paprika pepper
½ teaspoon salt
Freshly ground black pepper, to taste

Garnish

2 hard-cooked eggs, shelled and quartered
2 scallions, chopped
Lemon wedges, optional

Boil noodles for just 2 minutes. Drain; rinse with cold water and drain again. Put noodles in a bowl with 1 tablespoon oil and mix well. Set aside.

Using moderate heat, place 1 tablespoon oil in a wok or heavy skillet. Add noodles, stirring to brown on all sides. Set aside and wipe pan clean with paper towels.

Fry garlic in 1 tablespoon oil until brown. Add pork and fry for 5 minutes. Add chicken and shrimp and stir-fry on high heat for 2 minutes. Remove from pan and set aside.

Wipe pan clean again with paper towels. Return pan to heat for 1 minute. Put in remaining oil, onion, and cabbage. Stir-fry for 4 minutes. Onion should be transparent and cabbage crunchy.

Add the remaining ingredients and the cooked meat and fish mixture to the pan. Stir constantly for 2 minutes. The juices will evaporate while you stir. Return noodles to pan, stirring and tossing gently until all is hot. Transfer to serving dish and garnish with eggs, spring onions, and lemon wedges. Serve at once.

Soft-fried Noodles with Mushrooms

CHINA *Yield 8 servings*

1 5-ounce package fine egg noodles
2 tablespoons safflower oil
1 cup bamboo shoots

1 cup fresh mushrooms, sliced
1 cup sliced almonds
½ cup chicken broth
3 tablespoons soy sauce
Salt to taste

Cook noodles in a large pot in boiling, lightly salted water for 8 minutes; drain well.

Heat oil in a wok or skillet over low heat. Add noodles; stir-fry 4 minutes. Stir in bamboo shoots, mushrooms, and almonds; mix thoroughly. Stir in broth, soy sauce, and salt. Reduce heat to low; simmer, covered, 20 minutes or until liquid is almost absorbed.

Deep-fried Crispy Noodles

CHINA *Yield 4 to 5 cups*

1 5-ounce package fine egg noodles
Vegetable oil

Place noodles in a large saucepan in enough water to cover; bring to boil. Cook, stirring occasionally, 5 minutes; drain well.

Fill deep-fat fryer half full with oil; heat to 350°F. Drop noodles into basket in oil; cook 2 minutes. Remove from oil; drain well on paper toweling. Heat oil to 375°F. Return noodles to fryer; cook until golden brown and crisp. Drain well on paper toweling; separate noodles if necessary.

"Sizzling" Rice

CHINA *Yield 5 to 6 servings*

To get the "sizzling" effect, food, rice, and containers must be hot.

1 cup long-grain rice
4 cups water
2 teaspoons salt
Oil for deep frying

At least a day in advance, combine rice, water, and salt in a 2-quart saucepan. Let stand 30 minutes. Bring to boil; cover. Simmer 30 minutes; drain. Spread evenly on heavily greased cookie sheet. Bake in 250°F oven 8 hours, turning occasionally with spatula. Break crusty rice into bite-size pieces. Can be stored in airtight containers in refrigerator several weeks.

Just before serving time, heat oven to 250°F; warm serving platter. Pour oil about 2 inches deep in a 6-quart saucepan (or deep-fryer). Heat to 425°F. Fry rice, stirring with slotted spoon, until golden brown, approximately 5 minutes. Drain quickly; place in warmed serving platter.

Fried Rice with Mushrooms

CHINA   *Yield 10 servings*

½ cup dried mushrooms, sliced
¼ cup olive oil
¼ cup green onions, sliced
2 cups long-grain rice
4 cups chicken stock
⅛ teaspoon dry mustard
1 tablespoon soy sauce
½ cup white bean curd, cut into cubes
¼ cup safflower oil
¾ cup cooked fresh green peas
Radish flowers for garnish

Soak mushrooms in cold water 5 minutes; drain well.

Heat olive oil in a wok or deep skillet over medium heat. Add onions; stir-fry until onions are limp and transparent. Add rice; stir-fry until rice is

golden. Add 1 cup stock and mustard; stir-fry 2 to 3 minutes or until liquid is absorbed. Add 1 cup stock and soy sauce; stir-fry until liquid is absorbed.

Add 1 more cup of stock; reduce heat to low. Stir in bean curd; cook, stirring occasionally, until liquid is absorbed. Add remaining stock, safflower oil, peas, and mushrooms. Cover; cook, stirring occasionally, about 20 to 25 minutes or until rice is tender. Spoon into serving dish; garnish with radish flowers.

Fried Rice I

CHINA   *Yield 4 to 6 servings*

Chinese roast pork, available from Chinese food stores, is ideal for this dish.

1 cup long-grain rice
Boiling salted water
2 strips bacon, diced
½ pound cooked pork, thinly sliced
2 eggs
2 tablespoons water
½ teaspoon salt
Generous dash of pepper
6 tablespoons oil
6 shallots, finely chopped
1 teaspoon ginger, grated
½ pound shrimp
1 teaspoon soy sauce

Cook rice in boiling salted water for 12 minutes. Drain well. Spread on tray; allow to dry out overnight.

Finely dice bacon; slice pork thin. Beat eggs with water. Season with salt and pepper.

Heat 1 tablespoon oil in pan. Pour in enough egg mixture to make 1 pancake. Turn and cook other side; remove from pan. Repeat this with remaining mixture, using 1 tablespoon oil for each pancake. Roll egg pancake; slice into thin strips.

Finely chop shallots. Shell and devein shrimp. Fry diced bacon until crisp. Add remaining 2 tablespoons oil to pan. When oil is hot, add rice, pork, ginger, shallots, and shrimp. Add egg strips last. Stir lightly. When completely heated through, add soy sauce; mix well.

Fried Rice II

CHINA *Yield 4 servings*

½ pound long-grain rice
½ pound cooked ham, cut into strips
1 6-ounce can shrimp, drained
3 tablespoons oil
2 tablespoons soy sauce
1 leek, sliced
4 eggs
Freshly ground black pepper

Cook rice according to package directions. Cut ham into strips. Drain shrimp.

Heat oil in a large skillet. Add ham and shrimp; cook until lightly browned, approximately 5 minutes. Add rice and soy sauce; cook for another 5 minutes. Add leek; cook for 5 minutes more, stirring occasionally.

Lightly beat eggs with pepper. Pour over rice; cook until eggs are set. Serve on a preheated platter.

Rice Salad

CHINA *Yield 6 to 8 servings*

3 tablespoons oil
2 cups long-grain rice
3¾ cups chicken stock
1 teaspoon salt
1 pound shrimp, shelled, deveined, and cooked

6 shallots or spring onions, chopped
½ green cucumber, chopped
1 small green pepper, diced
1 small red pepper, diced
2 sticks celery, sliced
⅓ cup French dressing
1 teaspoon soy sauce

Heat oil in a large saucepan. Add rice; stir until golden brown. Add soup stock and salt. Cover; simmer gently 12 minutes or until rice has absorbed all liquid. Turn out onto a large tray; allow to cool. When rice has cooled completely, add shrimp, shallots, cucumber, peppers, and celery. Mix gently.

Combine French dressing and soy sauce; pour over salad. Toss gently to mix.

Pot Roasted Rice

INDOCHINA *Yield 4 to 6 servings*

2 cups medium-grain rice
2 tablespoons peanut oil
1¾ cups hot water

Wash rice well and drain thoroughly until quite dry. Heat oil in a heavy saucepan. Put in rice and stir with a metal spoon until rice is golden, about 10 or more minutes. Add hot water and bring to a boil. Place a tight-fitting lid on the pot; reduce heat and simmer for 20 minutes. This basic rice recipe goes with many of the main dishes from Indochina.

Molded Rice

INDOCHINA *Yield 4 servings*

½ cup pork fat, chopped
½ cup lean pork, chopped
½ cup chicken meat, chopped

3 cloves garlic, peeled and finely chopped
3 spring onions, finely sliced
4 cups hot cooked rice
Fish sauce to taste
Hearty dash of freshly ground black pepper

Heat a wok or large skillet and cook pork fat until it is crisp and fat melted. Add pork, chicken, garlic, and onions and stir-fry until everything is well cooked. Add cooked rice and season with fish sauce and pepper. Toss with a large fork to mix well.

Press rice mixture into a greased mold. Cover with foil and keep warm until ready to serve. Turn out onto a platter and serve with extra fish sauce if desired.

Long Rice with Chicken and Bamboo Shoots

INDOCHINA   *Yield 6 servings*

1 pound chicken pieces
1 clove garlic, peeled and crushed
8 ounces cellophane noodles, soaked in hot
　　water 15 minutes
1 tablespoon peanut oil
1 medium onion, peeled and cut into wedges
2 cans bamboo shoots, cut into strips
1 tablespoon fish sauce
¼ teaspoon black pepper
½ cup chicken stock

Cut chicken meat from bones and use bones to make stock. Meat should be prepared in bite-size pieces, as should the skin. Mix with crushed garlic.

Place presoaked noodles in lightly salted boiling water and cook for 5 minutes. Drain and cut into 2-inch lengths.

Fried rice I

Fried rice II

179

Rice salad (China)

Use a wok or skillet to heat the peanut oil. Stir-fry chicken in the oil until meat is white. Push cooked chicken to side of pan. Add onion and bamboo shoots and fry for 1 minute, then mix with chicken. Add fish sauce, pepper, and stock and cook for 2 more minutes. Last, add the well-drained noodles and stir until very hot. Serve from heated platter.

Rice and Bean Sprouts

KOREA *Yield 4 to 6 servings*

1 cup canned bean sprouts, drained
1 clove garlic, peeled and minced
2 green onions, chopped
2 teaspoons sesame seeds
1 teaspoon sesame oil

2 cups rice
3 tablespoons soy sauce
3 cups cold water

Mix bean sprouts, garlic, onions, sesame seeds, and oil together in a large saucepan. Stir constantly over medium heat for 5 minutes. Add rice, soy sauce, and water. Cover the saucepan tightly and bring to a boil. Reduce heat to a simmer and allow to steam for 30 minutes. Do not remove lid or stir rice during this cooking period.

Remove from heat, stir with a fork, and put in a serving dish; serve at once and very hot.

Rice and Dates

KOREA *Yield 4 to 6 servings*

The addition of dates to the rice makes this a delightful taste contrast to other Korean foods. The sweetness of the rice will complement other more spicy dishes.

½ cup dates, pitted
2 cups rice, washed and drained well
3 cups water

Cut dates into small pieces. Place in a large saucepan with the rice and water. Bring to a quick boil. Then cover the pan with a tight-fitting lid and reduce heat to a simmer. Allow to steam for 35 minutes. Do not lift lid or stir rice until 35 minutes are up.

Rice with Mushrooms

KOREA *Yield 6 servings*

½ pound fresh mushrooms, washed and sliced
1 tablespoon vegetable oil
1 tablespoon sesame oil
2 medium onions, peeled and finely sliced

½ cup lean steak, finely shredded
1 pound short-grain rice
3 cups hot water
1 teaspoon salt
¼ teaspoon ground black pepper
2 tablespoons toasted, ground sesame seeds

Prepare mushrooms and dry on paper towels. Heat both oils in a large saucepan. Fry onions, steak, and mushrooms for 2 minutes, stirring constantly. Add rice and stir-fry for another minute. Put in remaining ingredients and bring to a boil.

Cover the saucepan and reduce heat to a simmer. Allow to steam for 20 minutes. Do not lift lid or stir during this time. Fluff with a fork when cooking time is over and transfer to a serving dish.

Rice with Potatoes

KOREA   *Yield 4 to 6 servings*

1 cup potatoes, peeled and cubed
2 cups rice, washed well and drained
1 teaspoon salt
3 cups cold water

Place all ingredients in a large saucepan in the order given. Cover the pan with a tight-fitting lid and allow to come to a boil. Then reduce heat to a simmer and cook for 30 minutes. Do not lift lid or stir rice until steaming time is complete.

Crab and Pork Fried Rice

KOREA   *Yield 4 servings*

While fried rice is often served with a main dish, this combination is good enough to be a meal by itself.

2 tablespoons oil
1 clove garlic, peeled and grated
1 teaspoon fresh ginger, finely grated
½ cup cooked crab meat, flaked
½ cup cooked pork, chopped
4 cups hot cooked rice
½ cup spring onions, chopped
1 teaspoon salt to taste

Using a wok or heavy skillet, heat the oil. Add garlic, ginger, crab, and pork and stir-fry until hot and well mixed. Add rice and continue to stir until rice is crisp and brown. Last, put in spring onions and sprinkle with salt. Mix well and add more salt if desired. Transfer to warmed serving dish and serve at once.

Compressed Rice Cakes

MALAYSIA   *Yield 6 servings*

Here is a simple Western way of preparing Malaysian rice cakes.

1 pound short- or medium-grain rice
4 cups water
Aluminum foil

Allow water and rice to come to a boil in a large saucepan. Cover the pan and reduce heat to a simmer. Cook for 35 minutes or until all the water is absorbed. Stir with a wooden spoon. Press rice into a pie plate until it is in an even layer about 1-inch high.

Cover pie plate with greased aluminum foil, which should be resting on the rice. Weight this down with a plate and press firmly. Add more weight on top of the plate and let stand at room temperature several hours. When very firm, remove weights and foil. Cut with a wet knife into 2-inch squares.

White Rice in Coconut Milk

MALAYSIA	*Yield 4 to 6 servings*

1½ cups long-grain rice, washed and drained
2½ cups coconut milk
½ teaspoon salt

Place rice and coconut milk in a heavy saucepan. Add salt and bring to a boil. Then lower heat and simmer uncovered until liquid has been absorbed. Stir once or twice to prevent rice from sticking to bottom of pan. Cover saucepan with tight-fitting lid and reduce heat to simmer. Cook for 10 minutes more. Serve at once.

Fried Rice Noodles

MALAYSIA	*Yield 6 to 8 servings*

2 pounds fresh rice noodles
¼ pound barbecued pork
½ pound small raw shrimp
2 Chinese sausages
1 cup fresh bean sprouts
4 tablespoons lard or oil
4 small onions, peeled and sliced
2 cloves garlic, peeled and finely chopped
4 fresh red chilies, seeded and chopped
2 tablespoons dark soy sauce
2 tablespoons light soy sauce
1 tablespoon oyster sauce
Pepper and salt to taste
3 eggs, beaten
4 spring onions, chopped

Cut rice noodles into ¼- to ½-inch widths. Thinly slice the pork. Shell and devein shrimp. Steam the sausages and cut into thin, diagonal slices. Pinch tails off bean sprouts.

Using a wok or skillet, heat half of the oil; fry onions, garlic, and chilies over medium heat until they are soft. Add pork, shrimp, and sausage and stir-fry until seafood is cooked, just a few minutes. Add bean sprouts and mix well. Remove from wok.

Put in remaining oil. When very hot, stir-fry the rice noodles until they are heated through. Add seasonings and mix well. Pour in beaten egg, stirring constantly until egg is set and firm. Return the fried mixture to the wok and toss well until it is hot. Garnish with spring onions and serve at once.

Glutinous Yellow Rice

MALAYSIA	*Yield 6 servings*

1 pound glutinous rice, washed and drained
2 cups water
2 teaspoons salt
1 clove garlic, peeled and crushed
1 teaspoon ground turmeric
½ teaspoon ground black pepper
1 pandanus leaf
2 cups hot coconut milk
Crisp fried onion flakes for garnish

Place rice, water, salt, garlic, turmeric, pepper, and pandanus leaf in a large saucepan. Allow mixture to come to a boil; reduce heat and cover. Simmer for 10 minutes. Do not lift lid during this time.

Uncover and stir in hot coconut milk with a fork. When rice is mixed with coconut milk, cover and simmer for 10 more minutes. Transfer to a serving bowl and garnish with onion flakes.

Fried Rice with Catsup

JAPAN	*Yield 3 to 4 servings*

2 cups cooked leftover rice
½ tablespoon oil
Leftover meat or seafood, cut into small pieces

182

1½ tablespoons catsup (more or less, to taste)
2 tablespoons frozen or fresh peas

Heat rice in oil for 5 minutes, stirring occasionally. Add rest of ingredients; mix thoroughly, while heating, for another 3 minutes.

Chilled Noodles

JAPAN *Yield 4 servings*

This unusual way of serving noodles is particularly good during the hot summer months, served with bowls of your favorite sauce as a dip.

1 pound wheat vermicelli
6 or more cups boiling water

Sauce

2 cups chicken broth
½ cup light soy sauce
¼ cup sake
1 tablespoon sugar

Garnish

A few ice cubes
Cherry tomatoes, quartered
Scallions, finely shredded

Cook wheat vermicelli in boiling water for 5 minutes until just tender. Drain and rinse under cold running water. Drain again. Then place in a large shallow serving dish, preferably glass, and chill in the refrigerator for at least 1 hour.

Put all sauce ingredients in a pan and bring to a boil, stirring constantly. Reduce heat and simmer for 2 minutes; allow to cool. Divide into individual bowls and chill in the refrigerator for at least 1 hour.

When ready to serve, garnish vermicelli with ice cubes, tomatoes, and scallions. Serve bowls of sauce separately.

Chicken Rice

JAPAN *Yield 4 servings*

6 ounces chicken meat
3½ tablespoons soy sauce
2 tablespoons mirin (sweet rice wine)
4 cups chicken stock
4 cups rice

Thinly slice the chicken; marinate it for 30 minutes in a sauce made from the soy sauce and mirin. If substituting sherry for the mirin, add 1 tablespoon sugar to the sauce.

Remove the chicken; mix the sauce with the chicken stock. Use this mixture, instead of water, to boil the rice in, adding a little water if necessary to thin the mixture.

Serve the rice in 4 individual bowls, with the chicken slices on top.

Rice Balls

JAPAN *Yield 4 large rice balls*

2 cups hot cooked rice
Goma sio (black sesame seeds and salt)
Raw or smoked fish, optional, cut into thin strips

Cook rice and allow it to become cool enough to handle. Wet your hands and form a ball with ½ cup of the rice. When firm and about 3 inches in diameter, insert 1 strip of fish into the center of the rice ball, molding the rice around it. Roll the finished rice ball in goma sio. In Japan, rice balls frequently take the place of bread and are a good picnic item.

Shrimp Crisps

INDONESIA	*Yield as many as you fry*

Krupuk or shrimp crackers are pink and measure about 4 inches in length. They are obtainable in Oriental stores.

Shrimp crackers
1¼ cups vegetable oil

Heat oil in a wok or deep frying pan. Separate crackers and drop one at a time into the hot oil. They will swell up several times their original size. Flatten immediately with a spatula. Fry each cracker for a few seconds only and remove from the pan. Drain on paper towels. Allow to cool before serving.

Peanut Brittle

INDONESIA	*Yield about 50 pieces*

These unusual snacks are made with very fine rice powder. They will keep in an airtight container for two weeks.

2 kemiri, chopped
1 clove garlic, peeled and chopped
2 teaspoons coriander powder
1 teaspoon salt
1 cup rice powder
1 cup water
1 cup whole, shelled peanuts, halved if large
1¼ cups vegetable oil

Pound the kemiri and garlic to a very smooth paste. Add coriander and salt and stir well to mix. Add rice powder and water and stir until batter is smooth and liquid. Last, add the peanuts.

Heat 5 tablespoons of oil in a heavy skillet. Drop batter by spoonfuls into the oil. Fry for 1 minute. Remove from pan with a slotted spoon and drain on paper towels. Continue in this way, adding oil as needed, until all the batter is used. Stir batter from time to time, adding a little water if it gets too thick.

Pour remaining oil into the skillet for deep frying. Fry the peanut brittle again for 1 minute until golden brown, turning during the frying time. Drain again on paper towels and allow to completely cool before storing.

Banana Cake with Cashews

INDONESIA	*Yield 8 or more servings*

3 eggs
1 cup sugar
¾ cup cream
1½ cups flour
4 pounds of ripe bananas
1 cup fresh cashews, coarsely chopped
1 cup fresh coconut, grated

Use an electric mixer on low to beat eggs and sugar together. When thick and pale, add cream and mix for 1 minute more. Add sifted flour to the bowl and blend in with a wooden spoon. Peel and very coarsely mash bananas and add them and the nuts and coconut to the batter. Do not overstir. Mix only until all the ingredients are combined.

Grease two 8-inch pans and dust lightly with flour. Pour mixture into pans and bake in a preheated oven at 350°F for 1 hour. When cake is done, it will be golden brown and springy on top. Serve warm or cold.

Steamed Banana Pudding

INDONESIA	*Yield 4 servings*

3 eggs, well beaten
1 cup sugar
1 cup coconut milk
1 teaspoon vanilla
3 bananas, sliced

Add sugar, coconut milk, and vanilla to beaten eggs and mix well. Stir in the bananas. Put this mixture in a heavy saucepan with a lid. Steam on low heat for about 30 minutes or until the sauce has thickened. Dish into individual serving bowls and serve hot.

Banana Fritters

INDONESIA	*Yield 4 to 6 servings*

This can be served as an accompaniment to a meal, but it is a delicious dessert as well.

4 ripe bananas, mashed
¾ cup flour
½ teaspoon salt
3 tablespoons sugar
Oil for deep frying
Cinnamon sugar (1 teaspoon cinnamon to ⅓ cup sugar)

Make a batter of the mashed bananas, flour, salt, and sugar. Mix well until the batter is fairly smooth. Heat oil in a deep frying pan. Drop 1 tablespoon of the batter into the fat for each fritter. Cook a few at a time, being sure not to crowd the frying pan, until golden brown on both sides. Drain on paper towels. Sprinkle with cinnamon sugar and serve at once.

Fruit Salad

INDONESIA	*Yield 4 to 6 servings*

This can be served with the main course or as a dessert.

2 cups honey
2 tablespoons peanut butter
1 teaspoon vinegar
1 teaspoon salt
1 teaspoon red pepper
4 cups shredded carrots, apples, pears, and cucumbers

Combine honey, peanut butter, vinegar, salt, and pepper and stir until well mixed. Last, put in the shredded vegetables and fruit. Mix again so that the flavors blend; refrigerate for at least 1 hour. Serve chilled.

Sweet Potato Balls

INDONESIA	*Yield 4 to 6 servings*

2 cups mashed, cooked sweet potatoes
1 tablespoon flour
1½ tablespoons sugar
1 egg
Oil for deep frying
Confectioners' sugar

Mix potatoes, flour, sugar, and egg in a bowl. The mixture should be stiff. If it is not stiff enough, add extra flour by teaspoons. Roll the mixture into 1-inch balls. Heat oil in a deep frying pan and fry the sweet potato balls until golden brown. Remove from pan and drain on paper towels.

These may be served hot or cold and should be sprinkled lightly with confectioners' sugar.

Fried Pineapple

INDONESIA	*Yield 4 servings*

2 tablespoons flour
1 egg
Dash of salt
6 to 8 slices of pineapple, ½ inch thick, drained
Oil for deep frying
Cinnamon sugar (1 teaspoon cinnamon to ⅓
    cup sugar)

Use a whisk to mix the flour, egg, and salt in a bowl. Dip each pineapple slice in this mixture. Heat oil in a heavy skillet or deep-fryer and fry the pineapple until golden brown. Drain on paper towels. Sprinkle with cinnamon sugar and serve.

Golden Bean Cakes

THAILAND

8 ounces mung beans
1 cup white sugar
½ cup water
Confectioners' sugar

Sugar syrup

⅓ cup sugar
1 tablespoon water

Soak beans for 24 hours in cold water. Wash the soaked beans several times until all the green skins float away. Put them into a saucepan with water and cook until soft. Drain and mash cooked beans into a smooth paste.

Heat white sugar and water over medium heat until sugar is dissolved. Add bean paste. Stir occasionally in the beginning; when the paste begins to thicken, you must stir constantly. When the mixture pulls away from the side of the pan, it is ready. Allow it to cool. When cool, roll the mixture into small balls. Make a syrup of the sugar and water.

Dip cooled balls in sugar syrup and roll in confectioners' sugar. Allow them to dry fully before putting them in small paper cases or a cookie tin.

The amount this recipe makes depends on the size of the balls.

Sweet Coconut Rice

THAILAND	*Yield 6 to 8 servings*

1 pound glutinous rice
Water
2½ cups coconut milk
⅔ cup sugar

Soak rice overnight in enough water to more than cover it. When ready to begin cooking, drain and steam the rice for 45 minutes until very tender. Place rice in a saucepan. Add coconut milk and sugar and simmer until all liquid is absorbed.

Turn the rice mixture out onto a plate and press down with the back of a spoon or a spatula. Allow to cool. Cut into squares or diamond shapes. Serve as a dessert or as an accompaniment to fruit.

Steamed Custard in Pumpkin Shell

THAILAND	*Yield 4 to 6 servings*

To enrich this dish, use milk instead of water when making the coconut milk.

¾ cup thick coconut milk
½ cup palm sugar or substitute
3 eggs
Few drops rose water
1 medium-size pumpkin

Beat eggs slightly; mix them with the sugar and coconut milk. Stir until sugar is completely dissolved; then add rose water.

Cut a hole in the top of the pumpkin. Remove seeds and pulpy tissue, leaving the shell about 1 inch in thickness.

Pour custard almost to the top of the pumpkin. Place pumpkin in a dish that fits into a steamer. Steam the custard for 1 hour or until a knife inserted in the center comes out clean. Cool and chill. Slice into individual portions and remove the pumpkin skin from each piece. Serve chilled.

Sweet Rice with Black Beans

THAILAND	Yield 4 servings

1 ¼ cups thick coconut milk
1 ¾ cups water
½ cup dried black beans, soaked in cold water for 12 hours
¼ cup glutinous rice
2 tablespoons coconut sugar or brown sugar

Place coconut milk and water in a saucepan on low heat. Stir frequently.

Put drained beans, rice, sugar, and coconut milk in a bowl and mix well. Pour into a baking dish and cover. Bake at 250°F for about 3 hours. Stir after 2 hours. Serve hot.

Sweet Rice and Custard

THAILAND	Yield 4 servings

Custard

2 tablespoons rose water
2 tablespoons brown sugar
1 ¾ cups thick coconut milk
4 eggs, beaten

Sweet Rice

1 cup glutinous rice
1 ¾ cups coconut milk
1 teaspoon salt
1 tablespoon sugar
Lime slices to garnish

Mix rose water and brown sugar with the thick coconut milk. Stir in eggs and beat well. Put in an ovenproof bowl. Place bowl in a baking dish of water and bake at 275°F for about 1½ hours or until custard has set.

Use a bowl on top of a steamer or a double boiler to make the sweet rice. Mix coconut milk with salt and sugar and pour over the rice. Steam for 30 minutes or until rice is cooked.

To serve, put cooked custard on top of the rice and garnish with lime slices. This dish can be served either hot or cold.

Banana Dessert

BURMA	Yield 6 servings

2 tablespoons water
1 cup sugar
6 large firm bananas
Pinch of salt
1 ⅓ cups coconut cream

Make a syrup of the water and sugar by cooking them over low heat, stirring. Peel the bananas and place in the bottom of a deep saucepan. Pour the syrup over the bananas. Bring this to a boil. Add the pinch of salt and coconut cream and simmer gently until the liquid is absorbed. Turn the bananas while they cook. Serve at once.

Ginger Mix

BURMA   *Yield 4 to 6 servings*

This can be offered as a sweet snack or a dessert. In Burma, they eat it with the fingers.

4 ounces very tender fresh ginger
4 to 6 tablespoons lemon juice
2 tablespoons peanut oil
1 tablespoon sesame-seed oil
12 garlic cloves, peeled and sliced
2 to 3 tablespoons sesame seeds
Salt to taste

Scrape the skin off the ginger and slice with a very sharp knife. The younger the ginger, the better the snack will be. Cut the slices even finer into slivers. Soak in lemon juice for 1 hour.

Heat both oils in a small skillet and fry garlic until it is golden. Remove from skillet with slotted spoon and drain on paper towels. Using a clean, dry skillet, fry the sesame seeds until golden brown, stirring constantly. Turn out to a plate to cool.

When ready for dessert, drain ginger and put it in a bowl. Add salt to taste and sprinkle garlic and sesame seeds over all. Toss to mix and serve.

Seaweed Jelly

BURMA   *Yield 6 to 8 servings*

1 ounce dried agar-agar
½ cup thick coconut milk
1 cup granulated sugar
5 cups water

Place the agar-agar in enough water to cover and soak it for 3 hours. Strain and discard the water. Then measure the agar-agar. Set aside ¼ of the thick coconut milk.

Put the remaining coconut milk in a pan. Add the agar-agar and sugar. In another pan, bring water to a boil. You'll need 5 cups of water for every 2 cups of agar-agar. Add the water to the first pan and simmer gently for about 10 minutes. When the mixture is smooth, it is ready. Transfer to a shallow square dish and allow to cool slightly. Pour over the reserved coconut milk. Leave in a cool place for at least 1 hour until jelly is set. Cut into diamond shapes and arrange on a serving dish.

Sesame Semolina Pudding

BURMA   *Yield 6 to 8 servings*

1⅓ cups semolina
1 cup dark brown sugar, firmly packed
½ teaspoon salt
¾ cup thick coconut milk
5 cups boiling water
¼ cup butter or margarine
2 teaspoons vegetable oil
2 medium eggs, beaten
½ cup seedless raisins
4 tablespoons sesame seeds

Use a heavy pan to cook semolina over low heat for 10 minutes, stirring from time to time. Do not let the semolina burn, but it should be toasted.

Remove from the heat and stir in brown sugar, salt, coconut milk, and water. Allow this to stand for about 30 minutes. Then return to heat and allow to simmer for 15 minutes until quite thick. Remove from heat.

Stir in butter or margarine until melted. Add oil and allow to cool for a few minutes. Stir in the beaten eggs. Return to heat and simmer for 5 minutes, stirring constantly. Add raisins and continue to cook for 5 minutes more or until the mixture is thick but not solid. Pour this into a greased, ovenproof, square dish. Sprinkle with sesame seeds.

Bake at 400°F for about 1½ hours. When the pudding shrinks away from the side of the dish, it is ready. Remove from oven and allow to cool. When completely cold, cut into squares and serve.

Tapioca Pudding

BURMA *Yield 6 to 8 servings*

1⅓ cups tapioca
1 cup dark brown sugar, firmly packed
½ teaspoon salt
3¾ cups water
1⅓ cups coconut, freshly grated
2 teaspoons confectioner's sugar

Bring the tapioca, brown sugar, salt, and water to a boil. Reduce heat and simmer for about 10 minutes. Stir constantly. The mixture will be thick and the tapioca soft and transparent.

Remove from heat and pour into a greased shallow dish. Allow to cool completely.

Using a tablespoon, scoop out the mixture and roll it in coconut and then in confectioners' sugar.

Teething Cake

BURMA *Yield about 6 servings*

This cake is so named because it is served to celebrate when a baby gets his first tooth.

1 cup flour
1 cup rice flour
Pinch salt
½ teaspoon baking soda
1 tablespoon light sesame oil or corn oil
Scant ⅔ cup water

Banana dessert I

1 cup fresh coconut, grated
½ cup palm sugar, grated
4 cups coconut milk
1 tablespoon or more sugar

Mix flours, salt, and baking soda. With your hands, rub in the oil. Add just enough water to make a paste and then knead well to form a smooth dough. Mix the grated coconut and palm sugar together. Pull off pieces of the dough and flatten to a circle. Dot the center with a little of the coconut and palm mixture and roll up to make a ball.

Bring the coconut milk and sugar to a boil in a large saucepan. Drop in the balls. They will sink to the bottom but, as they cook, will slowly rise to the top. Stir gently in case some of the balls stick to the bottom of the pan. Allow to simmer for 10 minutes after the balls float. Serve hot or cold with a little of the liquid in which the balls were cooked.

189

Carrot dessert and banana dessert

Add the water and mix to a firm dough. Knead for at least 10 minutes, the longer, the better. Form the dough into a ball; cover and let stand for at least 1 hour. (If possible, do this much the night before, so that chapati will be as light and tender as possible.)

Shape the dough into balls about the size of a walnut. Sprinkle reserved flour on a board and thinly roll out each ball into a circle. When all balls are rolled, heat a griddle or heavy frying pan. Place each chapati on the griddle for 1 minute. Turn and cook the other side, pressing down edges to form air bubbles and make the chapati light. Keep warm until all the chapati are finished cooking. Serve with butter.

Baked Leavened Bread

INDIA	Yield 6 to 8

2 cups flour
½ teaspoon baking powder
1 teaspoon salt
1 teaspoon sugar
1 teaspoon active dry yeast (1 package)
⅔ cup milk
⅔ cup unflavored yogurt
1 egg, beaten
2 teaspoons poppy seeds

Unleavened Bread

INDIA	Yield 20 to 24

Known as chapati in India, this bread is made with ata or whole-wheat flour.

3 cups fine whole wheat flour
1½ teaspoons salt
1 tablespoon ghee or oil
1 cup lukewarm water

Set aside ½ cup flour. Place remainder in mixing bowl with salt. Then rub in ghee with your fingers.

Indian nut heaps

In a large bowl, sift flour, baking powder, salt, and sugar. Take 2 tablespoons of milk and mix them with the yeast to make a smooth paste. Use a whisk to beat yogurt into the remaining milk and heat until lukewarm. Stir in the yeast paste. Gradually, add the liquid to the dry ingredients and mix to a dough. Knead well and then add the egg. Knead again, cover with a damp cloth, and allow to rise until doubled in size, at least 2 hours.

Divide dough into 8 pieces, rolling each piece into a small ball. Flatten each ball with your hand and press poppy seeds into top. Bake at 450°F for 12 minutes; bread will be puffed and blistered. Serve hot.

Fried Besan Bread

INDIA   *Yield 4 to 6*

Besan is chick-pea flour and must be kneaded well to form the smooth dough for this bread.

2 cups besan
1 teaspoon salt
1 cup water
½ cup ghee
¾ cup melted butter

Sift flour into a bowl, straining out lumps with a spoon pressing through sieve. Add salt. Gradually add water. The mixture will be stiff. Use hands to knead in the ghee and work until dough is very smooth. Divide the dough into 4 to 6 pieces and shape into 3-inch balls. Roll on a lightly floured surface to ¼ inch thickness.

Heat melted butter in a skillet. Cook each rolled ball separately for 3 minutes on each side, using a low heat. Keep finished balls warm in oven while you continue to cook. Brush all with melted butter on top when ready to serve.

Banana Dessert I

INDIA   *Yield 4 servings*

4 large bananas
3 tablespoons butter or margarine
Juice of 1 lemon
3 tablespoons grated coconut
4 tablespoons raspberry preserves

Peel and slice the bananas and place in a pudding dish that has been well greased. Dot with butter. Sprinkle with lemon juice and cover with grated coconut.

Bake at 350°F for 10 minutes. Remove from oven and divide dessert into individual serving dishes. Top each portion with 1 tablespoon preserves and serve warm.

Indian Nut Heaps

INDIA   *Yield about 60 cookies*

2 tablespoons flour
2 tablespoons sugar
Pinch of salt
2 egg yolks
6 tablespoons butter or margarine
4 ounces candied ginger, finely diced
4 ounces grated cashew nuts
Pinch of ground cardamom

Put flour in a bowl. Make a hollow in center. Place sugar, salt, and egg yolks into the hollow and mix well. Cut butter into this mixture. Knead into a smooth dough on a floured board. Mix ginger, cashew nuts, and cardamom into the dough. Cover and refrigerate for 30 minutes.

Grease a cookie sheet. Shape the dough into small balls about 1 inch in diameter. Place on cookie sheet. Bake at 350°F for about 10 minutes. Let cookies cool on a rack after baking.

Carrot Dessert

INDIA	Yield 4 to 6 servings

1½ pounds carrots, grated or finely mashed
2½ cups milk
Pinch of saffron
6 tablespoons butter
1 teaspoon cardamom
3 tablespoons sugar (or to taste)
2 tablespoons raisins
2 tablespoons honey
1 cinnamon stick
2 tablespoons chopped almonds

Put grated carrots in a bowl; add just enough milk to cover them and soak for 30 minutes. Heat remaining milk in a saucepan and add carrots. Allow to come to a boil and cook for 90 minutes, stirring occasionally. Add saffron, 3 tablespoons butter, cardamom, sugar, raisins, honey, and cinnamon stick. Cook on medium heat for 15 minutes more. Add remaining butter and cook for 15 more minutes. The dish is done when it is a nice orange color. Remove cinnamon stick and put carrot dessert into large bowl for serving. This tastes good hot or cold and, once made, can be reheated.

Banana Dessert II

INDIA	Yield 4 to 6 servings

8 bananas, peeled and sliced
6 tablespoons butter
2 cups water
½ cup sugar
3 tablespoons rose water
1 heaping teaspoon cardamom
Pinch of saffron
3 tablespoons chopped almonds

With a fork, mash banana slices in a bowl. Heat butter in saucepan. Stir bananas into butter and cook for 5 minutes. Add 5 tablespoons water and boil lightly for 3 minutes, using medium heat.

In another saucepan, melt sugar in remaining water. Stir this into the bananas and simmer for 10 minutes, stirring occasionally. Add the rose water. When mixed and hot, place in a preheated serving dish. Mix cardamom, saffron, and almonds in a bowl and sprinkle this over the top. Serve at once, hot.

This dessert can be made ahead of time, stored in the freezer, and thawed when ready to serve. Slightly frozen, it has a very delicate taste.

Deep-Fried Whole Wheat Bread

INDIA	Yield 8 to 10

1½ cups whole wheat flour
½ teaspoon salt
¾ cup water
⅓ cup melted ghee or butter
Vegetable oil for deep frying

Sift flour and salt together and gradually add water. Blend well into a firm dough. Add the ghee and knead well. Allow dough to rest for 20 minutes.

Divide dough into 8 or 10 pieces and shape into 1-inch balls. On lightly floured surface, roll into rounds about ⅛-inch thick.

Heat oil and deep-fry the rolled-out balls, one at a time. Cooking time is about 1½ minutes or until bread puffs up and floats on surface. Remove and drain on paper towels. Transfer to a warmed platter and keep hot in oven until ready to serve. Serve hot with your favorite chutney.

Stuffed Puri

INDIA   *Yield about 10*

Mix dough as for deep-fried whole wheat bread (puri; see preceding recipe), rolling it into smaller balls. You may want to double the recipe to make more stuffed puri.

Cauliflower filling

2 cups cauliflower, finely chopped
2 teaspoons salt
¼ teaspoon ground cloves
¼ teaspoon ground cinnamon
¼ teaspoon ground cardamom
¼ teaspoon pepper
½ teaspoon ground cumin
¼ ounce grated ginger, dried or fresh

Mix finely chopped cauliflower with spices in a bowl. Take 1 rolled-out ball and put stuffing in center. Cover with a second rolled-out ball and seal edges tightly. Deep-fry until bread puffs up and floats on surface. Remove and drain on paper towels. Keep hot in oven until ready to serve.

Almond Balls in Syrup

INDIA   *Yield 20 to 25 balls*

2 cups all-purpose flour
2 cups ground almonds
½ cup butter
1 teaspoon baking powder
⅔ cup unflavored yogurt
Vegetable oil for deep frying

Syrup

3¾ cups water
4 cups sugar
Pinch of cream of tartar
5 whole cloves

5 whole cardamoms
½ teaspoon rose water

Mix flour and almonds in a bowl and rub in the butter with your hands. Stir in baking powder and gradually add the yogurt until mixture becomes a firm dough. Cover and let stand for at least 2 hours.

While the dough is standing, make the syrup. Place all ingredients in a saucepan except the rose water. Do not boil. Heat gently until all sugar is dissolved. Remove from heat and stir in the rose water.

When ready to cook, divide the dough into 25 pieces and roll into 1-inch balls. Use a deep-fat fryer and heat the oil. Deep-fry the balls until they are golden brown. Remove from the pan and drain on paper towels. Drop the balls into syrup while still warm. Serve either hot or cold.

Carrot Pudding

INDIA   *Yield 4 servings*

This pudding, known as kheer in India, is a very rich dessert, but very delicious and easy to make.

1 pound carrots, peeled and grated
1 cup sugar
6¼ cups milk
6 whole cardamoms
1 tablespoon seedless white raisins
1 tablespoon slivered almonds

Sprinkle grated carrots with sugar and set aside. Place milk and cardamoms in a saucepan and bring to a boil. Allow to boil for about 45 minutes or until the milk is reduced by half. Add the carrots and reduce heat to a simmer. When the mixture has thickened, remove from the heat. Allow to cool slightly. Stir in the raisins and almonds. This pudding may be served either hot or cold.

Baked Coconut Pudding

INDIA	*Yield 4 servings*

2 whole coconuts
2 cups boiling water
1 cup sugar
1½ cups rice flour
2 eggs, beaten
½ cup slivered almonds

Break the coconuts in half, reserving the thin liquid inside. Grate the coconut meat into a large bowl and cover with boiling water. Allow to steep for 15 minutes. Then strain the liquid to get the thick coconut milk. Mix this with the liquid from the coconut and beat in the remaining ingredients in the order given.

Pour this into a saucepan and bring it to a boil. Stir constantly. Lower the heat and simmer until it thickens. Then pour into a well-greased, 8-inch, round baking tin. Bake at 350°F for about 30 minutes, until the top is lightly browned. Serve at once.

Ice Cream

INDIA	*Yield 4 servings*

3¾ cups milk
½ cup rice flour
1¼ cups light cream or evaporated milk
½ cup sugar
1 tablespoon pistachios, chopped
1 tablespoon almonds, chopped and blanched
Green food coloring, optional
Pistachio nuts and varak to garnish, optional

Allow the milk to come to a boil. Reduce heat and simmer until it is reduced to ⅔ original volume. Gradually stir in rice flour followed by the cream. Return this to a boil. Then reduce heat and simmer for 15 minutes. Add sugar, stirring until it is well dissolved. Set aside to cool.

When mixture has cooled, stir in nuts and food coloring if desired. Transfer to freezer containers and freeze until partially frozen. At this point, beat ice cream vigorously, then return to freezer until firm. Serve garnished with nuts and varak.

Rice Pudding

INDIA	*Yield 4 servings*

If you can't buy rice flour, make your own. Grind rice with a mortar and pestle or in your electric blender or food processor.

2½ cups milk
½ cup sugar
½ cup rice flour
2 teaspoons pistachios, chopped
2 teaspoons almonds, blanched and slivered
½ teaspoon rose water

Bring the milk to a boil in a heavy saucepan. Stir in the sugar and then gradually add the rice flour. You cannot leave the stove while this pudding is cooking, because you must stir continuously. Add the nuts and allow mixture to thicken. Remove from the heat and stir in the rose water. Turn out mixture into a serving bowl and allow to cool. This pudding should be served cold.

Spiced Fruit Salad

INDIA	*Yield about 4 servings*

2 oranges
2 bananas
2 pears
1 apple

Dessert fruit platter

2 guavas, optional
Juice of 1 lemon
2 teaspoons chili powder
1 teaspoon ginger powder
1 teaspoon garam masala
1 teaspoon salt
½ teaspoon freshly ground black pepper

Peel the oranges and bananas and cut into pieces. Core the pears and apple, leaving skin on for color and texture. Chop pears and apple with guavas, including the guava seeds.

Place prepared fruit in a bowl and sprinkle lemon juice over all. Mix the spices and seasonings and sprinkle them over the fruit. Toss gently to cover the fruit with the spices. Refrigerate for at least 2 hours before serving.

Spiced Semolina Dessert (Halwa)

INDIA	*Yield 4 servings*

1 ⅓ cups semolina flour
¼ cup coconut, shredded
2 cups sugar
1 tablespoon poppy seeds
Seeds of 6 cardamoms
2 ½ cups water
½ cup melted ghee

In a heavy pan, mix the semolina, coconut, sugar, poppy seeds, and cardamom. After this is

Fruit salad

well mixed, stir in the water. Bring to a boil, still stirring. Lower the heat and allow to simmer for 1 hour until the mixture is consistently soft. Stir frequently during the cooking process. Last, add the ghee and mix well.

Transfer the mixture to a shallow pan, spreading it out evenly. Allow to cool. Then cut into triangles. The halwa should be about ¼ inch thick. It may be stored in an airtight container.

Lichees

Vermicelli and Nut Dessert

INDIA	*Yield 4 servings*

½ pound vermicelli
Water to cover
⅓ cup ghee
1 tablespoon seedless white raisins
1 tablespoon almonds, slivered
1 tablespoon pistachios
1 tablespoon rose water
2½ cups heavy cream
2 tablespoons coconut, shredded
Sugar for sprinkling

Cover the vermicelli with water in a large saucepan. Bring to a boil, then lower heat to simmer and cook for 10 minutes. Drain off just enough water to leave the vermicelli covered but not drowning.

Add ghee and return mixture to boil. Reduce heat and cover the pan. Allow to simmer for 10 minutes. Do not stir this, as you might break the vermicelli. Gently fold in raisins and nuts. Add the rose water and transfer to a serving dish. Pour the heavy cream over the mixture. Sprinkle with coconut and sugar and serve either hot or cold.

196

Spiced mandarin oranges

Honey shortbread

Crispy orange cookies

Rice dessert

Sweet Bread Rolls

PHILIPPINES   *Yield 18 rolls*

1 ounce compressed yeast
¼ cup lukewarm water
3 teaspoons sugar
4 cups flour
1½ sticks (6 ounces) butter or margarine
½ cup powdered sugar
6 egg yolks
½ cup milk
1 extra stick (4 ounces) butter, melted
4 ounces cheese (Dutch Edam preferred), finely
   grated
2 to 3 tablespoons extra powdered sugar

Dissolve yeast in warm water. Stir in sugar until dissolved. Sprinkle 1 spoonful flour on top and set aside in a warm place.

Cream butter and powdered sugar until light. Add egg yolks, singly, beating well each time. Alternate flour and milk with yeast mixture and beat until smooth. The dough should be soft but not sticky. Form into a ball and let stand on floured board for about 10 minutes. Wash a bowl in hot water, dry it, and grease it lightly. Place dough in bowl, cover, and let rise until doubled in size, about 1 hour.

Divide dough in half and roll into 2 rectangles, 18 x 15 inches. Brush with melted butter and sprinkle with half of the cheese. Cut each rectangle into 3 strips and roll from the long end. Cut each roll into 3 pieces. When both rectangles are rolled and cut, you will have 18 pieces.

Roll each piece on floured board until the width of a pencil. Twist well. Place on greased baking sheet, allowing space for them to rise; cover with a dry cloth and put in a warm place for 40 minutes.

Bake in a preheated 350°F oven for 10 minutes or until golden brown. Remove from oven; brush with melted butter and sprinkle with powdered sugar. Serve warm or at room temperature.

Banana Chips

PHILIPPINES	Yield 6 or more servings

1 cup sugar
⅓ teaspoon salt
20 unripe bananas, peeled and sliced
Fat for deep frying

Mix sugar and salt together. In another bowl, place 3 cups of the sliced bananas. Add 3 tablespoons of the sugar-salt mixture. Repeat until bananas are used up.

Heat fat in a deep-fryer. Drop a few banana slices in the hot fat and cook until golden brown. Remove and separate if the pieces are stuck together. Allow to cool before serving.

Small Brandied Cakes

PHILIPPINES	Yield 12 cakes

Syrup

½ cup sugar
½ cup water
1 tablespoon brandy

Cakes

¼ cup melted butter, allowed to cool
½ cup flour
½ teaspoon baking powder
Pinch of salt
2 large eggs
½ cup sugar
1 tablespoon brandy

Make syrup first by dissolving sugar in water in a small saucepan over low heat. Allow to boil for 2 minutes, then cool. Last, stir in brandy. Set aside.

Mix dry ingredients together in a large bowl. Beat eggs until frothy, gradually adding sugar. Add butter and brandy and fold in the dry ingredients. Use a spatula or wooden spoon for the folding process.

Drop by spoonfuls into greased muffin tins, filling them halfway. Bake at 400°F for 10 minutes or until cakes are golden brown. Remove from muffin tins and dip into syrup for just a few seconds. Allow to cool on a cake rack.

Coconut Custard

PHILIPPINES	Yield 6 to 8 servings

1 cup brown sugar
¼ cup water
2 cups coconut cream
6 egg yolks
4 egg whites, slightly beaten

1 cup sugar
1 teaspoon lemon rind, grated

Put brown sugar and water in a saucepan on moderate heat. When the sugar browns or caramelizes, pour ¾ of the sugar into a large mold. Rotate the mold so that its base and sides are coated.

Dissolve the remaining sugar with coconut cream over low heat, stirring constantly. Combine egg yolks and whites in a bowl and beat until mixed. Add sugar and lemon rind. Last, add the saucepan of coconut cream. Strain this mixture and pour it into the prepared mold.

Place the mold in a baking tin with hot water coming halfway up the mold. Bake at 300°F for 45 minutes to 1 hour, or until a knife comes out clean. When custard is done, allow it to cool, then refrigerate it for several hours. Unmold onto a serving plate and serve cold.

Mango Ice Cream

PHILIPPINES   *Yield 6 servings*

2 cups milk
2 eggs, separated
½ cup confectioners' sugar
1 teaspoon unflavored gelatin
1½ to 2 cups mango pulp, fresh or canned
2 tablespoons water
1 cup cream

Bring milk slowly to a boil in a saucepan. In a bowl, beat the egg yolks and half of the sugar. Stirring constantly, add a little of the hot milk to the yolks. Put yoke mixture in saucepan with the rest of the milk and cook over hot water on a very low heat. Stir constantly to prevent the custard from curdling. When mixture lightly coats the back of your spoon, remove from heat but continue to stir until it cools slightly. Pour into a freezer tray and freeze until mixture is mushy.

Put 2 tablespoons cold water in a cup and sprinkle gelatin on top. Place cup in a saucepan of water and bring water to a boil. When gelatin is dissolved, stir this into the mango pulp. Whip the cream until it holds soft peaks. Beat the egg whites until they hold in soft peaks as well. Add the remaining sugar to the egg whites and beat until well blended.

Remove half frozen custard from freezer tray into a bowl. Beat with a rotary beater until smooth but not melted. Fold in mango pulp, egg whites, and whipped cream and return to freezer. Freeze until firm.

Rice Fritters

PHILIPPINES   *Yield About 20*

These fritters can be served as a dessert or as a between-meal snack.

1 cup cooked medium-grain rice
2 eggs, beaten
3 tablespoons sugar
½ teaspoon vanilla extract
½ cup flour
1 tablespoon baking powder
Pinch of salt
¼ cup sweetened coconut, shredded
Vegetable oil for deep frying
Confectioners' sugar for sprinkling on top

Mix rice, eggs, sugar, and vanilla in a large bowl. Gradually stir in the flour, baking soda, and salt. Last, add the coconut.

Heat oil in a deep-fat fryer. Drop the rice mixture by tablespoons into the heated oil. Fry until golden brown on both sides. Drain on paper towels. Place cooked fritters on a heated platter until all are done. Sprinkle with confectioners' sugar and serve at once.

Almond Delight

CHINA   *Yield 4 servings*

1 envelope unflavored gelatin
3 tablespoons warm water
1 small can evaporated milk
1¼ cups cold water
6 tablespoons sugar
1 tablespoon almond extract
1 small can mandarin oranges (drain; reserve
   juice)

Orange syrup

¼ cup sugar
2 cups warm water
1 teaspoon almond extract
Juice from mandarin oranges

Dissolve gelatin in warm water. Heat milk with cold water and sugar to just below boiling. Add gelatin mixture; cool. Add almond extract. Pour into square or rectangular glass dish; refrigerate to set. Cut into squares; float in syrup with mandarin oranges.

To make the syrup dissolve sugar in water. Add almond extract and juice. Chill before serving.

Dessert Fruit Platter

CHINA

The Chinese, as a rule, do not eat many sweets, either as dessert or as snacks. After a meal it would be very correct to offer a platter of fresh fruit, as shown. On page 195 is an assortment of fruit, including mandarin oranges, strawberries, raspberries, bananas, grapes, honeydew melon, cherries, and peach slices, all attractively arranged. Guests always welcome a dessert of fresh fruit artistically presented. Delicious served with small pitcher of Fruit Dressing (see Index).

Lichees

CHINA   *Yield about 4 servings*

1 can lichees

For a totally unique and delightful taste treat, try a dessert of lichees. This is a canned fruit in syrup, usually imported from Hong Kong. They can sometimes be purchased in your local supermarket, for sure at a Chinese food store. Try lichees mixed with other fruits: experiment with different combinations.

Fruit Salad

CHINA   *Yield about 12 servings*

All the fruits in this recipe are available at Oriental food stores. Some may be available at your supermarket.

1 4-ounce jar ginger in syrup, drained
1 11-ounce can lichees in syrup, drained
1 8-ounce can kumquats, drained
1 20-ounce can longans, drained
1 12-ounce can water-lily roots, drained
1 16-ounce can mangos, drained
1 round watermelon, chilled, cut in half, meat
   and seeds removed, meat cut into balls or
   cubes
1 18-ounce can white nuts
1 lemon, sliced

Place ginger, lichees, kumquats, longans, lily roots, and mangos in a large bowl; mix well. Chill until cold.

Cut slice off base of each watermelon half; place each half on serving dish. Place melon balls or cubes back into shells. Spoon mixed fruit on watermelon balls. Serve with nuts and lemon.

Sesame Cookies

CHINA	*Yield about 3 dozen cookies*

1 cup sifted cake flour
½ stick butter
½ cup sugar
¼ teaspoon salt
1 egg
1 egg yolk mixed with 1 tablespoon water
Sesame seeds

Combine flour, butter, sugar, salt, and egg in bowl and knead well until it forms a soft dough. Place on well-floured board and form into a long roll about 1½ inches in diameter. Cut into approximately 36 pieces and flatten each with bottom of a glass dipped in flour.

Brush one side of cookie with egg-yolk and water mixture. Sprinkle sesame seeds on brushed side and press sesame seeds into cookie. Place on greased cookie sheet and bake at 350°F for 10 to 12 minutes.

Spiced Mandarin Oranges

CHINA	*Yield about 4 servings*

1 small tangerine (an orange may be
   substituted)
2 11-ounce cans mandarin oranges
¼ cup water
⅓ cup firmly packed brown sugar
1 2-inch piece of stick cinnamon

Cut the peel from the tangerine in paper-thin strips. Squeeze the juice and strain. In medium-size saucepan, combine the peel and juice with the rest of the ingredients. Simmer for 15 minutes. Remove from heat and remove the peel and cinnamon. Chill for several hours. Serve in small dessert dishes.

Honey Shortbread

CHINA	*Yield about 2 dozen*

2½ cups flour
Pinch of salt
½ cup butter
½ cup honey

In a medium-size bowl, place flour and salt. Mix the butter into the flour with the fingers until mixture is like fine meal. Add the honey gradually and, still working with the fingers, blend until dough is smooth and leaves the side of the bowl. From a piece of cardboard, cut a fan-shaped pattern. Roll out the dough on lightly floured surface to about ¼ inch thick and cut into fan shapes.

Place on baking sheet that has been lightly floured and cut 6 deep slashes lengthwise as shown in picture. Bake in preheated 350°F oven until lightly browned, about 12 minutes.

Almond Cookies

CHINA	*Yield about 4 dozen*

1 cup shortening
1 cup sugar
1 egg, beaten
3 cups sifted flour
1½ teaspoons baking soda
3 tablespoons almond extract
4 tablespoons honey or corn syrup
1 cup blanched almonds

Cream the shortening and sugar together. Add the egg. Slowly add flour, baking soda, almond extract, and honey and blend until smooth. Take a small piece of dough and roll it into a ball. Repeat until all the dough is used. Flatten each ball to about ½ inch thickness. Place an almond in the center of each. Bake on greased cookie sheet in a preheated 375°F oven for about 15 to 20 minutes.

In China lard is the usual ingredient in Almond Cookies, but you may substitute margarine.

Caramel bananas

Almond Torte

CHINA	*Yield 6 servings*

Orange-cup dessert

2 eggs
1½ cups sugar
¼ cup sifted flour
2½ teaspoons baking powder
¼ teaspoon salt
2 teaspoons almond extract
½ cup almonds, slivered
1 medium apple, finely chopped

Preheat oven to 350°F.

Beat eggs until light. Gradually add sugar; beat until thick and lemon-colored.

Sift flour, baking powder, and salt together. Fold into egg mixture. Add almond extract, nuts, and apple; fold in gently. Pour into 8-inch-square greased baking pan. Bake 25 minutes.

Rice Dessert

CHINA *Yield about 4 servings*

1 cup leftover rice
1 cup drained fruit (canned or frozen, thawed, may be used) such as pineapple, peaches, oranges, berries, mixed fruit, etc.
2 cups whipped cream
Nuts for garnish, optional

Mix rice with drained fruit (cut up if necessary); fold in whipped cream. Serve in dessert dishes. Garnish with fruit and/or nuts, if desired.

Fruit dressing

Crispy Orange Cookies

CHINA *Yield about 36*

1 ¼ cups flour
¼ cup rice flour
½ cup butter or margarine
³/₈ cup white sugar
Grated rind of 1 large orange
1 egg, separated
½ cup brown sugar

Preheat oven to 350 °F.
Sift flour and rice flour into bowl. Rub in the butter until the mixture resembles fine bread crumbs. Add sugar, orange rind, and egg yolk; mix well. Knead until smooth; wrap in foil. Refrigerate ½ hour.
Roll dough to about 12 inches square. Brush with lightly beaten egg white; sprinkle with brown sugar. Fold corners to center. Form into ball; knead lightly. Cut in half; shape each half into roll about 9 inches long. Cut rolls into slices about ½ inch thick; place on greased baking sheets. Bake about 20 minutes; remove to cooling trays. Store when quite cold.

Bananas Cooked in Coconut Milk

INDOCHINA *Yield 6 servings*

6 to 8 large, ripe bananas
2 cups thick coconut milk
2 tablespoons sugar

Peel the bananas and cut into 2-inch pieces, about 3 or 4 pieces per banana. Put coconut milk and sugar in a saucepan and simmer until thick and creamy. Add bananas and cook on low heat until bananas are soft but not mushy. Transfer to individual serving dishes and serve warm.

Fruit bowl

Banana Cake with Cashews

INDOCHINA	*Yield 16 to 20 servings*

3 eggs
1 cup sugar
¾ cup cream
1½ cups flour
4 pounds very ripe bananas
1 cup fresh cashews, coarsely chopped
1 cup fresh coconut, grated

Beat eggs and sugar together using low speed on electric mixer. When mixture is thick and pale, add cream and beat just until mixed. Put aside mixer and use a wooden spoon to gradually add the flour. Peel bananas and soften or smash them slightly. Do not mash. Add bananas, cashews, and coconut, stirring only to blend in together.

Grease 2 8-inch pans and dust lightly with flour. Divide cake batter into these pans. Bake at 350°F for 1 hour or until the cake is golden brown on top. Serve warm or cold.

Orange Shaped Cakes

INDOCHINA	*Yield 12*

Filling

¾ cup yellow mung beans
¾ cup water
½ cup sugar

Wrapping

2 cups glutinous rice flour
1 teaspoon baking powder
½ teaspoon salt
½ cup sugar
2 medium potatoes, boiled, peeled, and mashed
½ cup boiling water

½ cup toasted sesame seeds
2 cups oil for deep frying

Use cold running water to rinse mung beans thoroughly. Place beans and ¾ cup water in a small saucepan and bring to a boil. Cover the pan, reduce heat, and simmer for about 30 minutes. When the beans are tender and dry, and the water cooked away, remove from heat. Mash well; add sugar and mix well. Set aside.

Mix well the dry ingredients for the wrapping, including the mashed potatoes. Gradually add the boiling water. Then knead well until dough forms a smooth ball.

Form a small ball from about 2 tablespoons of the dough. Flatten this into a 3-inch circle. Place 1 teaspoon of the filling mixture into the center and cover this as you reshape the dough into a sealed ball. Repeat this wrapping procedure until all balls are made.

Toast sesame seeds in a dry skillet by stir-frying until they are well browned and not oily at all. Roll prepared balls into the seeds until well coated.

Heat oil in a small skillet; cook only a few balls at a time. Drop the balls into the oil and flatten slightly with a circular motion of a spoon or spatula. Cook for about 10 minutes until golden brown. Remove from the pan and drain on paper towels. Keep warm until all the balls are fried and serve at once.

Caramel Bananas

KOREA	*Yield 4 servings*

4 bananas, peeled and cut into 1-inch rounds
2 tablespoons flour
2 egg whites, beaten with a fork
2 tablespoons cornstarch
Oil for deep frying

Caramel sauce

¼ cup sugar
2 tablespoons butter

2 tablespoons water
2 tablespoons sesame seeds

After preparing bananas, place flour on a plate. Combine beaten egg whites with cornstarch. Roll bananas first in flour and then in egg-white mixture. Heat oil in skillet. Fry bananas for 3 minutes to a golden brown color. Remove and drain on paper towels.

In a pan, allow sugar and 1 tablespoon butter to become golden brown. Stir in water and sesame seeds. Gently place bananas in this and turn to cover with the sauce. Use remaining butter to grease serving dish. Place bananas on greased serving dish and serve at once.

Chestnut Balls

KOREA	*Yield 4 to 6 servings*

5 cups chestnuts in the shell
Water
¼ cup sugar
4 tablespoons honey
2 teaspoons cinnamon
4 tablespoons pine nuts, chopped

Place chestnuts in a saucepan and cover with water. Bring to a boil and cook until the nuts are tender. As soon as you can handle the nuts, remove shells and skins. Mash the nuts into a fine paste.

Mix sugar, honey, and cinnamon with the chestnuts. When flavors are all blended, roll into small balls, about 1 inch in diameter. Roll each ball in the chopped pine nuts and serve when desired.

Date Candy

KOREA	*Yield 6 to 8 servings*

1 cup pitted dates
3 tablespoons honey
½ teaspoon cinnamon
Pine nuts, whole
½ cup pine nuts, chopped

Chop the dates in a bowl until they are very sticky. Add the honey and cinnamon and stir until well mixed. Use a teaspoon to take out portions of this mixture. The shapes will be somewhat rounded. Put 1 pine nut into the center of the date mixture. Then roll it in the chopped pine nuts and put on a serving dish. Continue in this way until all the candies are made.

Fried Cakes

KOREA	*Yield 4 to 6 servings*

1 cup flour
1 teaspoon baking powder
½ teaspoon salt
3 tablespoons sugar
Water
6 dates, shredded
Small amount of oil for frying

Put the dry ingredients in a bowl. Add only enough water to make a firm dough. When the dough is firm, roll it out on a floured board to ⅛-inch thick. Cut into 2-inch circles.

Press bits of the dates into the circles of dough. Heat oil in a skillet and brown the cakes on each side. These delicacies are best served hot, so keep the cooked ones warm until all are fried.

Coconut Custard

MALAYSIA   *Yield 4 to 6 servings*

6 eggs
¼ teaspoon salt
2 cups sugar
2 cups coconut cream
½ cup fresh coconut, grated

Mix eggs, salt, and sugar together in a bowl until light. Add coconut cream and mix well. Last, stir in the coconut.

Pour this mixture into buttered custard cups or a buttered casserole. Place in a shallow dish filled with cold water. Bake at 350°F for 25 minutes or until a knife comes out of the custard clean. Allow to cool or chill before serving.

Spiced Fruit Salad

MALAYSIA   *Yield 4 to 6 servings*

In Malaysia, this is made with native fruits, such as kedondong and jeruk bali. Here, fruits that are available in the West are substituted.

1 underripe mango
2 crisp dessert apples
½ fresh pineapple
½ teaspoon salt
1 pink meat grapefruit
¼ cucumber, peeled and sliced

Seasonings

¼ teaspoon chili powder
1 slice trasi, broiled, optional
⅔ cup palm sugar
Pinch of salt
1 tablespoon tamarind water

Peel and slice the mango into a bowl. Peel, core, and slice the apples into the same bowl. Peel pineapple and cut into chunks as well. Add enough cold water to cover and stir in the salt. Peel the grapefruit and divide it into segments, keeping it separate from the other fruit for the time being.

Blend the seasonings, using a mortar and pestle, until very smooth. Add salt and tamarind water and stir to mix. Drain the water from the fruit; place it in a serving bowl and add grapefruit and cucumber. Pour the seasonings on top and stir the fruit gently to mix well. Chill until ready to serve.

Orange-cup Dessert

JAPAN

This is a very pretty and refreshing dessert.

Oranges with unblemished skin, as many as are
   needed, 1 per person
Fruit such as:
   Pineapple
   Orange sections
   Grapefruit sections
   Bananas
   Maraschino cherries
   Walnuts

Cut slice from top of orange so that the insides may be scooped out.

Combine any of the above fruits, or others of your choice, and spoon into the orange shells; refrigerate until serving time. The same thing may be done with grapefruit or bananas, as pictured on page 203. If desired, a small amount of your favorite liqueur may be added to the fruit.

Sponge Cake

JAPAN   *Yield 1 9-inch cake*

5 eggs, beaten
⅔ cup sugar
¼ cup honey
¾ cup flour
¾ teaspoon baking powder
2 tablespoons confectioners' sugar

Beat eggs, sugar, and honey together for about 10 minutes until thick and pale. The electric beater helps here. Sift flour and baking powder and fold into the egg mixture.

Pour this into a greased and floured 9-inch square pan. Bake at 350°F for 30 minutes. Allow the cake to cool in the pan for 10 minutes. Then remove from pan and place on a wire rack. Cool completely. When ready to serve, dust with confectioners' sugar and cut into squares.

Fruit Bowl

JAPAN   *Yield 2 servings*

1 can mandarin oranges, drained
1 apple, peeled and sliced
1 banana, sliced and sprinkled with lime or lemon juice
6 dates, cut in half
⅛ cup walnut chips

Place drained mandarin oranges in glass bowl. Combine with apple, banana, and dates. Sprinkle with walnut chips.

Fruit Dressing

JAPAN   *Yield about 1 pint*

This is delicious poured over any kind of fruit.

1 cup sugar
1 egg, well beaten
Juice and grated rind of 1 orange, 1 lime, and 1 lemon

Combine all ingredients in saucepan and blend well. Cook over medium heat, stirring constantly, until mixture comes to a boil. Boil 1 minute. Remove from heat, cool, and store in refrigerator in covered jar. Serve as an accompaniment to a dessert of fresh fruit.

Fruit Kabobs

JAPAN

This is a nice dessert for guests to make themselves.

Pineapple chunks, canned or fresh
Bananas, cut into large pieces
Mandarin oranges
Brandied peaches, cut into halves, or large pieces
Spiced crab apples, left whole

Skewer fruits; cook on a hibachi. There is an endless list of fruits suitable for this. Use the fruits that appeal to you and that are available to you. Make approximately 6 to 8 pieces of fruit per serving.

Although this section comes at the end of the book, these diverse foods and sauces may be some of the most interesting in the entire book. Just reading the various ingredients included in the recipes provides a trip through the Orient. As you read, you may decide you want to complement your Western cooking with an Eastern relish or chutney. This is an excellent way to include taste delights from far away in your own menus.

In some of these miscellaneous recipes, the yield has been omitted. Most of the time, the yield is for 4 servings; but since accompaniments are dished by the individual and depend on his own taste as to how much he uses, it is difficult to say exactly how far a given sambal, let's say, will go. Once you have made it and served it, you will know how much to make for your own needs.

Coconut Milk

Yield 1⅔ cups thick coconut milk

Since so many countries in the Orient include coconut milk in their recipes, this particular recipe cannot be attributed to any one country. Some Oriental stores carry canned coconut milk. This is not the fluid that comes out of the coconut when the husk is broken. Coconut milk is made directly from the flesh of fresh coconuts. In the absence of fresh coconut meat, dried coconut or desiccated coconut may be used.

2 cups coconut meat, grated
2½ cups hot water

In a large bowl, pour water over the coconut. Set aside until it cools to lukewarm. Knead the mixture firmly with your hands for a few minutes. Strain through a fine strainer or fine cheesecloth, being sure to squeeze out as much liquid as possible.

Use the same coconut to make thin coconut milk by adding 2½ cups hot water to the same flesh of the coconut. Repeat the process above and the yield will be about 2 cups thin coconut milk.

Coconut milk should not be stored for more than 24 hours.

Toasted Coconut

ORIENTAL *Yield ½ cup*

½ cup coconut, grated
1 tablespoon butter
2 tablespoons confectioners' sugar

Mix the coconut with butter and sugar; spread on baking sheet. Bake in preheated 350°F oven 8 to 10 minutes, until browned.

Hot Relish

INDONESIA *Yield 4 servings*

20 red chilies, seeded and chopped
10 shallots, peeled and chopped
2 cloves garlic, peeled and chopped
5 kemiri, chopped
1 slice trasi
2 tablespoons vegetable oil
1 teaspoon ginger powder
1 teaspoon brown sugar
3 tablespoons tamarind water
Salt to taste
⅔ cup thick coconut milk

Use a mortar and pestle to pound chilies, shallots, garlic, kemiri, and trasi to a fine paste.

Heat oil in a skillet and fry this smooth paste for 2 minutes, stirring constantly. Add all remaining ingredients except the coconut milk and stir well. Last, add the coconut milk and simmer for 15 minutes. Stir occasionally. When the relish is thick and oily, increase the heat and stir-fry for 3 minutes. Serve hot or cold.

Sambal Tomat

INDONESIA *Yield 4 servings*

This spicy hot tomato sauce is particularly tasty served cold over fish, shrimp, or chicken.

2 tablespoons crushed red peppers
1 tablespoon water
2 tablespoons fresh tomatoes, chopped
1 teaspoon shrimp or anchovy paste
½ teaspoon salt

After you have crushed the peppers, soak them for 10 minutes in water. Add the remaining ingredients and mash them together until all flavors have blended. You can do this with your electric blender, food processor, or mortar and pestle.

Peanut Sauce

INDONESIA *Yield about 1 cup*

6 tablespoons peanut butter (smooth or crunchy)
1 cup water
¾ teaspoon garlic salt
2 teaspoons palm sugar or substitute
2 tablespoons dark soy sauce
Lemon juice to taste
½ teaspoon shrimp paste
Coconut milk or water for thinning

Place peanut butter and water in a saucepan and stir constantly. When well blended, remove from heat. Add the remaining ingredients and blend well until the sauce is a paste consistency but is able to be poured. Add more salt and lemon juice to taste if desired.

This sauce will keep for several weeks in a bottle in the refrigerator.

Nuoc Cham

INDONESIA *Yield 4 servings*

This hot, tangy sauce can be safely kept in the refrigerator for a week.

2 cloves garlic, peeled
4 dried red chilies or 1 fresh red chili
5 teaspoons sugar
Juice and pulp of ¼ lime
¼ cup fish sauce
⅓ cup water

Use a mortar and pestle to pound the garlic, chilies, and sugar. Add the juice and pulp of the lime; then add fish sauce and water. Mix well to combine all the ingredients.

Peanut Wafers

INDONESIA

These crunchy snacks can be served as hors d'oeuvres or with dinner.

½ cup rice flour
2 tablespoons ground rice
½ teaspoon ground cumin
¼ teaspoon ground turmeric
¾ teaspoon salt
1 cup coconut milk
1 clove garlic, peeled and very finely crushed
1 small onion, peeled and finely chopped
¼ pound roasted, unsalted peanuts
Oil for frying

Combine flour, ground rice, and seasonings in a small bowl. Stir in the coconut milk and beat until the batter is very smooth. Stir in garlic, onion, and peanuts and continue to stir until all spices are evenly spread throughout the batter.

Heat about ½ inch of oil in a skillet. Drop the batter by tablespoons into the oil. Each spoonful should spread into a lacy wafer as it cooks. If it is too thick, add an extra spoonful of coconut milk and stir well. Fry the wafers until golden brown on both sides, turning once. Cool wafers on paper towels over a wire rack to allow air to come through them. Store in an airtight container.

Shrimp Paste Sambal

THAILAND

3 tablespoons dried shrimp paste
2 tablespoons onions, finely chopped
1 tablespoon garlic, finely chopped
2 tablespoons dried shrimp powder
¼ cup lime or lemon juice
1 tablespoon palm sugar or substitute

Fish sauce to taste
1 teaspoon lime or lemon rind, finely shredded
Fresh red chilies, chopped for garnish

Make a flat cake of the shrimp paste and wrap it in foil. Roast under a hot grill for 5 minutes per side. Allow to cool completely.

Using mortar and pestle, make a paste of the onions, garlic, dried shrimp paste, shrimp powder, and lime juice. When the paste is smooth, add the sugar and fish sauce. Place on a serving plate in a large, rounded mound. Garnish with citrus rind and chilies.

Shrimp Sauce

THAILAND   *Yield about 1 generous cup*

This can be used as a dip or over white rice as a main course.

2 tablespoons dried shrimp
Hot water
1 teaspoon dried shrimp paste (kapi)
4 cloves garlic, peeled and quartered
2 teaspoons ground chilies or 2 fresh red chilies
2 teaspoons palm sugar or substitute
2 tablespoons lemon juice
1½ tablespoons soy sauce
3 tablespoons water

Soak washed shrimp in hot water for 20 minutes. Rinse thoroughly. Wrap shrimp paste in foil and grill for 3 minutes on each side.

Place shrimp, shrimp paste, garlic, chilies, sugar, lemon juice, soy sauce, and water in blender. Cover and blend until smooth. If blender is unavailable, use mortar and pestle to pound these ingredients into the needed texture.

Garlic and Vinegar Sauce

THAILAND

2 or 3 fresh red chilies
3 cloves garlic
2 tablespoons sugar
4 tablespoons vinegar
Salt to taste

Finely chop or crush the chilies and garlic. Add the remaining ingredients and mix thoroughly. This sauce is best made several hours before using and left to blend at room temperature. If a blender is used, the sauce must be made well ahead of time.

Oily Balachaung

BURMA

Once made, this will keep for weeks.

20 cloves garlic, peeled and thinly sliced
4 medium onions, peeled and finely sliced
2 cups peanut oil
1 8-ounce packet of shrimp powder
2 teaspoons chili powder, optional
2 teaspoons salt
1 teaspoon dried shrimp paste
½ cup vinegar

After garlic and onions are prepared, heat oil in a skillet. Fry garlic separately until it is golden. Lift out with slotted spoon and set aside. Repeat this procedure for the onions, setting them aside as well. When cool, onions and garlic will be crisp and dark.

Fry the shrimp powder in the same oil for 5 minutes. Mix remaining ingredients together and add to shrimp powder. Stir well and fry until crisp.

Add the onion and garlic and stir well to mix. When cool, store in an airtight container.

Cucumber Pickle

BURMA   *Yield 6 servings*

2 large, green cucumbers, peeled
½ cup malt vinegar
2 cups water
1 teaspoon salt
¼ cup peanut oil
2 tablespoons sesame oil
8 cloves garlic, peeled and sliced
1 medium onion, peeled and finely sliced
2 tablespoons sesame seeds

Cut peeled cucumbers in half the long way. Scoop out the seeds and cut the cucumbers into strips about ½ inch thick. Then cut the strips into 2-inch pieces.

Put vinegar, water, and salt in a saucepan and bring to a boil. Add cucumber pieces and allow to boil until just transparent. Drain and allow to cool.

Heat the oils in a skillet and fry the garlic until golden. Drain and set aside. Fry the onion until golden and drain. Allow oil to cool. Toast sesame seeds in a dry skillet, stirring constantly until they are golden brown. Turn out on a plate to cool.

When the oil is completely cool, pour 3 tablespoons of it over the cucumbers. Mix gently with your fingers. Put it in a small serving dish with the onion, garlic, and sesame seeds. Toss lightly. Chill if desired.

Peach chutney

stantly as the mixture comes to a boil. Add sugar and continue to stir.

Reduce the heat to a simmer for 20 minutes or until all the agar-agar is dissolved. Last, add the rose flavoring. Take a square, 8-inch, ovenproof dish and rinse it with cold water. Then pour the mixture into the chilled dish and allow it to set. Cut it into squares and serve.

Garam Masala

INDIA

Garam masala is a combination of spices and is not usually found in a food store. Variations from individual cooks range from the sweet to the hot. The recipe included here can be adjusted to your personal taste.

4 tablespoons coriander seeds
2 tablespoons cumin seeds
1 tablespoon whole black peppercorns
2 teaspoons cardamom seeds (measure after removing pods)
3-inch cinnamon stick
1 teaspoon whole cloves
1 whole nutmeg

Roast each of the spices above, except the nutmeg, separately. To roast, place the spices on a small pan in a moderate oven and let them roast until you begin to smell a delicate fragrance. Turn out on a plate to cool. Remove the pods from the cardamom and discard, keeping only the seeds.

When the roasting process is over, blend the spices into a fine powder with a mortar and pestle or an electric blender or food processor. Last, finely grate the nutmeg and mix in. Place the spice mixture, well mixed, in an airtight jar and store until needed.

Seaweed Jelly

BURMA   *Yield about 18 pieces*

This very firm jelly can be picked up with the fingers — it's a popular accompaniment in Burma.

¼ ounce agar-agar strands
4 cups coconut milk
½ cup sugar
Few drops rose flavoring

In cold water, soak the strands of agar-agar at least 1 hour, preferably overnight. Drain and measure. You should have about 1½ cups. Place this with coconut milk in a saucepan and stir con-

Cumin and Tamarind Water

INDIA   *Yield 4 to 8 servings*

This is frequently served at the start of a meal, much the same way as tomato juice is served here.

½ cup dried tamarind pulp
2 cups hot water
3 teaspoons fresh ginger, finely grated
2 teaspoons ground cumin
Pinch of chili powder, optional
½ teaspoon garam masala
3 teaspoons sugar, or to taste
Salt to taste
Ice water and crushed ice for serving
Mint sprigs for garnish
Lemon slices for garnish

Cover the dried tamarind pulp with 2 cups hot water and allow to stand overnight. Squeeze to dissolve the pulp. Strain through a sieve, discarding the pulp and seeds. Add the ginger, cumin, chili, garam masala, sugar, and salt to the tamarind water, stirring well to be sure all flavors are blended. Strain again through a fine sieve or muslin. Refrigerate until ready to use. Dilute this with desired amount of ice water and pour over crushed ice. Garnish with mint and lemon.

Yogurt Drink

INDIA   *Yield 4 servings*

½ cup yogurt
2½ cups ice water
Pepper and salt to taste
Ice cubes

Beat the yogurt well until it is rich and creamy, with no lumps. Gradually add the water, mixing well. Season the mixture with salt and pepper and pour over ice cubes in a large glass.

This drink may be made with sugar if you prefer, and soda water may be substituted for ice water to make it seem like a frothy milk shake.

Potato Straws

INDIA   *Yield 4 to 6 servings*

4 large potatoes
Ice water
Oil for frying
1 teaspoon salt
½ teaspoon chili powder
½ teaspoon ground cumin
½ teaspoon garam masala

Peel the potatoes and slice very thin. Then cut them into matchstick strips. Cover the straws with ice water. Drain and dry well on paper towels.

Heat the oil in a skillet and fry a few of the potatoes at a time until they are golden and crisp. Lift out with a slotted spoon and drain on paper towels. When all are fried, mix the salt and spices together and sprinkle over the potato straws. Gently shake to spread the spices all around.

Peach Chutney

INDIA   *Yield 2 or 3 jars*

2 pounds thoroughly ripe peaches
½ cup seedless raisins
3 onions, peeled and finely chopped
1 cup dark brown sugar
½ teaspoon saffron

1 cup wine vinegar
1 teaspoon ginger
1 teaspoon chili powder

Peel peaches and cut into thin slices. Cut slices in half again. Pour hot water over raisins in a sieve and drain.

Place peaches together with raisins, onions, sugar, and saffron in a pot. Stir and bring to a boil. Allow to boil for 10 minutes. Add wine vinegar and ginger. Cover and reduce heat to simmer. Simmer for 30 minutes. Last, season with chili powder. Fill jars that have been rinsed with hot water. Seal with paraffin and allow to cool completely. Store in a cool place for up to 3 months.

Indian Relish

INDIA   *Yield 3 to 3⅔ pints*

2 quarts green tomatoes, peeled, chopped
½ cup salt
3 cups cabbage, finely chopped
3 cups vinegar
½ cup onion, finely chopped
½ cup green pepper, chopped
¼ cup pimiento, diced
1½ cups sugar
1½ teaspoons celery seed
1½ teaspoons mustard seed
1 teaspoon whole cloves
Small piece (¼ inch) cinnamon stick

Sprinkle tomatoes with salt; leave overnight. Strain off liquid. Put tomatoes into a kettle. Add cabbage and vinegar; boil gently 25 to 30 minutes.

Add onion, pepper, pimiento, sugar, celery seed, and mustard seed. Add cloves and cinnamon tied loosely together in piece of cheesecloth. Mix well; cook over gentle heat until the onion is tender and the relish a good consistency. Pack in hot sterilized jars; seal at once.

Mint Chutney

INDIA   *Yield 4 servings*

This refreshing chutney goes well with most dishes—and it is easy to put together.

⅔ cup unflavored yogurt
3 cups mint, chopped
2 green chilies, finely chopped
Juice of 1 lemon
½ teaspoon salt
Pinch of chili powder for garnish

Mix all of the ingredients in the order given except for the garnish. Stir well to blend the flavors. Chill well in the refrigerator. When ready to serve, garnish with chili powder.

Tomato Chutney

INDIA   *Yield 2 half-pints*

1 tablespoon salad oil
1 whole red chili pepper, crumbled
½ teaspoon cumin seed
¼ teaspoon nutmeg
¼ teaspoon mustard seed
4 tomatoes, peeled, sliced ⅛ inch thick
½ lemon, quartered
⅓ cup raisins
½ cup sugar

Heat oil; add chili pepper. Add cumin, nutmeg, and mustard seed. When seeds start to jump, add tomatoes and lemon. Simmer 15 minutes; stir frequently. Stir in raisins and sugar. Simmer, stirring frequently until thickened, about 30 minutes; chill. Pack in sterilized jars; seal.

Note: This chutney is from Bengal. It is sweeter and milder than most. If made ahead of time and refrigerated, allow it to warm to room temperature before serving.

Guava Jelly

PHILIPPINES　　*Yield several jars of jelly*

4 pounds slightly underripe guavas
4 green cooking apples
Sugar (¾ cup to each cup of juice)
Lemon juice

Wash guavas and cut into quarters. Core and quarter apples. Place in a large saucepan with enough cold water to cover. Allow to cook uncovered for at least 1 hour or until fruit is soft and colorless. Wet 3 layers of muslin and wring it out. Then strain the cooked liquid through the muslin. Measure how much liquid there is and discard the fruit or use it to make guava paste. (See next recipe.)

For each cup of juice, allow ¾ cup sugar. Put no more than 5 cups liquid in a saucepan and bring to a boil. Add sugar and 2 tablespoons lemon juice and stir until all sugar is dissolved. Allow the jelly to cook without stirring, but skin off any froth that rises to the top. When the liquid thickens on the side of a spoon, it is ready. Pour into sterile jars and seal with paraffin.

Guava Paste

PHILIPPINES

To make guava paste, you must reserve the pulp of the fruit used to make jelly. This is a tasty sweetmeat.

Guava pulp
Sugar
Juice of 1 lemon

Strain the pulp through a nylon sieve, discarding seeds and skins. Weigh the pulp and add ¾ of its weight in sugar. Heat pulp and sugar with the juice of 1 lemon and allow to thicken, stirring con-

stantly. Use a long-handled spoon and cook over low heat, as this spatters while cooking.

When the mixture is stiff and pulls away from the sides of the pan, turn it out onto a well-greased dish. Flatten it with a buttered spoon and allow it to cool and become firm. Using a sharp knife, cut into thin slices and serve.

Hot-Pot Cooking

CHINA　　*Yield 4 servings*

Choose from the following:

Flank steak, cut into thin slices
Boneless lean lamb
Boned chicken breast
Shrimp, shelled, deveined
Scallops
Oysters
Celery cabbage
Spinach
Fresh mushrooms
Pea pods
Hot mustard sauce (dry mustard mixed to a
　　paste with water)
Soy sauce
Chinese oyster sauce
Hoisin sauce
Teriyaki sauce
Chinese plum sauce

"Hot-Pot Cooking" is a one-pot meal that is cooked at the table, similar to Swiss Fondue. The hostess presents an artistically arranged platter of selected meats, seafood, and vegetables. These are passed around. Each diner selects from the platter and cooks his or her meal in a pot of chicken broth, which is later eaten as soup with rice or noodles added to it. A "hot-pot" meal might consist of the following: chicken broth; white rice or thin noodles; selection of meats, seafood, and vegetables; sauces for dipping the meats, seafood, and vegetables. For 4 people, select 6 to 8 foods (variety of meat, seafood, and vegetables).

Sweet-and-Sour Sauce

CHINA   *Yield about 2 cups*

1 tablespoon oil
1 medium onion, finely sliced
1 medium carrot, sliced
½ green pepper, diced
½ red pepper, diced
1 15-ounce can pineapple chunks
1 small cucumber, peeled and diced
1 tablespoon cornstarch
2 teaspoons fresh ginger, grated
½ cup white vinegar
2 teaspoons sugar
3 teaspoons tomato sauce
2 teaspoons soy sauce
1 cup liquid (juice from pineapple chunks plus
   chicken stock)
Salt and pepper to taste
2 shallots or spring onions

Heat oil; sauté onion, carrot, and pepper 2 to 3 minutes. Drain pineapple, reserving liquid. Add pineapple chunks and cucumber to pan. Stir to combine vegetables; remove; set aside.

Blend cornstarch and ginger with vinegar, sugar, tomato sauce, and soy sauce. Combine this with the liquid; add to pan. Stir constantly until sauce boils and thickens. Season with salt and pepper. Return vegetables to pan; reheat thoroughly. Last, add sliced shallots to sauce. Cook for 2 minutes more.

Spiced Kumquats

CHINA   *Yield about 3 pints*

1 quart kumquats
3 cups sugar
1 cup vinegar
1 stick cinnamon
1 tablespoon whole cloves
1 tablespoon whole allspice

Wash and slit kumquats; place in a pot. Cover with water; bring to a boil. Cook 10 minutes; drain. Combine sugar; vinegar, and 3 cups of water in a large saucepan; bring to a boil.

Tie spices in a small piece of muslin; drop into syrup. Cook 5 minutes. Add kumquats; cook 10 minutes. Discard spice bag. Let kumquats stand overnight. Bring to a boil; cook until syrup is thick. Pack kumquats into hot sterilized jars; cover with syrup. Place lids on jars; screw bands tight. Process jars 10 minutes in boiling water.

Pickled Crab Apples

CHINA   *Yield about 5 pints*

4 pounds ripe crab apples
4½ cups sugar
2½ cups vinegar
2 cups water
1 teaspoon salt
½ tablespoon whole cloves
½ tablespoon allspice
1 1½-inch piece fresh gingerroot
2 sticks cinnamon
Red food coloring (optional)

Wash and rinse apples; drain. Remove stem end; prick apples with a large needle. Place sugar, vinegar, water, and salt in a saucepan.

Tie spices in a muslin bag; drop into pan. Cook, stirring constantly, until sugar dissolves. Add one layer of apples; boil gently 7 minutes. Remove from pan; place in a large bowl. Repeat until all crab apples are cooked; add a few drops of color to the syrup. Pour syrup over crab apples; add spice bag. Cover; let stand in cool place 48 hours. Pack crab apples to within ½ inch of top of hot sterilized fruit jars.

Heat syrup to boiling; pour over crab apples. Place lids on jars; screw bands tight. Process pints and quarts 20 minutes in boiling water.

Sweet-and-sour sauce

Pickled Figs

CHINA	*Yield about 6 pints*

5 quarts firm ripe figs
1 cup soda
4 to 5 cups sugar
2½ cups vinegar
1 teaspoon salt
¼ teaspoon ground nutmeg
2 teaspoons whole cloves
2 teaspoons whole allspice
1 medium piece fresh gingerroot
3 sticks cinnamon
Green food coloring (optional)

Pickled fruits (China)

Place figs in a large bowl; sprinkle with soda. Add 6 quarts boiling water; let stand 5 minutes. Rinse figs thoroughly in cool water; drain.

Combine 2½ cups sugar and 2 quarts water in a kettle; bring to a boil. Add figs; cook 30 minutes or until tender. Add remaining sugar, vinegar, salt, and nutmeg.

Tie whole spices in a bag; drop into the syrup. Cook until figs are clear. Let stand in a cool place overnight. Add coloring if desired. Pack figs to within ½ inch of top of pint jars.

Bring syrup to a boil; pour over figs. Place lids on jars; screw bands tight. Process 15 minutes in boiling water.

Pickled Watermelon Rind

CHINA	Yield 4 quarts

5 pounds watermelon rind
1 tablespoon salt
8 teaspoons alum
9 cups sugar
1 quart cider vinegar
2 lemons, sliced thin
4 2-inch pieces cinnamon stick
2 teaspoons whole allspice
2 teaspoons whole cloves

Cut off and discard green and red portions from watermelon rind; leave only white inner rind. Cut into 1-inch pieces, about 4 quarts. Place rind in a large stainless-steel or enamel pot. Add water to cover. Stir in salt; bring to a boil. Reduce heat; simmer 20 minutes or until the rind can be easily pierced with a fork. Remove from heat. Stir in alum; cool. Cover; let stand 24 hours. Pour off water. Rinse; drain well. Add sugar, vinegar, lemon, and cinnamon sticks.

Tie allspice and cloves in a cheesecloth bag. Add to rind mixture; mix well. Bring just to boil, stirring constantly. Remove from heat; cool, uncovered. Cover; let stand 24 hours.

Drain off syrup into a large pan; bring just to boil. Pour over rind; cool. Cover; let stand 24 hours. Heat rind in syrup, but do not boil. Remove and discard spice bag. Pack rind and cinnamon in hot sterilized jars. Heat syrup to boiling; fill jars with boiling syrup. Seal immediately. Store 4 weeks or longer before serving.

Glazed Chestnuts

CHINA	Yield about 24

2 cups chestnuts
¾ cup honey
2 cups sugar

Place chestnuts in a bowl with water to cover. Soak overnight; drain. Remove shells; dry on paper toweling.

Combine honey and sugar in a saucepan. Cook over low heat for 1 hour, stirring often. Add chestnuts; cook 2 hours, stirring often. Separate chestnuts on cookie sheets; cool.

Garlic, Chili, and Fish Sauce

INDOCHINA

Since this is used in small quantities, it goes a long way. Serve it with any Indonesian main dish.

2 ripe red chilies
1 clove garlic, peeled
1 teaspoon sugar

1 lemon
1 tablespoon vinegar
1 tablespoon water
4 tablespoons fish sauce

Remove stalks from chilies and cut the chilies down the center. Remove seeds and center membrane and discard. Cut chilies into pieces; add the garlic and grind to a paste with a mortar and pestle. Add the sugar and a peeled, seeded lemon gradually, continuing to pound to a pulp. Last, stir in vinegar, water, and fish sauce. Place in a small serving bowl.

If an electric blender is used, the mixture will be frothy. While the taste will be the same, it will look slightly different.

Pickled fruits (Japan)

Sesame-Seed Sauce

KOREA

This is a delicious dipping sauce for cooked or raw vegetables—and it can be made several days in advance.

½ cup sesame seeds
1 tablespoon sugar
3 tablespoons vinegar
4 tablespoons light soy sauce

Place sesame seeds in a dry frying pan over medium heat and stir constantly until toasted. After about 5 minutes, they will be brown in color. Crush the seeds with a mortar and pestle or in an electric blender or food processor. Mix the toasted and ground sesame seeds with sugar, vinegar, and light soy sauce. Store in a bottle, shaking well before serving.

Soy Sauce

KOREA   *Yield 4 servings*

This enriched soy sauce can be used as a dip with many kinds of Oriental food.

3 tablespoons soy sauce
1 tablespoon scallions, chopped
1 teaspoon sesame seeds
1 teaspoon sesame-seed oil
1 teaspoon garlic, peeled and crushed
½ teaspoon sugar
1 teaspoon vinegar
Pinch of chili powder

Mix these ingredients together and let stand for an hour until the flavors blend. Serve in individual shallow dishes as a side accompaniment to other foods.

Sweet Fruit Drink

KOREA	Yield 4 to 6 servings

Although this is called a drink, it is usually served in individual bowls with a spoon.

1 grapefruit
1 cup sugar
5 cups water
¼ cup whole pine nuts
Fresh or maraschino cherries

Peel the grapefruit; remove the pulp and put it in a bowl. Add ¼ cup sugar and set aside for a half hour.

Bring the remaining sugar and water to a boil in a saucepan until all the sugar is dissolved. Allow to cool. Place 1 tablespoon of grapefruit pulp in a glass bowl, making a portion for all those at the table. Add about 1 cup of sugar-water mixture to each bowl. Top with pine nuts and some cherries.

Strawberry Drink

KOREA	Yield 4 to 6 servings

2 cups strawberries, washed, stemmed, and
    sliced
1½ cups sugar
1 quart water
3 tablespoons whole pine nuts

Sprinkle the prepared strawberries with 1 cup of sugar and set aside. Make a syrup of the water and remaining sugar by bringing them to a boil until the sugar is fully dissolved. Divide the berries into dessert bowls and add sugar syrup to each bowl. Top with pine nuts and serve with a spoon.

Coconut Relish

MALAYSIA	Yield 4 servings

1 slice dried shrimp paste, fried or broiled
2 cloves garlic, peeled and chopped
3 to 5 lombok rawit (hot chilies), chopped
1 small piece brown palm sugar
1 tablespoon tamarind water
7 tablespoons white coconut flesh, freshly
    grated
Salt to taste

Make a very smooth paste of the dried shrimp paste, garlic, chilies, and sugar. Use a mortar and pestle, electric blender, or food processor to make the paste. Stir in the remaining ingredients except for the salt. When well mixed, add salt to taste. Chill and serve on the same day made.

Chili Sauce

MALAYSIA	Yield 4 to 6 servings

3 tablespoons dark soy sauce
2 shallots, peeled and finely sliced
1 garlic clove, peeled and crushed
1 green chili, finely chopped, or ¼ teaspoon
    chili powder
Juice of ½ lemon
1 teaspoon olive oil, optional
½ teaspoon brown sugar

This chili sauce does not have to be cooked. Place all the ingredients in a bowl and mix thoroughly. When all flavors are blended, put it in a serving bowl to accompany your main dish.

Peanut Sauce

MALAYSIA   *Yield 4 to 6 servings*

5 tablespoons vegetable oil
4 ounces whole shelled peanuts
3 shallots, peeled and chopped
1 clove garlic, peeled and chopped
1 slice trasi (shrimp paste)
Pinch of chili powder
Salt to taste
1 tablespoon peanut oil
1½ pints water
1 tablespoon tamarind water
1 teaspoon brown sugar

Heat the vegetable oil in a skillet. Fry the peanuts for about 5 minutes or until lightly browned, shaking the pan to prevent sticking. Remove; allow to cool. Using an electric blender, food processor, or mortar and pestle, grind peanuts to a powder.

Pound shallots, garlic, and trasi to a smooth paste. Add chili powder and salt and mix well.

Heat the peanut oil; add the spice paste and fry gently for 30 seconds, stirring constantly. Add water to the spice paste and bring to a boil. Put in ground peanuts, tamarind water, and brown sugar. Stir and check seasonings, adding more salt if needed. Continue cooking until the sauce thickens, stirring all the while. Serve at once.

Vegetable Pickle

MALAYSIA   *Yield about 6 servings*

This pickle can be made and stored for a week or two in the refrigerator.

1 cup carrot sticks
1 cup green beans
10 fresh red and green chilies
1 green cucumber
2 tablespoons peanut oil
2 cloves garlic, peeled and finely grated
2 teaspoons fresh ginger, finely grated
3 candlenuts, grated
1 teaspoon ground turmeric
½ cup white vinegar
½ cup water
2 teaspoons sugar
1 teaspoon salt
1 cup cauliflower sprigs

The carrot sticks should be cut in julienne strips. Cut the green beans into uniform pieces and slice in two the long way. Remove stems from the chilies but keep them whole. Peel the cucumber and cut in half the long way. Remove seeds and slice into the same-size pieces as the green beans.

Use a large saucepan and heat the oil. Fry the garlic and ginger on low heat for 1 minute. Add the grated nuts and turmeric and fry for 30 seconds more, stirring well. Put vinegar, water, sugar, and salt into the saucepan and bring to a boil. Add all of the vegetables except the cucumber and bring back to a boil. Then boil for 3 minutes. Last, put in the cucumbers and allow to boil for 1 minute. Place pickle in a glass bowl or jars for storage. Allow to cool completely. Chill before serving.

Tempura Cornstarch Batter

JAPAN   *Yield about 2 servings*

The kinds of food suitable for dipping in tempura batter and frying crisply can range from small pieces of seafood to vegetables to ice cream. This recipe and the ones to follow show a number of ways to make tempura batters and sauces, and give a number of suggestions for tempura ingredients.

1½ cups cornstarch
¾ teaspoon salt
¾ cup cold water
1 egg
Peanut or vegetable oil for frying

Blend ingredients together, but do not overmix. Dip fresh vegetables or seafood into the batter, then fry in hot peanut or vegetable oil. The foods you are frying should be cut into bite-size pieces. You may use a frying pan or a wok.

Tempura Flour Batter

JAPAN *Yield about 2 servings*

2 eggs, beaten
1 cup cold water
¾ cup flour
Pinch of salt

Beat the eggs with cold water until frothy. Blend in flour. Add salt. Blend well. Keep batter cool while using it by setting it in a bowl of ice.

Use a variety of vegetables, or seafood, cut into bite-size pieces. Dip into batter and fry in hot peanut or vegetable oil in wok or frying pan.

Extra-light Tempura Batter

JAPAN *Yield about 2 servings*

1 egg, separated
½ cup sifted flour
2 tablespoons cornstarch
¼ teaspoon salt
½ teaspoon pepper
½ cup cold water

In a small bowl, beat the egg white until stiff peaks form. In another bowl, sift the flour, cornstarch, salt, and pepper together.

In a separate bowl, beat the egg yolk and water until frothy. Gradually add the flour mixture to the egg yolk and water, mixing constantly. Blend until smooth. Fold egg white into yolk mixture. Blend thoroughly.

Tempura Dipping Sauce

JAPAN *Yield about 3 to 4 servings*

2 teaspoons soy sauce
¼ teaspoon salt
½ teaspoon sugar
½ cup white radish, grated
2 cups dashi (broth made from dried bonito and
  seaweed)
1 tablespoon scallions, chopped

Mix soy sauce, salt, sugar, and grated radish together. Blend in dashi; then add scallions. This sauce can be used with any food that has been fried in a tempura batter.

More Tempura Sauces

JAPAN *Yield about 2 cups*

Any of the following may be used for dipping tempura-fried foods:

Grated white radish
Hot (or mild) mustard
Catsup
Soy sauce
Sweet-and-sour sauce

Sweet-and-sour sauce

1 tablespoon butter
1 cup water
½ cup cider vinegar
3 tablespoons soy sauce
¼ cup sugar
1 tablespoon cornstarch
3 tablespoons sherry

Melt the butter in a saucepan over medium heat. Blend in water, vinegar, soy sauce, and sugar. Bring to a boil. Lower heat; simmer for 10 minutes.

Make a paste of the cornstarch and sherry; slowly blend it into the rest of ingredients, stirring constantly until thickened.

Vegetable Tempura

JAPAN	Yield about 2 servings

Vegetables

Use a variety of the following, or whatever is available to you:
   Eggplant
   Green pepper
   String beans
   Mushrooms
   Onion
   Potato

Tempura batter

1 egg
½ cup ice water
1 cup sifted flour

Oil for deep-frying

Slice vegetables into thin strips, keeping them separate, and set aside.

To mix the batter, beat the egg; add cold water and sifted flour all at once. Blend thoroughly, but do not overmix.

Heat oil in a deep pan (or wok) until a drop of water dropped into the oil sizzles. Dip vegetables, a few at a time, in batter; then fry them until crisp, using tongs to turn them. Take them out of pan or wok with a slotted spoon. Drain on paper towels.

Dip vegetables in soy sauce before enjoying.

Shrimp Tempura

JAPAN	Yield 4 servings

1 pound fresh large shrimp
8 ounces bamboo shoots
4 peppers, green, red, and yellow
4 small onions
2 sugared or candied ginger

Tempura batter

2 ounces rice flour
6 ounces flour
1 cup water
4 jiggers rice wine or sherry
8 egg whites

4 cups oil for frying

Rinse shrimp. Drain bamboo shoots; cut into ½-inch pieces. Cut green peppers into ½-inch strips. Cut onions into thick slices; separate into rings. Slice sugared ginger. Arrange these ingredients in separate, small bowls.

To prepare the batter, place the flour in a bowl. In a separate bowl, combine water and rice wine or sherry and egg whites until well blended. Gradually stir into flour to form loose batter.

Heat the oil in a fondue pot or wok. Each person places a shrimp or piece of vegetable on a fondue fork, dips it in batter, and deep-fries it in hot oil.

Dessert Tempura

JAPAN	Yield 4 servings

This is a fun dessert to do at the table in a fondue pot or wok.

Fruit for 4 (apples, bananas, pears)
Tempura batter
Powdered sugar

Peel the fruit; cut it into chunks. Dip it into tempura batter; fry it in oil. Drain on paper towels. Sprinkle with powdered sugar. Delicious with hot tea.

Tempura Ice-cream Balls

JAPAN	Yield 4 servings

Oil for frying
4 ice-cream balls frozen very, very hard
 (vanilla, or another flavor of your
 choice)
Tempura batter
Sugar and cinnamon or powdered sugar

Heat oil to medium high. Remove balls from freezer; immediately dip them into tempura batter, and fry until golden brown.

Serve immediately, sprinkled with cinnamon and sugar or powdered sugar.

Pickled Fruits

JAPAN	

½ pound canned pineapple slices
½ pound canned apricots
½ pound canned figs
½ pound canned peaches
1 ¼ teaspoons allspice
1 clove (whole)
2 pieces stick cinnamon, about 4 inches long
4 tablespoons sugar
½ cup vinegar
Pinch of salt
1 small jar maraschino cherries (4 to 5 ounces)
2 jiggers brandy

Drain fruits thoroughly, reserving juices. Place spices in a cheesecloth, tie securely, and place in saucepan together with reserved fruit juices. Add sugar, vinegar, and salt; boil for 10 minutes. Add fruits and maraschino cherries; simmer over very low heat for 1 hour.

Remove cheesecloth with spices. Pour in brandy. Cover saucepan, remove from heat, and let cool. When cooled, place in refrigerator for at least 24 hours before serving. Will keep for 3 weeks when refrigerated.

Green Tea

JAPAN	Yield 4 cups

Green tea
Boiling water

Place a good-size pinch of tea into a teapot. You may have to experiment with the amount that is palatable for you. Add enough boiling water for 4 cups; let steep for a few minutes. Have another pot of just-boiled water on the table, so that when you pour the tea your guests may add more water, if necessary.

A

Aburage. A Japanese fried bean curd, which comes in thin sheets, square or rectangular. This is usually sold frozen and can be stored in the freezer for several months.

Agar-Agar. A type of seaweed widely used in Asia. Available in strands or in powdered form. It is used in small quantities, as a little makes a lot of liquid. It can be found in Oriental stores and in health food shops.

Ajowan. Used in Indian cooking, particularly in lentil dishes. The seeds resemble parsley but give the flavor of thyme.

Akamiso. Japanese soy-bean paste, which is reddish in color. See Miso.

Anise pepper (Chinese pepper or Szechwan pepper). This is used in Five Spice Powder and comes from dried berries. Roasted over heat in a dry skillet, pounded and mixed with salt, anise pepper makes a good seasoning by itself.

Annatto seeds. Small red seeds used in the Philippines for color as well as for flavor. Paprika and turmeric serve as good substitutes.

Asafetida. Endowed with the medicinal property of preventing flatulence, this is used in minute quantities in Indian cooking. In addition, it adds a special flavor of its own.

Ata. A fine whole-wheat flour used in making Indian unleavened breads. Can be purchased at stores specializing in Oriental foods.

Azuki. Beans that vary in color from dark red to cream. Available in cans. As a substitute, use red kidney beans.

B

Bamboo shoots, dried. No substitute for fresh or canned bamboo shoots, dried bamboo shoots have their own special flavor. Available in cans at your Oriental store; can be stored for 2 weeks in a bowl in refrigerator if water is changed daily.

Basil. Herb sometimes called Sweet Basil and used primarily in Indonesian cooking.

227

Bean curd. A soft white, cheese-like cake made of pressed soy beans, which will keep refrigerated for several days if stored in water. Sometimes sold in instant powdered form in Oriental stores.

Yellow bean curd, also fresh, with a slightly different flavor, will also keep refrigerated.

Dried bean curd is available in flat sheets and must be soaked before using.

Beans, salted. Black soy beans that have been processed and preserved in salt. Available in cans and packets. Can be stored in the refrigerator in airtight container for up to 1 year.

Bean sauce. Made from yellow soy beans, which have been crushed and mixed to a paste with flour, vinegar, spices, and salt. Comes in jars and cans. Sometimes called yellow bean sauce or black or brown bean sauce.

Bean threads. See Mung bean threads.

Beni-Shoga. Pickled ginger, usually red and used as a garnish or for additional flavor.

Besan. Made from ground chick-peas, this fine flour tends to become lumpy and must be passed through a sieve before using. Because of its unusual flavor, ordinary wheat flour cannot be substituted.

Black beans, salted. These heavily salted soy beans are sold in cans and jars. Rinse before using to avoid over- seasoning your recipes. Will keep in the refrigerator in a covered jar for 6 months or longer.

Bombay duck. This salted and dried fish, sold in packets in Oriental stores, should be served in small 1-inch pieces. When deep-fried or grilled, it can be served with a meal of rice and curry. The diner should nibble very small pieces at a time.

Boo. A long white radish with very mild flavor but do not substitute Western radishes for boo. If unable to find in your Oriental store, white turnips will serve as a substitute.

C

Candlenut. Pale yellow nuts used in Indonesian and Malaysian curries, about the size of a chestnut. Since they are imported shelled and broken, when a recipe calls for 2 whole nuts, you will need to know the original size of the candlenut to approximate amount required.

Cardamom. A spice grown mainly in India and Ceylon and a member of the ginger family. Although they are expensive, both cardamom pods and ground cardamom are generally available. A little goes a long way in most recipes and adds a very special flavor.

Cashew nuts. This refers to raw cashews rather than roasted or salted ones. The nuts are usually available raw where Oriental ingredients are sold.

Cellophane noodles (also known as Bean thread vermicelli). Fine dried noodles made from mung bean flour, sold in packets. Must be soaked in hot water before using. Sometimes called transparent noodles.

Chili powder. Made from ground chilies and much hotter than the Mexican-style chili powder.

Chili sauce. Available in either the Chinese style or Malaysian. Both have a hot flavor and both are readily found at your Oriental store.

Chilies, bird's eye or bird peppers. Usually used for pickling but occasionally included where a very hot flavor is desired. Use with care.

Chilies, capsicum or peppers. A milder variety with a large enough pod to be used in stuffed meat or fish recipes.

Chilies, green. Used ground in sambals or sauces. Many times, the hot seeds are removed and not used. They can also be substituted or used with red chilies.

Chilies, red. Used for flavoring throughout the Orient. They may be served whole, finely chopped, or sliced for garnish.

Chinese bean sauce. Made of ground soybeans in a thick paste, about the consistency of ketchup. Available in bottles or cans.

Chinese parsley. See Coriander.

Chinese sausages. Dried and filled with spiced lean and fat pork. To cook, allow to steam for about 15 minutes when the fat is translucent. Serve by themselves, cut in thin slices, or include in recipe as indicated.

Chinese-style fish cakes. Available and ready to use at Oriental stores. Heat through and serve as is.

Chenna dal. See Dal.

Chrysanthemum choy. Edible chrysanthemum leaves available at Oriental stores. Use only the tender top leaves, before the plant has bloomed.

Cinnamon. A spice native to the Orient and best used in stick form rather than in ground form. The ground spice may lose its flavor if kept too long.

Cloves. A spice that has been used for more than 2,000 years. It not only flavors food but helps to preserve it as well.

Coconut cream. To make, use 2 cups of grated coconut. Pour over 1 cup of boiling water. Allow to stand for 30 minutes. Squeeze the flesh of the coconut and then strain before using. Use within 24 hours.

Coconut milk. To 1 cup of grated coconut meat, add 2 cups of boiling water. Allow to stand for 30 minutes. Squeeze the flesh of the coconut and then strain before using. Use, like the coconut cream, within 24 hours. Sometimes available in cans.

Coconut sugar. See Palm sugar.

Coriander. Sometimes called Chinese parsley or Cilantro, all parts of the coriander plant are used including leaves, roots, stems, seeds, and powder. While parsley is sometimes substituted for fresh coriander, it does not give the same flavor. Easily grown in a garden or a window box in a sunny location.

Creamed coconut. Sold in packets, tubs, slabs, and cakes, this is more concentrated than coconut milk. To use, cut up, heat with water and stir until melted. Then use as needed in recipe.

Cumin. An essential ingredient for curry powder and available in seed or ground form. Used throughout the Orient.

Curry leaves. Although used fresh in Asia, they are sold dried here and can be found where Oriental supplies are purchased.

D

Daikon. Large white radish used both raw and cooked in Japan.

Dal. The Indian name for a variety of pulses or edible seeds, which form the staple diet along with rice. Although there are several different varieties, the lentil is the most familiar.

Dashi. An essential for Japanese cooking, where it is used as a clear soup or as stock. Made from dried bonita flakes and seaweed and available in Oriental stores.

Daun pandan. Turmeric leaf.

Dried mushrooms. See Mushrooms, dried.

Dried shrimp paste. Although it has a different name in the countries of the East where it is used, it is always a pungent paste made from shrimp. It keeps indefinitely without refrigeration and is known as "blachan" commercially.

F

Fish paste. Made from fermented fish or shrimp and salt. Used frequently as a relish in the Philippines and Indochina.

Fish sauce. A thin, salty, brown liquid used to bring out the flavor of food in much the way salt is used in the West. Available in Oriental stores.

Five spice powder. Essential in Chinese and some Malaysian cooking. A reddish brown powder that includes anise, fennel, cloves, cinnamon, and Szechuan pepper. For best results, the powder should be ground from the ready-mixed whole spices sold in Oriental stores when ready to use.

Fried bean curd. See Aburage.

G

Garam masala. A mixture of ground spices necessary for Indian cooking. See index for recipe.

Garlic. Used throughout Asia for its flavor and health-giving properties. Many different varieties create flavors from strong to very mild.

Ghee. Clarified butter or pure butter fat with all milk solids removed. To make your own ghee, heat unsalted, sweet butter in a heavy pan. Skim off any floating impurities and maintain heat for 1 hour. Strain through several layers of cheesecloth and store in a cool place. Ghee will keep for several months. Also available in Oriental stores.

Ginger. A pungent-flavored root, which is used all over the Orient. When fresh ginger is called for, it should be used. The root can be kept by scraping the skin from the outside, dividing into sections and packing in a glass jar with lid. Pour dry sherry to cover the ginger, seal the jar and refrigerate.

Glutinous (sweet) rice. This short-grain rice becomes very sticky when cooked and is used in stuffings, cakes, and puddings. Sometimes known as "sticky" rice, it is available at Oriental stores.

Glutinous (sweet) rice flour. Made from ground glutinous sweet rice; has no real substitute. Can be purchased where Oriental foods are found.

H K

Hoisin sauce. Also known as barbecue sauce, it is made from soy beans, flour, sugar, spices, and red food coloring. Available in jars or cans at Oriental stores and keeps indefinitely in a closed container.

Kemiri nuts. See Candlenut.

L

Laos powder. Made from the root of a plant resembling ginger.

Lemon grass. The bulb-like base of the plant is used when chopped or sliced lemon grass is required. Dried lemon grass can be purchased at Oriental stores. Twelve strips dried are equal to 1 fresh stem. A good available substitute is 2 strips of thin lemon rind.

Lentil flour. When needed, this can be made from ground or pounded lentils. An electric blender works well but if you do not have one, use mortar and pestle.

M

Mint. A refreshing flavor for many curries and sambals. Although there are several varieties, spearmint is usually preferred.

Miso. Japanese name for soy-bean paste. See Soy-bean paste.

Moong dal. See Dal.

Mung beans. Small, green in color with green husks. When husks are removed, beans are yellow. Dried split peas may be used as a substitute but mung beans are usually available at health food stores.

Mung bean flour. Used basically in the making of sweets, this fine smooth flour is made from mung beans.

Mung bean threads. See Cellophane noodles.

Mushrooms, dried. Used in both Chinese and Japanese cooking as well as in the cuisine of other Oriental countries. They must be soaked in warm water for 30 minutes before using and there is no substitute for them. Available where Oriental foods are sold.

N O

Nam pla. The Thai name for fish sauce. See Fish sauce.

Noodles, Japanese. Several different varieties of noodles are used ranging from very fine, made from bean starch, to thick wheat-flour noodles.

Oyster sauce. Made from oysters and soy sauce and used to add delicate flavor to all kinds of dishes. Keeps indefinitely.

P

Palm sugar. A strong-flavored dark sugar from the sap of coconut palms and Palmyrah palms. Usually sold in round, flat cakes or in a ball shape. Substitute dark brown sugar if unavailable.

Peppers, red and green. Known as capsicums, sweet or bell peppers, they are used in many vegetable and salad dishes.

Plum sauce. Used primarily as a dip in China, this sauce keeps indefinitely in a covered jar.

Prawn powder. Finely shredded dried prawns or shrimp. Available in packets at specialty food stores.

Puri. Deep-fried whole wheat bread native to India.

R

Rice flour. Comes from ground rice and can be made at home with an electric blender or using a mortar and pestle.

Rice, ground. More granular than rice flour, this adds texture when used in batters. Available in many grocery stores and Oriental food stores.

Rice papers, dried. A thin pancake used as a wrapper for a variety of foods. Must be moistened with water to make them flexible and easy to use. Available at Oriental stores.

Rice powder. Finer than rice flour and when required in a recipe, there is no substitute.

Rice vermicelli. Known as rice sticks or rice noodles and come in a variety of sizes. Can be soaked in hot water for 10 minutes for most uses. Deep-fried, they can be used without soaking.

Rose water. Can be obtained commercially or made at home by floating rose petals in water overnight. Remove rose petals from liquid and use as directed in recipe.

S

Sake. Rice wine used primarily in Japan and Korea. Dry sherry can be substituted.

Salam. Native to Malaysia, these leaves are frequently used in Malaysian recipes. As a substitute, use bay leaves.

Sambal bajak. An accompaniment to rice and curry dishes made of chilies and spices. Commercially made sambal can be purchased where Oriental foods are sold.

Sambal ulek. Used widely in Indonesia as an accompaniment to main dishes and in cooking. Like Sambal bajak, this can be purchased at Oriental stores.

Santen. See Coconut milk.

Sereh powder. See Lemon grass.

Sesame seed. Easily available in most supermarkets, these seeds are used in sweet dishes in the Orient. To toast, dry fry in a skillet with no fat, shaking the pan until the seeds "jump."

Shrimp paste or shrimp sauce. Thick and gray in color, this is an essential flavor for Oriental foods. Anchovies mixed with vinegar may be substituted, but it's best to buy the real thing in jars from an Oriental store.

Shrimp paste, dried. See Dried shrimp paste.

Snow peas. Small flat pods, bright green in color and cooked for 1 or 2 minutes. Eaten whole. Available in supermarkets as well as Oriental stores.

Soy-bean paste. Called Miso in Japan. This is a basic seasoning used in China, Japan, and Korea. Made from cooked soy beans, malt and salt. Sold in plastic packs at Oriental stores.

Soy sauce. A basic ingredient in Asian cooking, which comes in several different forms. Light soy, dark soy, and sweetened soy are all available and keep well without need of refrigeration.

Szechwan vegetable. Preserved in salt and chili, this can be used as a relish or included in cooking for flavor. Available in cans.

T

Tamarind. An acid-tasting fruit, which is dried and sold in packets. To use, soak a small piece, size of a walnut, in ½ cup of hot water for 10 minutes. Squeeze until the tamarind mixes with the water, then strain out seeds and fibers. What remains is the tamarind liquid called for in so many recipes.

Tauco. See Beans, salted.

Terasi, trasi, or trassi. All names for dried shrimp paste. See Dried shrimp paste.

Transparent noodles. See Cellophane noodles.

Tree ears. Delicate, black mushrooms that are dried and sold in plastic bags. Will keep indefinitely without refrigeration.

V W

Vindaloo. A blend of spices similar to curry powder. Available at specialty food stores.

Wasabi. A strong, green horseradish used in Japan. Available in powdered form and can be reconstituted with cold water. If unable to obtain, substitute dry mustard mixed to a paste with water.

Water chestnuts. Can sometimes be purchased fresh but generally available canned at supermarkets and Oriental stores.

Wonton wrappers. Known sometimes as wonton skins, they come in paper-thin squares or circles of dough. Although they can be made at home, they are available in Oriental stores.

Wun sen. A transparent vermicelli made from mung beans.

Index

A

Abalone Appetizer, 16
Adobo Chicken with Coconut Cream, 74
Adobo, Pork, 109
Almond
  Balls in Syrup, 193
  Cookies, 202
  Delight, 201
  Torte, 203
Almonds, with Chicken, 90
Almonds and Mandarin Oranges with Chicken, 79
Appetizer, Abalone, 16
Appetizer, Simple Fish, 18
Appetizers Wrapped in Bacon, 11
Apple Rice, 162
Apple Salad, 130
Apples, Crab, Pickled, 218
Asparagus Salad, 140
Assorted Vegetable Salad, 133

B

Bacon
  Appetizers Wrapped in, 11
  Shrimp Wrapped in, 18
  with Water Chestnuts, 17
Baked
  Chicken Legs with Fruit, 89
  Coconut Pudding, 194
  Leavened Bread, 190
  Snapper, 41
  Spiced Fish, 48
Balachaung, Oily, 213
Balinese-Style Fried Chicken, 65
Bamboo-Shoot and Chicken Curry, 88
Bamboo Shoots
  with Beef, 115
  and Chicken, with Long Rice, 179
  and Mushrooms with Spinach, 138
  with Pork Soup, 23

Banana Cake with Cashews, 184, 206
Banana Chips, 199
Banana Dessert
  (Burma), 187
  I, 191
  II, 192
Banana Fritters, 185
Banana Pudding, Steamed, 185
Bananas, Caramel, 206
Bananas Cooked in Coconut Milk, 204
Banquet, Rice, 162
Barbecue, Pineapple Cocktail, 15
Barbecued Spareribs, 118
Basic Tempura Batter, 63
Batter, Tempura
  Basic, 63
  Cornstarch, 223
  Extra-Light, 224
  Flour, 224
Bean
  Cakes, Golden, 186
  Curd and Bean Sprouts, 145
  Curd, Fried, Peking-Style, 141
  Mung, and Cucumber Soup, 26
  Pancakes, 156
  Sauce, Brown, with Vegetables, Fish in, 41
  Soy, Cake, Stuffed, 7
  Yellow, Sauce, with Chicken, 69
Bean Sprouts
  and Bean Curd, 145
  with Beef and Pork, 114
  with Celery and Mushrooms, 138
  Marinated, 148
  and Rice, 180
  with Shrimp, 54
Beans
  Black, with Sweet Rice, 187
  Green, with Shrimp, 143
  and Shrimp, Cantonese, 55
  Spiced French, 129
  Spicy Fried, 134

Beef
    Balls with Noodles, 20
    with Bamboo Shoots, 115
    Braised Meat with Onions, 119
    with Bread, Fried, 8
    Curry, 98
    with Fried Cucumbers, 118
    Fried Meat Balls, 98
    Ginger, 113
    Grilled Steaks, 122
    Ground, Filling for Egg Rolls, 17
    Ground, with Fresh Peas, 106
    and Horapa, Fried, 97
    with Hot Salad, 97
    Marinated Steak, 120
    Meat and Potato Croquettes, 6
    Meatball Soup, 39
    and Mushrooms, Chinese Stir-Fried, 113
    Oriental Meatballs, 126
    Pepper Steak, 127
    Picadillo, 110
    and Pork Balls, 106
    and Pork with Bean Sprouts, 114
    and Potato Curry, 103
    Saté, 119
    with Sesame Sauce, 115
    Sliced, 96
    Sliced, in Sweet Sauce, 119
    Slices Peking, 112
    Soup with Vegetables and Meat Dumplings, 31
    Sour Soup of, 30
    Spareribs of, 97
    Stew, 127
    Stuffed Rolled, 110
    Sukiyaki, 125
    Tasty Fondue, 121
    Teriyaki Meatballs, 126
    Teriyaki Steak, 125
    Tokyo Steak, 126
    in Yogurt, Spiced, 103
Besan Bread, Fried, 191
Bintatok, 157
Black Beans with Sweet Rice, 187
Black-Mushroom Soup, 32
Boats, Indian, 73

Boiled Pork, 118
Bombay Shrimp, 50
Bouillon, 121
Braised
    Chicken with Mushrooms, 86
    Liver, Spiced, 120
    Meat with Onions, 119
    Okra, 134
Brandied Cakes, Small, 199
Bread
    Baked Leavened, 190
    Deep-Fried Whole Wheat, 192
    Fried Besan, 191
    Fried with Pork, Beef, or Shrimp, 8
    Rolls, Sweet, 198
    Unleavened, 190
Broth
    Noodles in, 21
Brown Bean Sauce with Vegetables, Fish in, 41

C

Cabbage
    in Coconut Milk, Spiced, 128
    Fried, 134
    Pickled Chinese, 144
Cake
    Banana, with Cashews, 184, 206
    Sponge, 209
    Stuffed Soybean, 7
    Teething, 189
Cakes
    Compressed Rice, 181
    Fried, 207
    Golden Bean, 186
    Orange Shaped, 206
    Small Brandied, 199
Candy, Date, 207
Cantonese Shrimp and Beans, 55
Caramel Bananas, 206
Carrot Dessert, 192
Carrot Pudding, 193
Carrots and Cauliflower, 129

Cashews, with Banana Cake, 184, 206
Cashews and Peppers, with Pork, 113
Catsup, with Fried Rice, 182
Catsup Sauce, 122
Cauliflower
  and Carrots, 129
  Chili-Fried, 145
  Filling, 193
  and Potatoes, Spiced, 135
  Salad, 147
  with Water Chestnuts and Mushrooms, 148
Celery and Mushrooms, with Bean Sprouts, 138
Celery Soup, 34
Cellophane Noodles, 169
Cham, Nuoc, 211
Chestnut Balls, 207
Chestnuts, Glazed, 220
Chestnuts, Water
  with Bacon, 17
  with Egg-Flower Soup, 40
  and Mushrooms, with Cauliflower, 148

Chicken
  Adobo with Coconut Cream, 74
  with Almonds, 90
  Balinese-Style Fried, 65
  Balls, Fried, 18
  and Bamboo Shoot Curry, 88
  and Bamboo Shoots, with Long Rice, 179
  Breasts Teriyaki, 95
  with Chinese Mushrooms, 80
  Chow Mein, 80
  with Coconut Milk, 82
  with Coconut Milk Gravy, 88
  with Dates, 75
  Deep-Fried Sweet-and-Sour, 77
  with Fresh Coconut, 71
  Fritada, 73
  and Fruit Filling, with Pancakes, 153
  Garlic, 68
  with Ginger, 81
  Ginger with Honey, 67
  Grilled, 72
  Grilled on Skewers, 65
  Indian Boats, 73
  Kai Yang, 67

  Legs with Fruit, Baked, 89
  with Lentils, 71
  Liver Teriyaki, 18
  Livers with Eggs and Noodles, 79
  Livers, Oriental, 11
  with Mandarin Oranges and Almonds, 79
  in Mild Sauce, 66
  with Mushrooms, Braised, 86
  and Mushrooms, in Eggs, 158
  with Mushrooms, Steamed, 82
  with Noodles and Coconut, 69
  Patties, 95
  Pieces, Skewered, 94
  with Pineapple, 81
  with Pork in Peanut Sauce, 74
  Rice, 183
  Salad, Curried, 72
  Salad with Lichees, 79
  Salted, 15
  Saté, 89
  Sesame, 90
  with Sesame Seeds, 95
  and Shrimp Salad, 135
  Skewered, 66
  in Soy Sauce, 87
  with Soy Sauce, 65
  Stew, 87
  Sukiyaki, 95
  Tarts, 89
  Teriyaki, 94
  Tinola, 74
  with Tomatoes, Steamed, 82
  with Vegetables, 87
  Wings, 11
  Wings in Oyster Sauce, 16
  with Yellow Bean Sauce, 69
Chicken Curry
  (Burma), 69
  I, 71
  II, 72
Chicken Soup, 19
  Cream, 28
  and Pork, 22
  Rice, 22
  Spiced, 38
  Vegetable, 34

Chili-Fried Cauliflower, 145
Chili, with Fried Steak, 96
Chili Sauce, 222
   Fried, Eggs in, 149
   Garlic, and Fish, 220
Chilled Noodles, 183
Chinese
   Cabbage, Pickled, 144
   Duck, 78
   Fish, 55
   Mushrooms, with Chicken, 80
   Stir-Fried Beef and Mushrooms, 113
   Style Mixed Vegetables, 140
Chop Suey, 111
Chow Mein, Chicken, 80
Chrysanthemum Soup, 35
Chutney
   Mint, 216
   Peach, 215
   Tomato, 216
Clam Soup (China), 34
Clam Soup (Japan), 39
Clear Soup (Burma), 24
Clear Soup (Japan), 39
Cocktail
   Barbecue, Pineapple, 15
   Kabobs, 17
   Meatballs, 11
Coconut
   Custard (Malaysia), 208
   Custard (Philippines), 199
   Dressing with Cooked Salad, 129
   Fish, Spiced, 62
   Fresh, with Chicken, 71
   and Noodles, with Chicken, 69
   Pancakes, 158
   Pudding, Baked, 194
   Relish, 222
   Rice, 170
   Rice, Sweet, 186
   Toasted, 210
Coconut Cream
   With Chicken Adobo, 74
   Fish in, 46
   with Fish, 58

Coconut Milk, 210
   Bananas Cooked in, 204
   Spiced Cabbage in, 128
   with Chicken, 82
   Gravy, with Chicken, 88
   Gravy, Eggs in, 152
   Rice in, 161
   Shrimp in, 52
   Soup, 37
   and Spices, Fish in, 42
   White Rice in, 182
Cod Fillets in Shrimp Sauce, 63
Cold Noodle Soup, 36
Compressed Rice Cakes, 181
Cooked Salad with Coconut Dressing, 129
Cookies
   Almond, 202
   Crispy Orange, 204
   Sesame, 202
Corn Fritters, 145
Cornstarch Batter, Tempura, 223
Crab
   Apples, Pickled, 218
   Omelet, 156
   and Pork Balls, 7
   and Pork Fried Rice, 181
   Rangoon, 56
   Soup, 33
Cream Chicken Soup, 28
Cream Sauce, 90
Cream, Coconut
   with Chicken Adobo, 74
   Fish in, 46
   with Fish, 58
Crepes, 154
Crisps, Shrimp, 6, 184
Crispy Fried Noodles, 55
Crispy Orange Cookies, 204
Croquettes, Meat and Potato, 6
Cucumber
   Hors d'Oeuvres, 17
   and Mung Bean Soup, 26
   Pickle, 213
   Salad, 130
   and Tomato with Yogurt Salad, 136

Cucumbers with Beef, Fried, 118
Cumin and Tamarind Water, 215
Curd, Bean, and Bean Sprouts, 145
Curd, Fried Bean, Peking-Style, 141
Curried
   Chicken Salad, 72
   Eggs with Mushrooms, 152
   Nuts, 8
   Shrimp (China), 56
   Shrimp (India), 48
Curry
   Beef, 98
   Beef and Potato, 103
   Dry Pork, 101
   Egg, 153
   Shrimp, 52
   Shrimp, with Tomatoes, 47
   Soup, 20
   Vegetable (Burma), 132
   Vegetable (Malaysia), 145
Curry, Chicken
   and Bamboo Shoot, 88
   (Burma), 69
   I, 71
   II, 72
Curry, Fish
   (Indonesia), 41
   (Malaysia), 60
   with Tomato, 49
Custard
   Coconut (Malaysia), 208
   Coconut (Philippines), 199
   in Pumpkin Shell, Steamed, 186
   and Sweet Rice, 187

D

Date Candy, 207
Dates, with Chicken, 75
Dates and Rice, 180
Deep-Fried
   Crispy Noodles, 176
   Fish with Vegetables, 57
   Sweet-and-Sour Chicken, 77
   Whole Wheat Bread, 192
Delight, Almond, 201
Dessert
   Carrot, 192
   Fruit Platter, 201
   Orange-Cup, 208
   Rice, 204
   Spiced Semolina (Halwa), 195
   Tempura, 226
   Vermicelli and Nut, 196
Dessert, Banana, 187
   I, 191
   II, 192
Dipping Sauce, Tempura, 224
Djakarta Salad, 128
Dosas (Pancakes), 154
Dressing
   Coconut, with Cooked Salad, 129
   Fruit, 209
   Salad, 146, 147
Dried Shrimp and Melon Soup, 35
Drink
   Strawberry, 222
   Sweet Fruit, 222
   Yogurt, 215
Dry Pork Curry, 101
Duck, Chinese, 78
Duck Soup, 35
Dumplings
   Dough for, 33
   Meat, and Vegetables with Soup, 31
   with Soup, 29

E

Eel Kabobs, 62
Egg
  Curry, 153
  Drop Soup, 31
  Flower Soup, 32
  Flower Soup with Water Chestnuts, 40
  Shirts, Leeks in, 143
Egg Foo Yong, 155
  Shrimp, 155
  Simple, 155
Eggplant
  Fried, 131
  and Prawn Soup, 21
  Stuffed (Japan), 146
  Stuffed (Philippines), 136
Egg-Roll Skins, 12
Egg Rolls
  Ground-Beef Filling for, 17
  I, 13
  II, 13
  Vegetarian, 12
Eggs
  Chicken and Mushrooms in, 158
  in Coconut Milk Gravy, 152
  Crab Omelet, 156
  Fish Omelet, 159
  in Fried Chili Sauce, 149
  Fried Stuffed, 151
  Marbled, 150
  with Mushrooms, Curried, 152
  and Noodles with Chicken Livers, 79
  Rolled Fish Omelet, 159
  Shredded Omelet, 150
  Son-in-Law, 152
  Zucchini and Mushroom Omelet, 159
Eggs, Scrambled
  (India), 153
  (Japan), 159
  with Shrimp, 156
  Unusual, 156
Extra-Light Tempura Batter, 224

F

Figs, Pickled, 219
Fillet of Sole, Pan Fried, 49
Filling
  Cauliflower, 193
  Chicken and Fruit, 153
  for Egg Rolls, Ground Beef, 17
Fish
  Appetizer, Simple, 18
  Baked Spiced, 48
  Balls, Hot, 6
  in Brown Bean Sauce with Vegetables, 41
  Chinese, 55
  in Coconut Cream, 46
  with Coconut Cream, 58
  in Coconut Milk and Spices, 42
  Fillets, 49
  Fried, 59
  Fried, with Tamarind, 45
  Garlic, and Chili Sauce, 220
  with Ginger, 51
  Hot Pickled, 52
  Meat, Skewered, 18
  Omelet, 159
  Omelet, Rolled, 159
  with Onions, Spiced Fried, 47
  Parcels, Steamed, 47
  with Peanut Sauce, 42
  and Radish Soup, 25
  Raw, Salad, 58
  in Red Sauce, 44
  Salted, 59
  with Simmered Pineapple, 58
  Soup, Spiced, 37
  Spiced Coconut, 62
  Steamed Whole, 64
  Sweet-and-Sour, 57
  with Sweet-and-Sour Sauce, 62
  Tempura, 63
  with Vegetables, Deep-Fried, 57
  Whole Fried, with Ginger Sauce, 43
Fish Curry
  (Indonesia), 41
  (Malaysia), 60
  with Tomato, 49

Flour Batter, Tempura, 224
Fondue, Tasty, 121
French Beans, Spiced, 129
Fresh
　Coconut with Chicken, 71
　Green Peas with Rice, 174
　Greens with Soup, 25
　Peas, with Ground Beef, 106
Fried
　Bean Curd Peking-Style, 141
　Beans, Spicy, 134
　Beef and Horapa, 97
　Besan Bread, 191
　Cabbage, 134
　Cakes, 207
　Chili, Cauliflower, 145
　Chili Sauce, Eggs in, 149
　Cucumber with Beef, 118
　Deep, Whole-Wheat Bread, 192
　Eggplant, 131
　Fillet of Sole, Pan, 49
　Meat Balls, 98
　Noodles, Crispy, 55
　Onions or Leeks, 135
　Oysters, 59
　Pineapple, 186
　Prawns, 8
　Steak with Chili, 96
　Stir, Beef and Mushrooms, Chinese,·113
　Stir, Mixed Vegetables, 142
　Stuffed Eggs, 151
　Vegetables, 137
Fried Chicken
　Balinese-Style, 65
　Balls, 18
　Deep, Sweet-and-Sour, 77
Fried Fish, 59
　Deep, with Vegetables, 57
　Spiced, with Onions, 47
　with Tamarind, 45
　Whole, with Ginger Sauce, 43
Fried Noodles, 161
　Deep, Crispy, 176
　with Mixed Meats, 175
　with Mushrooms, Soft, 176
　Rice, 182

Fried Rice, 168
　with Catsup, 182
　Crab and Pork, 181
　with Mushrooms, 177
　(Nasi Goreng), 160
　Noodles, 182
　I, 177
　II, 178
Fritada, Chicken, 73
Fritters
　Banana, 185
　Corn, 145
　Onion, 9
　Rice, 200
　Split Pea, 132
Fruit
　with Baked Chicken Legs, 89
　Bowl, 209
　and Chicken Filling, 153
　Dressing, 209
　Drink, Sweet, 222
　Kabobs, 209
　Platter, Dessert, 201
Fruit Salad
　(China), 201
　(Indonesia), 185
　(Korea), 144
　Spiced (India), 194
　Spiced (Malaysia), 208
Fruits, Pickled, 226

G

Galloping Horses, 7
Garam Masala, 214
Garlic
　Chicken, 68
　Chili, and Fish Sauce, 220
　with Sweet Spinach, 144
　and Vinegar Sauce, 213
Gelatin, Mandarin-Orange, 139

Ginger
 Beef, 113
 with Chicken, 81
 Chicken, with Honey, 67
 with Fish, 51
 Mix, 188
 Sauce, 43
Glazed Chestnuts, 220
Glutinous Yellow Rice, 182
Golden Bean Cakes, 186
Goreng, Nasi, 160
Gravy
 Coconut Milk, with Chicken, 88
 Coconut Milk, Eggs in, 152
 Sweet, Watercress in, 128
Green
 Beans with Shrimp, 143
 Peas, Fresh, with Rice, 174
 Tea, 226
Greens, Fresh, with Soup, 25
Grilled
 Chicken, 72
 Chicken, on Skewers, 65
 Steaks, 122
Ground Beef Filling for Egg Rolls, 17
Ground Beef with Fresh Peas, 106
Guava Jelly, 217
Guava Paste, 217

H

Halwa, 195
Heaps, Indian Nut, 191
Honey, with Chicken Ginger, 67
Honey Shortbread, 202
Horapa and Fried Beef, 97
Hors d'Oeuvres, Cucumber, 17
Hors d'Oeuvres, Shrimp, 15
Horses, Galloping, 7

Hot
 Fish Balls, 6
 Mustard Shrimp, 56
 Pickled Fish, 52
 Pot Cooking, 217
 Relish, 211
 Salad, with Beef, 97
 and-Sour Soup, 33

I

Ice Cream, 194
 Balls, Tempura, 226
 Mango, 200
Indian
 Boats, 73
 Nut Heaps, 191
 Relish, 216
 Style Lobster, 50

J

Jelly
 Guava, 217
 Seaweed, 188, 214

K

Kabobs, 104
 Cocktail, 17
 Eel, 62
 Fruit, 209
 Kati, 104
 Lamb, 104
 with Raisin Stuffing, 10
 Tasty, 105
Kai Yang, Chicken, 67
Kati Kabobs, 104
Kumquats, Spiced, 218

Index

L

Lacy Pancakes, 157
Lamb
   Kabobs, 104
   Kabobs Kati, 104
   with Saffron Rice, 105
   Skewered, 104
   Stew, 96
Leavened Bread, Baked, 190
Leeks in Egg Shirts, 143
Leeks or Onions, Fried, 135
Lentil and Vegetable Soup, 27
Lentils, with Chicken, 71
Lentils and Rice, 174
Lichees, 201
   with Chicken Salad, 79
Lily Buds, with Prawn Soup, 23
Lime Soup, 28
Liver
   Mandarin, 112
   Spiced Braised, 120
   Teriyaki, Chicken, 18
Livers, Chicken, with Eggs and Noodles, 79
Livers, Chicken, Oriental, 11
Lobster
   Indian-Style, 50
   Rock, Steamed, 64
   Soup, 38
Long Rice with Chicken and Bamboo Shoots, 179
Lotus Root and Pork Soup, 36

M

Mackerel
   Fish in Brown Bean Sauce with Vegetables, 41
   Fish in Coconut Milk and Spices, 42
   Salted Fish, 59
Mandarin
   Liver, 112
   Orange Gelatin, 139
   Oranges and Almonds with Chicken, 79
   Oranges, Spiced, 202

Mango Ice Cream, 200
Marbled Eggs, 150
Marinated Bean Sprouts, 148
Marinated Steak, 120
Masala, Garam, 214
Meat
   Balls, Fried, 98
   Braised, with Onions, 119
   Dumplings and Vegetables with Soup, 31
   Platter Szechwan, 111
   and Potato Croquettes, 6
   and Vegetables, with Noodles, 175
Meatball Soup, 39
Meatballs
   Cocktail, 11
   Oriental, 126
   Teriyaki, 122
Meats, Mixed, with Fried Noodles, 175
Medley of Vegetables, 133
Melon and Dried Shrimp Soup, 35
Mild Sauce, Chicken in, 66
Milk Soup, 19
Milk, Coconut, 210
   Bananas Cooked in, 204
   with Chicken, 82
   Gravy, with Chicken, 88
   Gravy, Eggs in, 152
   Rice in, 161
   Shrimp in, 52
   Soup, 37
   Spiced Cabbage in, 128
   and Spices, Fish in, 42
   White Rice in, 182
Mint Chutney, 216
Miso with Oyster Soup, 39
Miso Soup with Egg, 40
Mixed
   Meats, with Fried Noodles, 175
   Salad, 146
   Vegetables Chinese-Style, 140
   Vegetables, Stir-Fried, 142
Molded Rice, 178
Mulligatawny Soup, 26
Mung Bean and Cucumber Soup, 26
Mushroom, Black, Soup, 32

Mushroom and Zucchini Omelet, 159
Mushrooms
    and Bamboo Shoots with Spinach, 138
    with Braised Chicken, 86
    and Celery with Bean Sprouts, 138
    and Chicken in Eggs, 158
    Chinese, with Chicken, 80
    and Chinese Stir-Fried Beef, 113
    with Curried Eggs, 152
    with Fried Rice, 177
    with Rice, 180
    with Steamed Chicken, 82
    Stuffed, 10
    and Water Chestnuts, with Cauliflower, 148
Mustard, Hot, Shrimp, 56

N

Nasi Goreng, 160
Noodle Soup, Cold, 36
Noodles
    with Beef Balls, 20
    in Broth, 21
    Cellophane, 169
    Chilled, 183
    and Coconut, with Chicken, 69
    and Eggs with Chicken Livers, 79
    with Meat and Vegetables, 175
Noodles, Fried, 161
    Crispy, 55
    Deep, Crispy, 176
    with Mixed Meats, 175
    with Mushrooms, Soft, 176
    Rice, 182
Nuoc Cham, 211
Nut Heaps, Indian, 191
Nut and Vermicelli Dessert, 196
Nuts, Curried, 8

O

Oil Rice, 169
Oily Balachaung, 213
Okra, Braised, 134
Omelet
    Crab, 156
    Fish, 159
    Rolled Fish, 159
    Shredded, 150
    Zucchini and Mushroom, 159
Onion Fritters, 9
Onions
    with Braised Meat, 119
    or Leeks, Fried, 135
    with Spiced Fried Fish, 47
Orange
    Cookies, Crispy, 204
    Cup Dessert, 208
    Mandarin, Gelatin, 139
    Shaped Cakes, 206
Oranges, Mandarin, and Almonds, Chicken with, 79
Oranges, Mandarin, Spiced, 202
Oriental Chicken Livers, 11
Oriental Meatballs, 126
Oxtail Soup, 36
Oyster
    Sauce, Chicken Wings in, 16
    Soup, 40
    Soup with Miso, 39
Oysters, Fried, 59

P

Pan Fried Fillet of Sole, 49
Pancakes
    Bean, 156
    with Chicken and Fruit Filling, 153
    Coconut, 158
    Dosas, 154
    Lacy, 157
    Rice, 154
    Stuffed, 151
    Stuffed Savory, 150

Papaya Salad, 137
Parcels, Steamed Fish, 47
Paste, Guava, 217
Paste, Shrimp, Sambal, 212
Pastries, Savory, 8
Patties, Chicken, 95
Pea Pod Casserole, 137
Pea, Split, Fritters, 132
Peach Chutney, 215
Peanut Sauce
  with Fish, 42
  (Indonesia), 211
  (Malaysia), 223
Peanut Brittle, 184
Peanut Wafers, 212
Peas
  Fresh Green, with Rice, 174
  Fresh, with Ground Beef, 106
  and Pork, 121
Peking Beef Slices, 112
Peking-Style Fried Bean Curd, 141
Pepper Steak, 127
Pepper Water, 29
Peppers and Cashews, with Pork, 113
Picadillo, 110
Pickle, Cucumber, 213
Pickle, Vegetable, 223
Pickled
  Chinese Cabbage, 144
  Crab Apples, 218
  Figs, 219
  Fish, Hot, 52
  Fruits, 226
  Watermelon Rind, 220
Pineapple
  with Chicken, 81
  with Fish, Simmered, 58
  Fried, 186
  and Yams, Sweet-and-Sour, 138
Pineapples
  Galloping Horses, 7
Platter
  Dessert Fruit, 201
  Meat, Szechwan, 111
  Rice, 170
  Vegetable, 141

Plum Sauce, Sweet-and-Sour, 12
Pork
  Adobo, 109
  Barbecued Spareribs, 118
  and Beef Balls, 106
  and Beef with Bean Sprouts, 114
  Boiled, 118
  with Bread, Fried, 8
  with Chicken in Peanut Sauce, 74
  Chop Suey, 111
  Cooked with Sugar, 114
  and Crab Balls, 7
  and Crab Fried Rice, 181
  Curry, Dry, 101
  Fried Meat Balls, 98
  Galloping Horses, 7
  Loaf, 115
  Meat Platter Szechwan, 111
  and Peas, 121
  with Peppers and Cashews, 113
  Red, 103
  Skewered, 127
  Skin Salad, 130
  in Soy Sauce, 120
  Sweet, 98
  Sweet-and-Sour, 114
  Tasty Kabobs, 105
  with Vegetables, 137
  Vindaloo, 106
Pork Soup
  with Bamboo Shoots, 23
  and Chicken, 22
  and Lotus Root, 36
Pot-Roasted Rice, 178
Potato
  and Beef Curry, 103
  and Meat Croquettes, 6
  Straws, 215
  Sweet, Balls, 185
Potatoes and Cauliflower, Spiced, 135
Potatoes with Rice, 181
Prawn and Eggplant Soup, 21
Prawn Soup with Lily Buds, 23
Prawns, Fried, 8

Pudding
  Baked Coconut, 194
  Carrot, 193
  Rice, 194
  Sesame Semolina, 188
  Steamed Banana, 185
  Tapioca, 189
Pumpkin Shell, Steamed Custard in, 186
Pumpkin or Squash Soup, 25
Puri, Stuffed, 193

R

Radish and Fish Soup, 25
Radish, White, Salad, 143
Raisin Stuffing, Kabobs with, 10
Rangoon, Crab, 56
Raw Fish Salad, 58
Red Pork, 103
Red Sauce, Fish in, 44
Relish
  Coconut, 222
  Hot, 211
  Indian, 216
Rice
  Apple, 162
  Balls, 183
  Banquet, 162
  and Bean Sprouts, 180
  Cakes, Compressed, 181
  Chicken, 183
  Coconut, 170
  in Coconut Milk, 161
  and Dates, 180
  Dessert, 204
  with Fresh Green Peas, 174
  Fritters, 200
  Glutinous Yellow, 182
  and Lentils, 174
  Long, with Chicken and Bamboo Shoots, 179
  Mixed with Fingers, 169
  Molded, 178
  with Mushrooms, 180

Oil, 169
Pancakes, 154
Platter, 170
Pot Roasted, 178
with Potatoes, 181
Pudding (India), 194
Saffron, 174
Saffron, with Lamb, 105
Savory Yellow, 162
"Sizzling," 176
Spiced, 174
Steamed, 168
with Vegetables, 172
Vermicelli with Sauce, 168
White, in Coconut Milk, 182
Rice, Fried
  with Catsup, 182
  Crab and Pork, 181
  with Mushrooms, 177
  (Nasi Goreng), 160
  Noodles, 182
  I, 177
  II, 178
Rice Salad
  (China), 178
  (Indonesia), 160
  (Japan), 147
Rice, Sweet
  with Black Beans, 187
  Coconut, 186
  and Custard, 187
Rind, Watermelon, Pickled, 220
Roasted Rice, Pot, 178
Rock Lobster, Steamed, 64
Rolled Beef, Stuffed, 110
Rolled Fish Omelet, 159
Rolls, Egg
  Ground-Beef Filling for, 17
  I, 13
  II, 13
  Vegetarian, 12
Rolls, Shrimp, 43
Rolls, Sweet Bread, 198

S

Saffron Rice, 174
  With Lamb, 105
Salad
  Apple, 130
  Asparagus, 140
  Assorted Vegetable, 133
  Cauliflower, 147
  Chicken, with Lichees, 79
  Chicken and Shrimp, 135
  Cooked, with Coconut Dressing, 129
  Cucumber, 130
  Curried Chicken, 72
  Djakarta, 128
  Hot, with Beef, 97
  Mixed, 146
  Papaya, 137
  Pork Skin, 130
  Raw Fish, 58
  Tomato, 132
  Water Chestnut, 131
  White Radish, 143
  Yogurt, with Cucumber and Tomato, 136
Salad, Fruit
  (China), 201
  (Indonesia), 185
  (Korea), 144
  Spiced (India), 194
  Spiced (Malaysia), 208
Salad, Rice
  (China), 178
  (Indonesia), 160
  (Japan), 147
Salted Chicken, 15
Salted Fish, 59
Sambal
  Shrimp Paste, 212
  Tomat, 211
Saté, Beef, 119
Saté, Chicken, 89

Sauce
  Brown Bean, with Vegetables, Fish in, 41
  Catsup, 122
  Chili, 222
  Chili, Fried, Eggs in, 149
  Cream, 90
  Garlic, Chili, and Fish, 220
  Garlic and Vinegar, 213
  Ginger, 43
  Mild, Chicken in, 66
  Oyster, Chicken Wings in, 16
  Red, Fish in, 44
  with Rice Vermicelli, 168
  Sesame, with Beef, 115
  Sesame-Seed, 221
  Shrimp (Japan), 63
  Shrimp (Thailand), 212
  Sweet, Sliced Beef in, 119
  Tartare, 122
  Tempura Dipping, 224
  Yellow Bean, with Chicken, 69
Sauce, Peanut
  with Fish, 42
  (Indonesia), 211
  (Malaysia), 223
Sauce, Soy, 221
  Chicken in, 87
  with Chicken, 65
  Pork in, 120
  Vinegar, 59
Sauce, Sweet-and-Sour, 12, 218
  with Fish, 62
  Plum, 12
  Tempura, 225
Sauces, More Tempura, 224
Savory
  Pancakes, Stuffed, 150
  Pastries, 8
  Yellow Rice, 162
Scallops, 12
Scrambled Eggs
  (India), 153
  (Japan), 159
  with Shrimp, 156
  Unusual, 156

Seaweed Jelly, 188, 214
Semolina Dessert, Spiced (Halwa), 195
Semolina Pudding, Sesame, 188
Sesame
    Chicken, 90
    Cookies, 202
    Sauce with Beef, 115
    Seed Sauce, 221
    Seeds, with Chicken, 95
    Semolina Pudding, 188
Sharks'-Fin Soup, 32
Shoots, Bamboo
    with Beef, 115
    and Chicken with Long Rice, 179
    and Mushrooms with Spinach, 138
    with Pork Soup, 23
Shortbread, Honey, 202
Shredded Omelet, 150
Shrimp
    Baked, 168
    Balls, 51
    with Bean Sprouts, 54
    and Beans, Cantonese, 55
    Bombay, 50
    Bread, 167
    with Bread, Fried, 8
    and Chicken Salad, 135
    in Coconut Milk, 52
    Crisps, 6, 184
    Curried (China), 56
    Curried (India), 48
    Curry, 52
    Curry with Tomatoes, 47
    Dried, and Melon Soup, 35
    Egg Foo Yong, 155
    with Green Beans, 143
    Hors d'Oeuvres, 15
    Hot-Mustard, 56
    Paste Sambal, 212
    Rolls, 43
    Sauce (Japan), 63
    Sauce (Thailand), 212
    with Scrambled Eggs, 156
    Tempura, 225
    Toast, 15
    Wrapped in Bacon, 18

Simmered Pineapple with Fish, 58
Simple Egg Foo Yong, 155
Simple Fish Appetizer, 18
"Sizzling" Rice, 176
Skewered
    Chicken, 66
    Chicken Pieces, 94
    Fish Meat, 18
    Lamb, 104
    Pork, 127
Sliced Beef, 96
    in Sweet Sauce, 119
Small Brandied Cakes, 199
Snapper, Baked, 41
Sole, Pan Fried Fillet of, 49
Son-in-Law Eggs, 152
Soup
    Beef Balls with Noodles, 20
    of Beef, Sour, 30
    Black-Mushroom, 32
    Celery, 34
    Chrysanthemum, 35
    Clam (China), 34
    Clam (Japan), 39
    Clear (Burma), 24
    Clear (Japan), 39
    Coconut Milk, 37
    Cold Noodle, 36
    Crab, 33
    Cucumber and Mung Bean, 26
    Curry, 20
    Duck, 35
    with Dumplings, 29
    Egg Drop, 30
    Egg-Flower, 32
    Egg-Flower, with Water Chestnuts, 40
    with Fresh Greens, 25
    Hot-and-Sour, 33
    Lentil and Vegetable, 27
    Lime, 28
    Lobster, 38
    Meatball, 39
    Melon and Dried Shrimp, 35
    Milk, 19
    Miso, with Egg, 40

Mulligatawny, 26
Noodles in Broth, 21
Oxtail, 36
Oyster, 40
Oyster, with Miso, 39
Pepper Water, 29
Prawn and Eggplant, 21
Prawn, with Lily Buds, 23
Pumpkin or Squash, 25
Radish and Fish, 25
Sharks'-Fin, 32
of Soybean Sprouts, 37
Spiced Fish, 37
Tapioca, 24
Transparent Vermicelli, 24
with Vegetables and Meat Dumplings, 31
Wonton, 33
Soup, Chicken, 19
Cream, 28
and Pork, 22
Rice, 22
Spiced, 38
Vegetable, 34
Soup, Pork
with Bamboo Shoots, 23
and Chicken, 22
and Lotus Root, 36
Soup, Vegetable, 21
Chicken, 34
and Lentil, 27
and Meat Dumplings, 31
Sour-and-Hot Soup, 33
Sour Soup of Beef, 30
Soy Sauce, 221
Chicken in, 87
with Chicken, 65
Pork in, 120
Vinegar, 59
Soybean Cake, Stuffed, 7
Soybean Sprouts, Soup of, 37
Spareribs
Barbecued, 118
of Beef, 97
Sweet-and-Sour, 16

Spiced
Beef in Yogurt, 103
Braised Liver, 120
Cabbage in Coconut Milk, 128
Chicken Soup, 38
French Beans, 129
Fruit Salad (India), 194
Fruit Salad (Malaysia), 208
Kumquats, 218
Mandarin Oranges, 202
Potatoes and Cauliflower, 135
Rice, 174
Semolina Dessert (Halwa), 195
Spiced Fish
Baked, 48
Coconut, 62
with Onions, Fried, 47
Soup, 37
Spices and Coconut Milk, Fish in, 42
Spicy Fried Beans, 134
Spinach with Garlic, Sweet, 144
Spinach with Mushrooms and Bamboo Shoots, 138
Split Pea Fritters, 132
Sponge Cake, 209
Sprouts, Bean
and Bean Curd, 145
with Beef and Pork, 114
with Celery and Mushrooms, 138
Marinated, 148
and Rice, 180
with Shrimp, 54
Squash or Pumpkin Soup, 25
Steak
Fried, with Chili, 96
Marinated, 120
Pepper, 127
Teriyaki, 125
Tokyo, 126
Steaks, Grilled, 122

Steamed
  Banana Pudding, 185
  Chicken with Mushrooms, 82
  Chicken with Tomatoes, 82
  Custard in Pumpkin Shell, 186
  Fish Parcels, 47
  Rice, 168
  Rock Lobster, 64
  Whole Fish, 64
Stew
  Beef, 127
  Chicken, 87
  Lamb, 96
Stir-Fried Beef and Mushrooms, Chinese, 113
Stir-Fried Mixed Vegetables, 142
Strawberry Drink, 222
Straws, Potato, 215
Stuffed
  Eggplant (Japan), 146
  Eggplant (Philippines), 136
  Eggs, Fried, 151
  Mushrooms, 10
  Pancakes, 151
  Puri, 193
  Rolled Beef, 110
  Savory Pancakes, 150
  Soybean Cake, 7
  Tomato Garnish, 125
Stuffing, 146
  Raisin, 10
Sugar, Pork Cooked with, 114
Sukiyaki, 125
  Chicken, 95
Sweet
  Bread Rolls, 198
  Fruit Drink, 222
  Gravy, Watercress in, 128
  Pork, 98
  Potato Balls, 185
  Sauce, Sliced Beef in, 119
  Spinach with Garlic, 144
Sweet Rice
  with Black Beans, 187
  Coconut, 186
  and Custard, 187

Sweet-and-Sour
  Chicken, Deep-Fried, 77
  Fish, 57
  Pork, 114
  Spareribs, 16
  Yams and Pineapple, 138
Sweet-and-Sour Sauce, 12, 218
  with Fish, 62
  Plum, 12
Szechwan Meat Platter, 111

T

Tamarind and Cumin Water, 215
Tamarind with Fried Fish, 45
Tapioca Pudding, 189
Tapioca Soup, 24
Tartare Sauce, 122
Tarts, Chicken, 89
Tasty Fondue, 121
Tasty Kabobs, 105
Tea, Green, 226
Teething Cake, 189
Tempura
  Dessert, 226
  Fish, 63
  Ice-Cream Balls, 226
  Shrimp, 225
  Vegetable, 225
Tempura Batter
  Basic, 63
  Cornstarch, 223
  Extra-Light, 224
  Flour, 224
Tempura Sauces
  Dipping, 224
  More, 224
  Sweet-and-Sour, 225
Teriyaki Meatballs, 122
Teriyaki Steak, 125

Index

Teriyaki, Chicken, 94
  Breasts, 95
  Liver, 18
Tinola, Chicken, 74
Toast, Shrimp, 15
Toasted Coconut, 210
Tokyo Steak, 126
Tomat, Sambal, 211
Tomato
  Chutney, 216
  and Cucumber with Yogurt Salad, 136
  with Fish Curry, 49
  Garnish, Stuffed, 125
  Salad, 132
Tomatoes with Shrimp Curry, 47
Tomatoes with Steamed Chicken, 82
Torte, Almond, 203
Transparent Vermicelli Soup, 24

U

Unleavened Bread, 190
Unusual Scrambled Eggs, 156

V

Vegetable
  Curry (Burma), 132
  Curry (Malaysia), 145
  Pickle, 223
  Platter, 141
  Salad, Assorted, 133
  Tempura, 225
Vegetable Soup, 21
  Chicken, 34
  and Lentil, 27

Vegetables
  with Chicken, 87
  with Deep-Fried Fish, 57
  with Fish in Brown Bean Sauce, 41
  Fried, 137
  and Meat Dumplings with Soup, 31
  and Meat, with Noodles, 175
  Medley of, 133
  Mixed, Chinese-Style, 140
  with Pork, 137
  with Rice, 172
  Stir-Fried Mixed, 142
Vegetarian Egg Rolls, 12
Vermicelli
  and Nut Dessert, 196
  Rice, with Sauce, 168
  Soup, Transparent, 24
Vindaloo, Pork, 106
Vinegar and Garlic Sauce, 213
Vinegar Soy Sauce, 59

W

Wafers, Peanut, 212
Water
  Chestnut Salad, 131
  Cumin and Tamarind, 215
  Pepper, 29
Water Chestnuts
  with Bacon, 17
  with Egg-Flower Soup, 40
  and Mushrooms, with Cauliflower, 148
Watercress in Sweet Gravy, 128
Watermelon Rind, Pickled, 220
Wheat, Whole, Bread, Deep-Fried, 192
White Radish Salad, 143
White Rice in Coconut Milk, 182
Whole
  Fish, Steamed, 64
  Fried Fish with Ginger Sauce, 43
  Wheat Bread, Deep-Fried, 192
Wonton, 10
  Soup, 33

X, Y, Z

Yams and Pineapple, Sweet-and-Sour, 138
Yellow
  Bean Sauce, with Chicken, 69
  Rice, Glutinous, 182
  Rice, Savory, 162
Yogurt
  Drink, 215
  Salad with Cucumber and Tomato, 136
  Spiced Beef in, 103
Zucchini and Mushroom Omelet, 159